HUMAN RIGHTS
AND
VALUES IN EDUCATION

HUMAN RIGHTS AND VALUES IN EDUCATION

Edited by

Dr. P.G. THOMASKUTTY
Reader in Economics
Mar Ivanios College
Trivandrum
(India)

&

Dr. MARY GEORGE
Reader in Mathematics
Mar Ivanios College
Trivandrum
(India)

DISCOVERY PUBLISHING HOUSE PVT. LTD.
NEW DELHI-110 002

First Published-2009
Reprinted-2011
ISBN 978-81-8356-487-8

Published by:
DISCOVERY PUBLISHING HOUSE PVT. LTD.
4831/24, Ansari Road, Prahlad Street
Darya Ganj, New Delhi-110002 (India)
Phone: 23279245 • Fax: 91-11-23253475
E-mail: dphbooks@rediffmail.com
dphtemp@indiatimes.com
web: www.discoverypublishinggroup.com

Printed at:
Mehra Offset Press
Delhi

Editors' Note

Mar Ivanios College, Trivandrum, Kerala, India, owes its existence to the far-reaching vision of the great visionary Servant of God Archbishop Mar Ivanios of Revered Memory. The College attained new heights under the patronage of the late Archbishop Benedict Mar Gregorios. The College strives to produce intellectually trained, morally upright, socially committed and spiritually inspired young men and women of India. It is in turn with the vision of the great founder, that the college undertakes such programmes, which ensure the integrated development of students.

In 2005 the University Grants Commission (UGC) granted a novel scheme to Mar Ivanios College entitled 'Human Rights and Values in Education'. As part of the scheme a National Seminar on 'Human Rights, Ethics and Values in Education' was held from 18th to 20th January 2007. The main objective of the seminar was to bring together Academicians, Practitioners, Research Scholars and students with research interest to discuss the emerging issues in Human Rights and Values in Education. Response to the seminar was remarkable in terms of the number of participants and the contents of discussion. The participants of the seminar urged for an edited volume of the seminar papers. This book is the first one in the series which contains some selected papers presented in the seminar.

Contributors include veterans like His Holiness Swami Paramanada Bharatiji of Bangalore and novices like Justin Thomas Panachakel, a first year BA (Hon.) student of St. Stephens College Delhi. The thrust areas of papers differ in its content and treatment. Some papers strictly adhere research methodology and style in presentation but a few, though original in content, appear journalistic in presentation. We have classified the papers into two broad category namely, Human Rights and related issues and Values in Education.

The Key note address of H.H. Swami Paramananda Bharatiji which is presented as the first article in this book titled 'Rights and Values' provides the reader with deep insight on the concept on Rights and Values. Swamiji defines rights and values unambiguously. *Everybody's ultimate aim has to be to get into one with God. That is, what the right and the value*. In his article 'Values Education in Curriculum', Samuel Sukumar highlights the need for value-based education which leads to the overall character and personality developments of students. It is the responsibility of educational centers to make education value-based and facilitate transformation and bring about a society which is free of all evils, ensures dignity to life and where equality and justice prevail. R Sathesh Kumar's article titled, 'Inculcation of Human Values in Education', highlights the decay in moral values in contemporary society and advocates for an approach in education which has sufficient room to acquire internal knowledge about themselves. Y. Bhaskaracharyulu and D. Pulla Rao stress on the positive role of teaches in value education. V. Chandrasekaran stresses on the need for religious and moral education which is very much essential for the development of true humanitarianism and improvement of moral, cultural, social and democratic qualities.

Mary George and P.G.Thomaskutty in their article titled 'The Role of Family Life Education in Impeding the Spread of the Pandemic HIV/AIDS' argue for scheduled family life education classes as part of value education. This according to the authors will have a tremendous impact on developing a positive attitude among youths on sex and sexuality. Value education will help to reduce the incidence of HIV/AIDS. Smitha S. Nair advocates for the use of appropriate proverbs and maxims in class rooms which can be convenient tools to impart value education. She illustrates her argument with examples of proverbs which can be used in Chemistry Classes. In the article titled, 'Institutional Role in Developing Values among Students', K. C Baiju and J. V. Asha present their view point on institutional role in developing values among students. Referring to reports on various Commissions, they underline the need for development of moral personality which will equip the student to understand the principles of 'right' and 'wrong' and act in the right way. Suggesting a learner-centered approach in imparting value education, P. N Faisal summarizes different approaches and the Jurisprudential Inquiry model of teaching for value inculcation among Higher Secondary students. Esther Gladiz advocates for a concerted, deliberate and broad-based effort to preserve and make available to modern generations what is humanly relevant and inspiring in one's own cultural tradition and to search and help others to discover the new to be found in emerging societies through her article, 'Higher Education: Value Free or Value Bound?'. Sajna Jaleel makes a comparison of the ethical aspects and its implications of different schools of philosophy and she observes that teachers can develop the value system if they are aware of the ethical aspects of different schools.

Aleyamma Vijayan, based on her experience as a social activist and as a feminist among the marginalized communities, observes in her article, 'Women and Human Rights', that gender equality remains as an abstract principle and that there exists a gap between the formal guarantee of gender equality and the substantive inequality experienced by women. She warns that there can be no peace, security or sustainable economic development in societies which deny human rights, including the human rights of women. Umid Abidhodjaev, an undergraduate student of Islamic Law from Uzbekistan, presents her arguments based on Islamic Studies and with the support of quotations from the Holy Q'uran. Her aim is to highlight the better status of women in Muslim societies which are often undermined by western writers. N. Sajeena Beevi's study focuses on Human Rights Violations on Dalit Women in India and she suggests various measures which can help to end the discrimination of the marginalized section. She is optimistic and advocates for collective efforts which can achieve the goal of elimination of caste-based discrimination and suppression and facilitate to establish a system in which every Dalit Woman will have equal rights, access to education, and a chance to succeed and prosper. Dhanya M. B observes that gender equality is an important issue of human rights and social justice. She supports effective implementation of empowerment programmes for women to ensure the attainment of the goal gender equality.

Sanjoy Kumar Mukherjee addressing the issue of Human Rights of Prisoners in his article, 'Right for the Rightless: Human Rights Scenario in Indian Prisons', and advocates for a proper balance between the security and preservation of human rights of the prisoners. Since majority of prisoners are not born criminals, they need and deserve care, sympathy and correct guidance. D. Sivankutty and Shan Eugene Palakkal evaluate the present scenario on Health Rights of prisoners and disclose various areas in which gross human right violations are taking place in prisons especially on the health rights of prisoners. Manoj K. John's article reveals various constitutional and other legal and judicial safe guards on the rights of prisoners in India. The author bases his studies and experience in legal profession and wonders how far these safeguards are put into practice. P.G Thomaskutty and Mary George in their article titled 'HIV/AIDS and Human Rights' presents a summary of Human Rights pertaining to HIV/AIDS infected and affected people, a summary of guidelines issued by UNAIDS and the need for strict compliance with international conventions and laws which safe guard the interest of people infected with HIV/AIDS. Sanoj Rajan in his article articulates the incidence of human rights violation during internal strife. Citing provisions of the Geneva Conventions and other international laws and conventions the author pays attention on the need for humanitarian remedies for averting the occurrence of human right violations during internal conflicts.

S. Visalakshi Rajeswari's paper deals with the need for healthy working milieu and advocates for an ergonomically designed working environment, which according to the author, contributes to a labour friendly setting. S. Prema and A. Venmathi describe the role of environmental education in ensuring ecological balance and facilitating sustainable development.

V.R. Dinkar addresses the issue of Genetic Privacy and Human Rights. His article highlights various risk factors related to human rights in more complex dimensions associated with genetic research. He warns that genetic research may lead to genetic discrimination which deserves special attention than any other discrimination like sex, religion or race. B. Sreejith pays attention to the rights of students and development of multiple intelligence. He observes that it is the duty of the teacher to arrange activities with special focus to multiple intelligence in the class room and thereby ensure the protection of rights of students in association with their overall development. Ajitha Nayar K. suggests that the right approach to realize the objective of Human Rights Education is not by creating a separate syllabus, separate curriculum or separate time schedule for imparting Human Rights Education, but to incorporate it within the time table and in the syllabus.

Neena Thomas' article 'Corruption and Human Rights' says that corruption denies people the fundamental economic and social rights guaranteed to them by the Universal Declaration of Human Rights. Justin Thomas Panachakel with illustrations from recent events tries to establish the fact that mounting corruption is a challenge to human rights. According to the author, extortions, robberies, assaults, crimes on women, children and the weak and even all that are associated with terrorism and the under-world are some of the outward expressions or manifestations of corruption that hurt human beings and their rights deeply and more. Bismi Gopalakrishnan underlines the power of right to information as a remedy to disease corruption. She lauds the Right to Information Act 2005 of Government of India as a very useful weapon to combat the menace of corruption.

Santhosh Areekkuzhiyil in his article lays emphasis on the need for a systematic human rights education programme at various levels of education. According to the author human rights education should include teaching about human right violations and it should also provide a value system that condemns those actions and upholds human dignity. T. Ravichandran in his article titled, 'Meaningful Inculcation of Human Rights Education through Class Room System' advocates for imparting human rights education in the class room in order to inculcate positive values among children especially on human rights. Aneeshya S. S. suggests the need for providing opportunities in school to young people to develop and practice the skills to respect human rights and citizenship. Rekha Nair. R in her article presents the issue of terrorism in Kashmir (India) from a human rights perspective. The article quotes from various sources and suggests measures to end instances of human right violations in Kashmir. M. Muralidharan Nambiar puts across the instance of human rights violations in one of the traditional sector, the Beedi manufacturing sector in Kerala. The low wages paid to the workers is a case of violation of right to live in dignity and the right to freedom is also curtailed by denying bargaining power and organizational activities.

Views expressed in the articles are the personal opinion of the respective authors and they neither embody the views of the editors nor the College to which they are attached.

Acknowledgements

We wish to place on record our sincere gratitude to all those who have facilitated us in bringing out this volume.

At the very outset we wish to place on record our sincere gratitude to His Highness Sree Padmanabha Dasa Uthradamthirunal Marthandavarma, Maharaja of Travancore, who reigns the hearts of thousands in this part of the country, who graced this book with his appropriate message. We also recall his presence on the occasion of the inauguration of the National Seminar and the value loaded inaugural address.

We are obliged to thank His Beatitude Moran Mor Baselios Cleemis Catholicos, Major Archbishop for blessing us with an appropriate foreword for this book and also for his gracious presence and enlightening benedictory address on the occasion of the seminar.

We are also thankful to His Holiness Swami Paramananda Bharathiji of Bangalore for his Holy presence in the seminar and also for granting permission to include his Key Note address in this Volume. We will be failing in our duty if we don't recognize the support and encouragement received from Dr. S Uma Devi, former Professor and Head, Department of Economics, University of Kerala, in organizing the Seminar.

We are indebted to the following Prelates in a very special way. Most Rev. Dr. Thomas Mar Kurilose, Metropolitan Archbishop of Thiruvalla for inaugurating the Seminar for University/College teachers; to Most. Rev. Dr. Joshua Mar Ignatios, Bishop of Mavelikara for presiding over the formal inaugural function of the Scheme and to Most. Rev. Dr. Joseph Mar Thomas for inaugurating the Seminar for School teachers.

The UGC Scheme is being implemented with the collaboration of St. Mary's Malankara Major Seminary, Trivandrum and we place on record our earnest gratitude to Very Rev. Dr. George Kalayil, Rector of the Seminary and to Rev. Dr. John Padipurakal, Dean of Theology of the Seminary. We are indebted to Prof. V. Ramdas, Secretary of Gandhi Smaraka Nithi for his guidance and help in implementing the Scheme.

Former Principals of Mar Ivanios College extended a very helping hand in the implementation of the UGC Scheme during their term and we place on record our gratitude to Rev. Fr. Daniel Kuzithadathil and Rt. Rev. Dr. Msgr. Samuel Kattukallil. The present Principal, Rev. Fr. Mathew Manakarakavil kindled our enthusiasm in making this volume a reality and our very special thanks to him.

Thanks are also due to the participants and paper contributors of the National Seminar from different parts of the Country and abroad. We thank the authors of the articles included in this volume for their willingness to include their work in this book. The Organizing Committee of the National Seminar is worthy of special mention and we thank all the members of the Committee. We thank all our colleagues at Mar Ivanios College for their encouragement in bringing out this Volume.

Thanks are due to Dr. P. J. Jacob of Department of English, Mr. Francis Kuriakose and Ms Deepa K.S, Junior members of the College for their help in editing and to our son Jerrin Thomas Panachakel for his secretarial assistance.

We are exceptionally grateful to the University Grants Commission (UGC), New Delhi for granting the Scheme 'Human Rights and Values in Education' to our College.

We record our special thanks to Mr. Tilak Wasan, Director of Discovery Publishing House Pvt. Ltd., Delhi, for bringing out this Volume in time.

Above all we bow before God Almighty in acknowledging all we received from His Bounty.

P.G. Thomaskutty
Mary George

Dedication

This Volume is dedicated to the
Glory of the Triune God
and to the Memory of Servant of God
Archbishop Mar Ivanios

Message

PATTOM PALACE

THIRUVANATHAPURUM-695004

28 September 2008

It is heartening to know that the Mar Ivanios College is bringing out a book on Human Rights and Values in Education incorporating selected papers presented in the National Seminar held at the College on 18-20 January 2007. The theme of the book is something that is most wanted in today's ethos, for Human Rights without Ethics and Values will be no Education at all.

Let Values and Human Rights

Be Equal for and to

All men for Good and

Benefits of Mankind

I congratulate the Mar Ivanios College and the Editors Dr. P.G. Thomaskutty and Dr. Mary George for their sincere efforts to bring out this book which will be of great use to educators as well as learners. It is hoped that this book will become a leading light and illumine many people and the young who are being educated.

Sree Padmanabha Dasa

His Highness Uthradom Thirunal Marthanda Varma

Foreword

THE SYRO-MALANKARA CATHOLIC CHURCH
MAJOR ARCHDIOCESE OF TRIVANDRUM

MORAN MOR BASELIOS CLEEMIS
MAJOR ARCHBISHOP-CATHOLICOS OF
THE MALANKARA CATHOLIC CHURCH &
MAJOR ARCHBISHOP OF TRIVANDRUM

THIRUSANNIDHI
MAJOR ARCHBISHOP'S HOUSE
PATTOM, TRIVANDRUM-695 004
KERALA, INDIA

I am pleased to know that a book is being published on human rights and values in education under the auspices of the Mar Ivanios College as the fruit of the UGC sponsored seminar on Human Rights and value Education conducted in the college. As I can recall, the seminar was a very unique experience in terms of the originality of the papers presented and the academic stature of the members participated. It is obviously a very good idea to make available the fruits of such a seminar to the reading public by publishing the papers presented.

The topic discussed in this book is of utmost importance in the confused times on which we live. As we know, the primary goal of education is to form the character of the students by imparting values. All academic enterprises, however sublime they may be, must be permeated by a radical concern for the perennial human values. Unfortunately, blatant violations of human rights and tragic disregard for human values have become a commonplace thing in our society. We are exposed to numerous instance of such violation everyday through the electronic and printed media. We live in a large culture of expediency and opportunism, which in the final analysis is the simple reflection of disgustful individualism and selfishness. Where selfishness, reigns, values will be on oblivion. In such a social situation, the task of the educator and the educated is of extreme significance. Education must be approached as a spiritual act aimed at influencing and in spring the intellect, will and heart of the student to imbibe values that are considered to be of eternal significance in all cultures and civilization. That is why it is maid that an educator is primarily an awakener. An integral system of education will equip and challenge the student to stand for human rights and values, even at the cost of many advantages that would have been otherwise available to him/her.

I am hopeful that the book will be a strong inspiration in this line. In this context I would like to place on record the academic commitment of Prof. Thomaskutty P.G and of Dr. Mary George and the pains that they have been taking to enhance the quality and effectiveness of the system of education, especially in Mar Ivanios College. Their value based approach to education and their readiness to stand and suffer for the same is a happy silver line in the otherwise cloudy educational scenario of our society. I take this opportunity to congratulate them wholeheartedly for the initiative that they have reflected in editing the seminar papers in book form and for the pains that they do take for the sake of their value based educational commitments. I thank and congratulate all their collaborators in this noble endeavor. I wish the book wide readership and all success. May GOD bless all of you abundantly.

+ Baselios Cleemis Catholicos

Major Archbishop of Trivandrum

Contents

List of Contributors

1. Ms. Aleyamma Vijayan, Sakhi Women's Resource Centre, Convent Road, Trivandrum - 35, Kerala.
2. Ms. Aneeshya S.S., M.Ed. Student, Dept. of Education, M.S University, Tirunelnelvely, Tamil Nadu.
3. Dr. Anitha Nayar K., Principal, St.Thomas Training College, Mukkolakkal, Trivandrum - 44, Kerala.
4. Dr. Asha J.V., Lecturer, Dept. of Education, University of Kerala, Kerala.
5. Dr. Baiju K.C., Reader in Economics, S.N College, Varkala, Kerala.
6. Dr. Bhaskaracharyulu Y., Professor & Head, Dept. of Adult and Continuing Education, Andra University, Visakhapatanam.
7. Dr. Bismi Gopalakrishnan, Lecturer, Dept. of Law, University of Kerala, Kariavattom, Kerala.
8. Mr. Chandrasekharan V., Lecturer in Education, Institute of Advanced Study in Education, Saidapet, Chennai.
9. Ms. Dhanya M.B., Research Scholar, Dept. of Economics, University College, Trivandrum, Kerala.
10. Dr. Dinkar V.R., Lecturer, Kerala Law Academy Law College, Trivandrum, Kerala.
11. Dr. Esthaer Gladiz, Sr. Lecturer, Mar Theophilus Training College, Trivandrum, Kerala.
12. Mr. Faisal, Research Scholar, Dept. of Education, University of Madras, Chepauk, Chennai - 600 005, Phone 09884576800.

13. Mr. Justin Thomas Panachakel, BA Economics(Hons), St. Stephens College, Delhi.

14. Adv. Manoj K. John, Asst. Public Prosecutor, Kottayam, Kerala.

15. Dr. Mary George, Reader, Dept. of Mathematics, Mar Ivanios College, Trivandrum, Kerala.

16. Mr. Muralidharan Nambiar M., Research Scholar, Dept. of Political Science, University of Kerala.

17. Ms. Neena Thomas, Lecturer in Physical Science, St. Thomas College of Teacher Education, Thodupuzha, Kerala.

18. His Holiness Swami Paramananda Bharati, Bangalore.

19. Dr. Prema S, Senior Lecturer, Nutrition & Dietetics, Dept of Resource Management, SRM Arts & Science College, Chennai.

20. Dr. Pulla Rao. D, Associate Professor, Dept. of Applied Economics, Andra University, Vishakhapatnam.

21. Mr. Ravichandran T. Lecturer, SNDP Yogam Training College, Adimali, Idukki, Kerala.

22. Ms. Rekha Nair R., Research Scholar, Dept. of Political Science, University of Kerala, Trivandrum, Kerala.

23. Ms. Sajeena Beevi N., Research Scholar, Dept. of Sociology, University of Kerala.

24. Ms. Sajna Jaleel, Lecturer, Dept. of Post Graduate Education, Mar Theophilus Training College, Trivandrum, Kerala.

25. Prof. Samuel Sukumar, Sr. Lecturer in Zoology, Convener, Value Education Program, Madras Christian College, Chennai.

26. Prof. Sanjoy Kumar Mukherjee, Scottish Church College, Dept. of Political Science, Kolkatta, West Bengal.

27. Mr. Sanoj Rajan, Lecturer, Kerala Law Academy Law College, Trivandrum, Kerala.

28. Mr. Santhosh A., Research Scholar, Dept. of Education, University of Calicut, Kerala.

29. Dr. Satheesh Kumar, Sr. Lecturer, Dept. of Development Economics, St. Pius X Convent, Kasaragod, Kerala.

30. Ms. Shan Eugene Palakkal, Research Scholar, Dept. of History, University of Kerala, Trivandrum, Kerala.

31. Dr. Shivankutty, Reader, Dept. of History, University of Kerala, Trivandrum, Kerala.

32. Ms. Smitha S. Nair, Research Scholar, Kerala University, Trivandrum, Kerala.

33. Mr. Sreejith B., Research Scholar in Education, University of Kerala, Kerala.

34. Dr. Thomaskutty P.G., Reader, Dept. of Economics, Mar Ivanios College, Trivandrum, Kerala.

35. Ms. Umid Abidhodjaev, Student of Islamic Law, Economy and Natural Sciences, Tashkent State Islamic University, Uzbekistan.

36. Dr. Venmathi A., Professor, Avinashilingam Deemed University, Coimbatore.

37. Dr. Visalakshi Rajeswari. S., Reader in Resource Management, Avinashalingam University, Coimbatore.

1

Rights and Values

H.H. Paramananda Bharatiji

When think about the topic of rights and values, I feel the subject is extremely complicated because both rights and values and their relationships are very intricate and as far as rights are concerned, sometimes they could even be crazy and as far as values are concerned they could be very hazy. However, I hope before the end of the article, I am able to delineate the concepts.

Now I want to demonstrate that the relationship between these two is rather complicated. I use the words rights and values as generally understood, but I will specify their meanings later. Now let us start with some examples where rights are in conflict with values.

1. Last year there was a problem in England. The garment industry produced a certain type of dress and they sold it. These were provocative dresses and when women wore them, there were a lot of attack on them, i.e. there were cases of molestation reported. Many people were disturbed by it and they asked the industry to stop the production of these garments as they said the modesty of women is disturbed, so it is not correct to produce it. The industry said, "We do our business, which is our right. To give protection to people is the responsibility of the police." We know in our heart of hearts that this is not correct and still we cannot do anything. So the concept of rights is a bit hazy.

2. The jurisdiction of rights is also very hazy – not well-defined. Take for instance freedom of speech. What happened sometime ago in the US was that journalists wrote certain things about some people, which were not true. So those people went to the Court with complaint about the press. The Supreme Court of US gave a ruling that some amount of lie is permissible in journalism. Now the question is who will define the permissible quality and the quantity of lies – and on what basis?

3. Let us take up another example where right conflicts with right. In Germany people were talking (though this did not actually happen) about going into a labourless economy by fully mechanizing the industry. But then what about the right to work? Is not the right of ownership of industry in direct conflict with the right of the common man in that situation?

4. Let me give you a fourth example, which is funny and crazy. About ten years ago I came across a small book in the US, "What children should know about their rights" written by two Ph.Ds in Psychology. A very small book of some 30 pages – half the page containing pictures and the other half of the page giving the lessons in big letters of some 4 or 5 sentences.

   Lesson No. 1: You have the right to your pocket money.

   Lesson No. 2: How you should spend your pocket money? You have the right to decide about a fraction of your pocket money. For the remaining part, you need permission of your dad or mom.

   Lesson No.3: You are free *to think* of hitting the nose of your sister, but not *actually* hit.

Imagine two psychologists writing a book for the age group of 7-10-15 year old children. You can guess the outcome.

In order to discuss rights, I go a step further. You cannot discuss rights and values. For what is the right? What for are values and what is the relationship between rights and values. Next step – here I do not want to be too international – only want to be national considering my own country.

In this country foregoing the right to help weaker people or some others is considered a great duty. Let me give you most startling statistical examples.

After the Indian independence, Sardar Vallabhai Patel, the great statesman, contacted all the kings and requested them to merge their kingdoms in the Union. Remember they abdicated their kingdoms and surrendered them. Compare this with revolution in France, in England and in Russia. Here while abdicating their kingdom and giving it to the Union, the Kings were surcharged with the idea that it is for the good of the country that they are giving up their kingdoms. But the people who promised privy-purse to them have withdrawn it. This gives you a stark contrast between the kings and the democratic rulers.

Next see the question of land reforms. In the Ninth Schedule of the Constitution Pandit Jawaharlal Nehru inserted the clause for land reforms according to which landlords had to give up their lands which was over and above the ceiling laid down. Why? - Because there were many weak people who did not have land for a long time. So they had to be given land. Except for a few skirmishes here and there, the land reform act was passed.

I remember a touching incident in the case of our own Mutt at Sringeri – a very highly respected organization. There the Ministers came and approached our Jagadguru Sri Abhinava Vidya Theerthaji and told the Swamiji that, "It pains us to take away the lands from the Mutt". So they started suggesting different ways of writing so that some land could be saved for the Mutt. Guruji said, "Please do not do anything like that, because right now we may be able to save some land, but the posterity would say later that the Pontiff (the Jagadguru) used his power over the Ministers and saved the land for the Mutt. That would be bad. So please do exactly as the law says."

So we have looked at the right to kingdom and the right to land and what happened. Now let us take up the question of right to education. Many backward classes have no education. Great leaders of this country have been shouting at the top of their voices that education has been denied to the backward classes for centuries. This is not correct. Education was there for everybody until 250 years all had the right to education. In fact some big educationists from England came here and gave a report saying that the system of education here is marvelous and that in England they should copy it. If you want to have an idea, have a look at the interview of Professor Nicholas Dirks by N. Ram in the Hindu of 15th January. British Government had given wrong facts. Many were declared robbers and were killed when most of them were actually freedom fighters.

Education was destroyed by closing the schools. Now they are asking for reservation. 50% has been reserved without any riots. When they wanted 69% reservation, then the Supreme Court intervened and said you cannot be so unreasonable.

The very psyche of the people is such that they are prepared to give up their rights to protect the rights of the weaker people. It is most important duty of the society to protect the rights of the weaker people. It is to be done. It has always been done. It has been our tradition. At no time people have been suppressed. Abduction of one's right is a duty and it the highest value. Now rights and values are getting somewhat distinguished. I shall further distinguish as we go forward. How are we to look at values? So much discussion is going on. It is there in Arrow's theory of Social Choice. It is an obvious theorem - if every individual is to be given freedom of choice, one cannot integrate all of them and arrive at the welfare of the society and make all happy. It is not possible to accommodate individual freedom and the good of the society. This is not only true of Social Sciences. It is also true in case of inanimate things. It is also true in sciences like Physics. Kurt Gordel has proved it long back. Here is a case of impossibility of accommodating the individual's choice and the good of the society.

Now let us see what exactly was the difficulty? We have no criterion to decide what is a right? Therefore, I say when people discuss animatedly about rights and values without a criterion, how one expects a sound conclusive theory to emerge. It is not at all possible. I will give you more examples gradually. In this background if you want to discuss what is right - notice that it is ego-centered i.e. it is me. Whereas, what is value? You are not exactly sure where it enters. For value you are forsaking your right – where is its centre? What is its purpose? We are not exactly clear. See the asymmetry between the two. Suppose you take roughly values as a sacrificing spirit – you will say it leads to somebody else's happiness – the spiritual happiness. What is the purpose of a right? Right is just mundane happiness – not even mundane happiness – it is a psychological craze like speech. Freedom of speech should never be restricted – there is no doubt about that – you can even tell lies, suppose there is a situation like that – what exactly do you gain by this? – Just that you have the pleasure of telling a lie - O.K. Therefore, you will see that the end product of right is also happiness and end product of value is also happiness, but the nature of happiness is different. Therefore, in order to know more, I will go a step further.

Let us take up what could be a value. Value is something wherein I am sacrificing something of my interest in the interest of someone else and that is his right. If we define value like this, it means you are not happy with the fact that you have to adjust, and somehow you are not able to resist the right of the other. So you are making an adjustment. There is a beautiful example given by Amartya Sen. He says there are two people. The elder one brought two apples and showed it to the youngster – the fellow took the bigger apple. The older fellow was not satisfied and accused the younger of being grabby. He also said, "If you had offered it to me I would have taken only the smaller one". The other fellow said, "So after all you have got what you would have chosen". What is happening in this case is that you are not happy with the so called value. You are sorry that you have given him a choice – you also want to pretend that you are at a higher level. Therefore this sort of an evaluation of value means – it is a sort of a maximization of rights and minimization of value. I want to have the maximum of that. Sometimes when tomorrow I want to fight for my right I will have to grab.

Therefore this definition or criterion of value is not good. So we would now be coming to the central theme, viz. How should we define rights and values? Remember, the end product intended of both is only happiness. We may say they are spiritual or mundane, we may say they are egoistical or worldly happiness etc. – but it is happiness.

Now let us look at the situation. You take any happiness whatsoever – the mundane are characterized by the following four features:

1. They are just minimal – you always find it is not sufficient – I want more – therefore it is not coming to your expectation.
2. It is not perennial.
3. It is always faulty – suppose you derive happiness in eating *jalebi,* then certainly you also have to defecate. This is the fault. Such happiness comes in packages. It is mixed with what you do not want.
4. It is not universal – something is happy for you something else is happiness for another.

Therefore, as long as we are dabbling only in this area, there is bound to be conflict. So how do we solve this problem? We have noted the four faults – minimal, faulty, not perennial, and not universal. Let us investigate whether there is some happiness, which is opposite to this happiness. That is, is there a happiness which is maximum, perennial (not temporal), absolutely faultless and universal?

Unless we ask these questions, all these powerful theorems of Arrow etc. mean nothing. Amartya Sen also uses another phrase. He says one who does not discuss, what serves my interest and what should I do for it is called a rational fool. He is speaking of right, but he is not asking what serves my right. In fact, according to me one who does not ask what *should* be his interest should be considered a rational fool. They seem to be talking big, but do not know what is good for them. Therefore, because we have been rational fools we have made a mess of our whole lives. Is it not very strange – there are a lot of cases pending in the Supreme Court; what happens is that there is a multi-bench and they give a judgment by just putting them for vote; all of them are not giving uniform judgment – six say yes and five say no- so the case wins. They are going by majority judgment. Recently, in the case where they were taking money for asking questions in the Parliament – three judges said the persons should be dismissed, one said they should not be. These judges are very good, very erudite and very experienced. They want to give a proper judgment. Top it all, they do not gain by giving a judgment nor lose by giving another judgment. So there is no vested interest. But still they are not able to give a uniform judgment. It only shows that in your jurisprudence itself, there is no criterion to decide what is right and what is wrong. The whole subject of jurisprudence is so shaky because we do not know what the criterion is. Since we have no criterion for deciding right and value we are simply rattling.

Coming back to our question, "Is there a happiness which is maximal, faultless, perennial and universal?" You will be surprised to know there is one. There is one such happiness. The scriptures tell that this is a fine sleep, a good sleep; sleep merely without dreams also. There is no happiness equal to that. Remember it is universal, fault free. Because if your sleep is disturbed you dislike your own spouse!

Now we are coming to the brass tax of the problem. The biggest, maximal and best happiness is in deep sleep, where there is absolutely no contact with this world. The moment you get up you are running after the world in search of happiness. Don't you think it is a paradox? Is it not funny? Therefore catch hold of this idea, then you would be able to arrive at the right decision. What is that? You analyze why is everyone happy in deep sleep? Its only fault is that it is not perennial, because you cannot always be sleeping - will have to get up. Therefore, the question arises that even when I am awake, I should be in the same state of happiness. So to get that I would have to understand exactly what is happening in deep sleep. Now I cannot go into the details of it because it is too subtle. I will simply make a statement and go ahead. The scriptures say, "My dear child you have maximum happiness because at that time you are one with the Supreme God." All of you digest this sentence. That is why you are all with faultless happiness then.

Therefore, the corollary to be drawn is that always being one with God even when I am awake is the only way I can be happy always faultlessly. Remember, in the state where God is there, there are neither rights nor values. In deep sleep there are neither rights nor values. But being one with God is the greatest value and your greatest right. Therefore, do not think rights and values are absent. Both rights and values have simply merged in that. The moment you get up and come to the mundane world, it is split – the right-value continuum is split like the space-time continuum. Rights and values get separated when you deviate from God and enter the mundane world.

Now I am going to define right and value unambiguously. Everybody's ultimate aim has to be the following – that is to be one with God. That is both the right and the value. But you may say, Sir I am not able to do it. At least keep that as aim. You can come down to the level of the world – but when you come down too do not forget that is your aim. Therefore, reaching that is the highest value and the highest right. So what should happen? You should not disturb this supreme right and supreme value in your activities. I should not claim anything as my right if it disturbs my own path and therefore, should practice all those values which assure me that I am going in the right direction.

Value is thus defined as follows: If I disturb the spiritual progress of myself and somebody else, then I will have to adjust my right to this, which also leads to the increase of value. Therefore, in our society values are given prime importance and rights are only derived quantities. We do not derive values from rights. We derive rights from values. Now what is happening – the moment this restriction is placed everybody would have to adjust his right. If they do not there should be a higher body which has vision and which can say this cannot be your right. Because you have been talking of rights, social well-being, money etc. old people are being sent to old age homes. Even today in this blessed country sturdy young men carry their old father and mother in baskets on a balance for hundreds of miles – the *right* of the old parents is served by the *value* of the son. The system is such that the rights and values are interdependent – my rights are served by your values and your rights are served by my duties. You have no time to study all types of scriptures, I have all the time before me because I am not earning. So I can study the scriptures, so it is my duty to tell you that, you have the right for that knowledge, but it is my right to get food from you.

Therefore, this society has been conceived by the great seers. I want to tell you one thing. I somehow feel that almost everybody sitting here respect values. I take it for granted. There may be Hindus, Muslims and Christians and there may be a difference of opinion. Forget about it. But we are common with regard to values. Therefore, all of us must have an alliance to fight against non-values. We have to jointly fight. They are making a mess of our lives in the name of rights. Let us all come together and work for protection of values.

Understanding things is our right. So let us discuss everything. Let us not be gullible. Just let us understand everything to get to know the truth. Because some Westerner has written a paper, we do not have to take it. We have lot of intelligence. Only be bold enough to keep your own independent step. The time is fast approaching. The country is changing everyday, it is progressing. All people in the rest of the world are looking at India and feel that the real message for peace could come from here. Therefore, it is the joint responsibility of all of us to look into this. I wish all success to your Workshop. Unless God is brought in the social sciences, your social sciences are not social sciences at all. God has to be brought in. That is an absolute necessity.

2

Value Education in Curriculum

Samuel Sukumar

Introduction

A 'Value' has been defined time and again, as a belief upon which an individual chooses to act in a given situation. Any ideal, or a moral, or a spiritual principle, which has an influence on our lives in specific circumstances, and based on which our behaviour is expressed, is a Value. Our decisions are based on our values.

The root word of 'education' comes from Latin, which means 'the development of character' or 'to make whole'. Education, apart from being a search for truth and enlightenment, is concerned with Values. Therefore, complete education of an individual involves an inseparable bond with values. The task of a Teacher (Educator) is a wholistic task – that of providing education with values, or value-based 'education'. Needless to say, that a teacher/educator should be a person with character, or else the very essence of education is lost, when a characterless educator tries to impart education without values he/she does not himself/herself possess.

What are Value?

Values can be addressed from three different dimensions:

- One's self;
- Self and the others with whom he/she interacts daily; and
- Social values.

In our everyday life, every individual's behaviour is determined by values based on these dimensions. For example, Self esteem and individual spiritual values govern a person's 'Self' dimension; our relationship with our parents, family and others is governed by values of interpersonal dimension; and, behaviour in society are governed by our respect to other's feelings.

Our life revolves around values such as Responsibility, Honesty, Politeness, Punctuality, Equality, Accountability, Concern, Love, Tolerance, Loyalty, Patriotism, etc., etc. These values come from our judgement of what is right and what is wrong. We imbibe them from our parents, who teach values and, more importantly, practice these values in their lives, which children observe and, in turn, practice. In the second circle, are elders and teachers who put values into youngsters. But finally, it is the individual himself/herself, who makes the choice between what he/she believes is right or wrong in a given situation, and acts according to his/her 'conscience' – parents, elders, religion, education, all have a role to play here.

Need for Value-based Education System

Today's youngsters have very little positive influence from parents or close relatives, thanks to the changing social order, with nuclear family system being the norm and both parents in the 'working class' bracket. To add to this, they have the privilege of being in the electronic age (e-age) of television, mobiles and internet, and a lot of free, lonely time available for them. They grow amidst confusion of what is right and wrong; good or bad; straight or crooked; healthy or unhealthy, due to the fact that they have no one on whom to depend, at an age when ideal are just forming in their minds.

Today, we also hear and read of highly placed, qualified and educated government officials, spiritual leaders, professionals, etc., who are involved in corruption, cheating, dehumanization, etc. Therefore, the student enters school, college or university with a total misunderstanding of values, because all around, the student hears people only preaching of values while they themselves do not practice what they preach. Power, greed, money, wealth, office, high connections are seemed to belittle values, without which 'prosperity' seems to flourish. Many questions are unanswered for the youngster and no one is able to spare time to answer these questions. Many youngsters, who could not find answers, have even taken the ultimate path of suicide, as statistics reveal to us.

It is at this juncture in his/her life that a Teacher with a strong belief in value-education comes in, and takes the role of a multiple personality of mother-father-teacher-leader-guide-hero. Therefore, o the question "Is there a need to introduce value education in our teaching?" the answer is a definite "YES"! But, care should be taken not to propagate any particular religious values – the values we are discussing here are general Human Values.

How do we Include Values in our Teaching?

The best method by which a youngster can learn values is for the educator (parents, teachers, elders), to practice them first, for that is the most effective method of value transfer. Secondly, parents can be the youngster's best educators – and all that is required of them is to spare a few minutes every day for their children. But it is the Teacher who can have a very great role to play in moulding the character of his/her students. Values need not be always taught in a regular classroom setup. The Teacher can device methods in his/her regular teaching. For example, a Commerce Teacher can highlight ethical practices in business; a Science Teacher can highlight ethical practices in experiments affecting human health; and a Humanities Teacher can touch upon negative aspects of unethical social practices.

Of course, today Autonomous Colleges have the option of including Value Education in their regular curriculum. Thanks to University Grants Commission, which has sponsored Refresher Courses in Value Education, this has served as an impetus for many Colleges in considering inclusion of Value Education in their regular curriculum.

Madras Christian College Model

Being an Autonomous College, Madras Christian College has been dealing with Ethical Studies or Value Education for over twenty years, as a mandatory course. Today, we feel that this course has indeed been useful to a vast majority of students in making them conscientious and prepared for life outside the College walls, in the wider arena of life.

Our Syllabus has been evolved by the Board of Studies in Value Education, consisting of senior faculty, as well as study material. The course is designed for all I year under-graduate students and the syllabus includes current topics of national and international importance including Family, Social Evils, Economy, Population, Pollution, Mass Media, Alternate Social Order, etc. Teachers of this course are chosen from each department and trained to teach not in a routine teacher-dominated classroom setup, but employing different methods of teaching and evaluation like, discussion, group discussion, term paper, field visits, group work, etc. A minimum pass is essential in the final examination for the award of degree. Preparation of individual project reports has been very useful to students as they have first-hand experience of contemporary issues, and the whole experience is a learning process not only for the students but also for the Teachers; a very rewarding experience, indeed.

Conclusion

Value-based education leads to overall character and personality development of students. It enables development of values in a youngster at an appropriate juncture of his/her life, and encourages him/her to grow out of inborn egocentricity to selflessness; from immaturity to maturity; from being a child to attaining adulthood; from being a silent listener to being empowered for dialogue encounter and problem solving.

Many Commissions including the Radhakrishnan Commission (1948), National Policy on Education (1968), New Educational Policy (1986), etc., have stressed the importance of value-based education. Today, thanks to Adult Literacy Program, Inclusion of Human Rights, Gender Issues, and Threats to Family Life, in our teaching, and the involvement of Organisations like, U.G.C., State Governments and Universities, inclusion of Value Education in curriculum is a much easier step. Therefore, training of Teachers is essential and organizing Seminars and Conferences and Refresher Courses in the same, like the present one, go a long way in helping our Society to become a value-conscious one with our youngsters growing into responsible citizens of tomorrow.

It is the responsibility of educational centers to make education value-based and facilitate transformation and bring about a society which is free of all social evils and there is dignity to life and equality and justice prevail. Finally, the words of our President should echo in our ears, "No amount of laws would be able to wipe out corruption in public life, unless education was made value-based".

REFERENCES

1. Barnabas, C.J. Value-based Education: An Instrument for Social Transformation. Proceedings of the International Conference on Developing Competitive Strength in Institutions of Higher Learning in the Changing Scenario, Chennai. 2004.
2. Daniel, J.T.K. Value Education Today. Viswanathan Printers, Madras. 1990.
3. Ignachimuthu, S. Values for Life. Better Yourself Books, Mumbai. 1999.
4. Jacob, M. (Ed), Recource Book for Value Education. Institute of Value Education, New Delhi. 2002.
5. Peace and Value Education for Schools. National Institute of Peace and Value Education. Secunderabad. 2002.
6. "University News" Issues. A Weekly Journal of Higher Education. New Delhi.
7. "Value Education in the New Millennium". Marie Mignon Mascarenhas. Bangalore. 1999.

3

Inculcation of Human Values in Education

Satheesh Kumar

The Need for Values in Education

Mankind is living in an era which witnesses unprecedented scientific progress. If 'speed' can be taken as a characteristic of this age, miraculous development is witnessed in the 'external' growth or outer conditions of man. Development in science and technology rapidly improves the living standards of even the common man. However, the same 'speed' is also operating in a negative direction. The 'inner' growth is the causality. Traditionally an ideal person is described as one with 'high thinking and low living', but now the ideal to many seems to be 'high living and low thinking'. Decay in inner growth and fall in morality is evident from the growing statistics of increasing divorces, old age homes, suicides, patients with mental illness, corruption, terrorism, drug addiction, alchaholism, crimes, and so on. This paradoxical situation of rising living standards and eluding peace of mind and happiness forces thoughtful people to ponder over this phenomenon. Persons with high level of formal education are reported behind many inhuman acts (Sharma, Kalpana -2008). Most of the educated are preoccupied with financial gains, sex, compulsive acquisition of more material goods and higher standards of living even at the cost of a conscientious living. Higher urges of humans such as goodness, contentment, peace, self satisfaction, aesthetics, self esteem, spiritual transcendence etc are neglected and lower urges like physical comfort, sex, prosperity, material possessions, power, position and recognition are given the top priority. (Mitra, Somenath – 2003)

Present moral degradation in all spheres of life signals to the fact that even though modern education succeeds in providing 'information' and bringing out 'greatness' in individuals but it fails in bringing out the humaneness and goodness in its recipients to the fullest extent and transform them to good humans. The experience of vast majority going through the present educational system reveals that it succeeds in making 'able' persons but not succeeding to make them "noble". Great scientist Albert Einstein once remarked that it is essential that the students acquire an understanding and lively feeling for values. He must acquire a vivid sense of beautiful and morally good. Otherwise, he with his specialized knowledge more closely resembles a well trained dog than a harmoniously developed person (Mitra, Somenath - 2003). Great educationist Kothari (Education Commisssion 1964-66), warns about the dangers of knowledge without essential values. Modern education system which gives over importance to the 'head' and bypasses the 'heart' is accused to be a major reason for many social evils and moral land slide. It becomes increasingly clear that intellectual development alone cannot transform children into a complete personality and responsible citizens. Hence an integral educational system which provides for the balanced development of both 'head' and 'heart', become essential.

Values - Meaning and Importance in Education

Dictionary meaning of value is 'worth' or 'having utility'. Values can be defined as "normative standards" which help in making choice out of alternative courses action. (Kapani, Madhu - 2000). From Mahatma Gandhi's life, we get many instances of taking decisions and behaving as per the prompting of well developed value system. For instance, one incident occurred in his school days is worth remembering in this context. When

Gandhiji misspelt the word 'kettle', he refused to copy the correct answer from the next boy, irrespective of the direction from the class teacher. He took a decision and acted on the basis of his own normal value system. Values can be treated as a set of desirable behaviour or special kind of attitudes following which it is good for the individual and the society.

The word 'education' is derived from the Latin derivative *educare* which means "to bring forth that which is within". Hence education should succeed in bringing out the truth, goodness, beauty and other human qualities latent in the student. What ever be the educational philosophy, whether it is pragmatic, idealist, naturalist or humanist all are concerned with the development of the student as a useful member of society. Education in human values is essential to develop a sense of self worth, self esteem, and character in students. Values education helps the evolution of a balanced and harmoniously developed person in three aspects- body, mind and spirit (Kapani, Madhu - 2000).

Core Values and Sub Values

In 1979 B.R.Goyal for N.C.E.R.T proposed a list of 83 values and in 1981 Dr. V.K. Gokak classified and grouped these values under five basic human values: Truth, Right conduct, Peace, Love and Non-violence. Table 3.1 gives a classification of core values and their sub values. (N.C.E.R.T.-1987)

Table 3.1

Truth	Right Action	Peace	Love	Non-violence
Truthfulness	Cleanliness	Abstinence	Sincerity	Kindness
Curiosity	Hygienic living	Freedom from six sins	Kindness	Courtesy
Quest for knowledge	Dignity of labour	Cultivation of six virtues	Sympathy	Good manners
Spirit of enquiry	Proper utilization of time	Discipline	Friendship	Helpfulness
Study of oneself	Regularity	Purity	Patriotism	Fellow feeling
Discrimination	Punctuality	Endurance	Devotion	Gentlemanliness
Secularism	Self help	Integrity	Tolerance	Unwillingness to hurt
Respect for all	Self support	Self discipline	Humanism	Consideration for others
				Readiness to cooperate

(Contd...)

Truth	Right Action	Peace	Love	Non-violence
religions	Obedience	Self control		Appreciation of the culture
Universal self existent truth	Duty and loyalty to duty	Self respect		others
	Simple living	Awareness of dignity of individual		Compassion Universal love
	Honesty			Awareness of responsibility
	Prudence	Concentration		citizenship
	Respect for others	Meditation		Democratic common good
	Reverence	Peace		National awareness
	Service to others			National unity
	Self confidence			Away from un-touchability
	Self reliance			and national property
	Initiative			Social service
	Resourcefulness			Social justice
	Courage			Secularism
	Leadership			Socialism
	Faithfulness			Solidarity
	Justice			
	Teamwork			
	Team spirit			
	Equality			
	Self sacrifice			

Core values are universally accepted values by all major religions. But they are abstract and sub values are more concrete and observable in the behaviour. Hence they help in the practical implementation and evaluation of the value education techniques. A brief description of the core values is attempted below: (N.C.E.R.T - 1987)

1. Truth

Truth is the unchanging reality. It is changeless in all three time periods-past, present and future. It represents the real "I" or the divine principle in each of us. The role of human intellect is to find out the truth. "When one realizes and experiences this truth, one sees that the same truth pervades every other person and object and in essence we are all one" (N.C.E.R.T - 1987).

2. Righteous Conduct

Truth in action can be considered as right conduct. It represents unity in thought, word and action of an individual. It cover all aspects of life and concerned not only in ones own welfare, but in the well being of all.

3. Peace

Peace is the end purpose of all human endeavors and it is a state of emotional equilibrium. Peace and love are closely connected. If love is blocked it will result in loss of peace. When flow of love is restored, then peace returns.

4. Love

Love is the supreme value. It is a form of energy which each individual transmits and receives. A special feature of love is that it grows by sharing. It is the mother value by developing this one value we get all other values. Hence the essence of value education is to train students to start the day with love, fill the day with love and to end the day with love (N.C.E.R.T- 1987)

5. Non-Violence

"Non –violence means not to injure others either by our thoughts, words, or action" (N.C.E.R.T - 1987). Non violence is based on the understanding of oneness or underlying unity of all beings. Fatherhood of God and brotherhood of man envisages the divine heritage of all beings and the common divine bondage. Non-violence is based on the understanding that beings –sentient and non sentient in the universe, even speck of dust to stars are connected and related. This means all are part of the same and hurting another by thought, word or deed amounts to hurting oneself. This is the basis of the principle of non-violence (N.C.E.R.T - 1987).

Approaches to Education in Human Values

Values can be inculcated in educational institutions by various methods. Three approaches are discussed below:

1. Integrated approach through curricular activities.

2. Integrated approach through co-curricular activities.
3. Direct approach.

The major approaches used in instilling and developing human values are presented in chart-3.1 below (N.C.E.R.T - 1987). In the class room or outside class room teachers can elicit and develop values inherent in the students by judiciously using one or more of the five techniques like silent sitting, story telling, prayers, group singing and group activities. An inspired teacher who is a true role model is essential for the effective functioning of this approach.

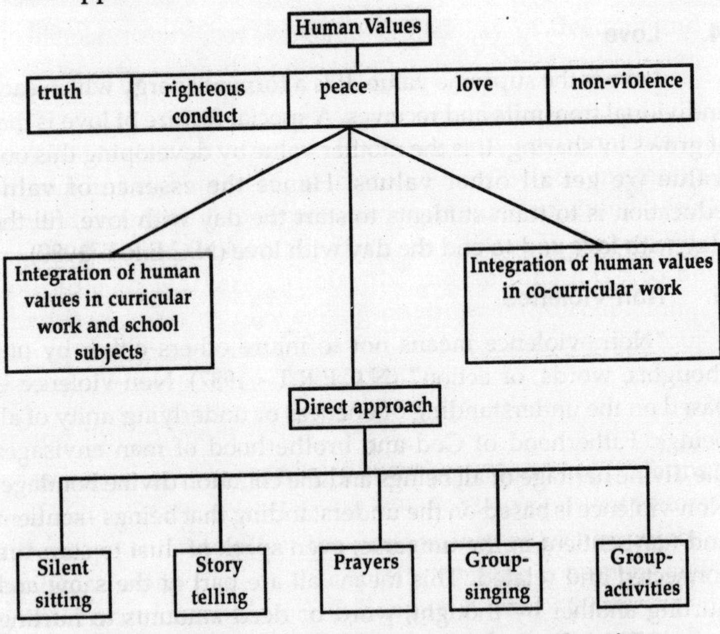

Chart - 3.1: **Approaches to human values in education**

Integrated Approach through Curricular Activities

In this approach, academic programmes and activities are utilized for inculcation of values. A trained teacher can apply his/her mind to identify and highlight values in academic subjects using various techniques. Two methods require special mention in this respect.

(i) Lesson plan preparation.

(ii) Integrating values in subjects.

Lesson Plan Preparation

Training in lesson plan preparation is a vital component in almost every teacher education programme. In this technique teachers are required to identify the core and sub values embedded in the curriculum portion intended to teach in the next class and prepare in advance various strategies, activities, and aids to elicit values. Here curriculum is used as a means to achieve the end of inculcation of human values in students.

Values are inherent in all subjects. For instance, teaching of life sciences and physical sciences help in the inculcation of various values such as keen observation, curiosity, love of nature, creativity and good habits. Mathematics help in the development of values like problem solving skill, self discipline, discrimination, commonsense, precision and thrift. Subjects like history, geography, and civics are useful in the development of values like tolerance, patriotism, love for cultural heritage, heroism, harmony, will power, perseverance, and qualities of a good citizen .Literature and languages help in the evolution of values such as aesthetic sense, truth, beauty, goodness, love, caring of other beings, value of wonderment, helpfulness, humility, non violence, peace and sense of unity.

Thus values inherent in academic subjects, if properly discovered and applied using lesson plan technique will help inculcation of values in students. May be the faith in the efficacy of this method can be a reason why value education failed to attract special emphasis till recently. The teacher training programmes provide training in lesson plan preparation exercises in all subjects. In this exercise teacher trainees master the art of identifying the objectives of each lesson and the methods available to attain these objectives. These objectives are related to values development. But the unfortunate thing is that only a limited number of teachers effectively utilize this method in their daily work. A vast majority of teachers neglect this daily lesson plan preparation method and take it for granted that whatever method they use will automatically develop values. The result is that we have a large number of "educated" youth with knowledge but without character. If teachers sincerely follow this method in their daily work, then without doing anything extra, education will succeed in producing value oriented generation. This points to the urgent need to motivate teachers to follow the daily preparation of lesson plans.

In this method teacher relates the current academic topic with values and uses the opportunity to inculcate those values. Assume a physics teacher is taking class about magnets. Here he can relate that an iron bit coming into contact with magnet may acquire qualities of magnet. Similarly friendship with good students will help to acquire good qualities and vice versa. The teacher may deviate from the academic subject for a few moments and relate it with some specific value. The advantage of this method is that special period for value education is not required. It goes along with academic exercise in a harmonious manner. But it is essential that the teacher should develop the value orientation needed to identify such opportunities in specific areas of the subject and the skill to tap it effectively. Now research is going on all over the world in this area. A number of illustrations of how to integrate or inter wind values in different academic subjects like mathematics, physical and natural sciences, statistics, economics, social studies , literature and languages etc are discussed by various researchers like Madhu Kapani(2000), Margarett Taplin(2004), and Lekshmi Seetharam et.al. (2005).

Integrated Approach Through Co-curricular Activities

School is a miniature society. In this method teachers consciously utilize co-curricular activities for value inculcation. Value eliciting activities can be planned in the Assembly hall, in play ground, in excursion trip, in free time etc. For instance, cultural activities like dance, drama, skit, role play, singing etc on value based topics help in value inculcation. Similarly play ground activities can also be tapped for value inculcation. Specially developed Value games are becoming popular and helpful in this respect. Since students are dynamic and enjoy games, this method ensures their full cooperation. A number of value games are discussed in book published by the Institute of Sathya Sai Education, India (2006). Various situations develop in the class can be utilized for the value inculcation. Using various methods in value education misdemeanors noted in students can be corrected (Margarett Taplin (2004). Co-Curricular activities like NCC, NSS, Scouts, various clubs, Associations, Forums etc provide immense opportunities for value inculcation. Cooperation, kindness, truthfulness, teamwork, leadership, service etc are some of the values which can be developed by these activities.

Direct Method

Direct method includes special period for value inculcation like moral science period, working of value clubs etc. A number of methods are available to elicit values. Five methods are very popular. Prayer/quotations, story telling, group singing, silent sitting, and group activities. Planned use of these methods is very effective in eliciting of values. Dr.R.Farmer and S.Farmer (2000) provide a good description of these methods.

Formation of a value club helps the institution to develop students who become good role models to others. Character formation is a time consuming process and requires sustaining programmes. Value club helps in this respect. A value club can be formed with 40 or 50 selected students who voluntarily come forward. A teacher who is inspired in value based living can become the 'teacher coordinator' of the Value club. He becomes the mentor of these students and act as the friend, philosopher and guide of the members. Necessary funds for the working can be raised with the help of Parent-Teacher Association. Club can plan and implement a number of activities for value inculcation. Some of the activities helpful in value inculcation are listed below:

(i) Debates on value based topics.

(ii) Essay competition on value topics.

(iii) Pick & speak-short elocution competitions.

(iv) Drawing competitions on value based topics.

(v) Recitation competition of value songs, generating patriotism, universal love and goodness.

(vi) Story telling &writing competitions on value topics.

(vii) Starting of manuscript magazines exclusively for value inculcation.

(viii) Organizing of value camps of short duration (one/two days).

(ix) Starting of value book corner in the library (old books in good condition can be collected free of cost from donors through a campaign).

(x) Starting of audio-visual club for value based movies, clippings etc.

(xi) Visiting of Orphanages, Old age Homes, Blind schools, Jails, etc.

(xii) Service activities.

(xiii) Value games.

(xiv) Silent sitting/meditation sessions.

(xv) Practicing of yoga methods.

(xvi) Interviewing and interactive sessions with value beacons in society (persons who put in to practice value based living and conducting humanitarian projects).

(xvii) Arranging of lectures on value topics.

Teacher As a Role Model

The most important and difficult part in value education demands that the teacher who is engaged in value inculcation programme should be a good role model. By practicing unity and purity in thought, word and deed he can easily ensure value inculcation in students.

Role of Parents

There are three pillars for a value education programme- they are students, teachers and parents. Hence awareness programmes on value based parenting play a crucial role in value inculcation programmes. Close co-operation between parents and teacher is imperative. Character formation requires long term effort and right environment in both schools as well as at home. Hence programmes like regular visits to students' home, parent meetings in the institution, etc., help values inculcation.

Conclusion

Along with development of skills required for earning a living, education should help the students to find the real meaning of "I". Along with knowledge of external world, students should acquire internal knowledge about them selves. Both types of explorations are essential for the fuller development of human beings. It is essential to find the ultimate goal of human existence-that is, attainment of existence, knowledge, bliss absolute.

Most of the ideas presented are taken from SSEHV(Sri Sathya Sai Education in Human Values) model developed by Sri Sathya Sai Seva Organisation, Prasanthi Nilayam, Puttaparthi, A.P, India. Detailed information about this model of Human values education can be obtained from publications of The Institute of Sathya Sai Education, Dhrmakshtra, Mahakali Caves Road, Andheri(East), Mumbai 400 093, India and other Institutes of sathya Sai Education in Human values all over the world.

Acknowledgement

This paper is indebted to the ideas generated by Sri Sathya Sai Baba and Sai Organisations all over the world. How ever for any mistakes or misinterpretations happened in the article the author alone is responsible and Sri Sathya Sai Organisation is not responsible in any manner. Also expresses deep gratitude to Dr. P.G. Thomaskutty, Reader, Dept. of Economics Mar Ivanios College, who permitted the presentation of this paper in the National Seminar on "Ethics and Values in Education" conducted in January 2007 at Trivandrum.

REFERENCES

1. Farmer R, and Farmer, S(2000): *Hand Book For Sai Teachers-The Sathya Sai Human Values Programme*, Institute of Human Values, Australia, Divine Print Publishers, Beenleigh 4207, Queensland, Australia.

2. Institute of Sathya Sai Education (2006): *Life is a Game Play it-90 Games Based on Human Values for Children and Teen agers*, Dharmakhetra, Mahakali Caves Road, Andheri East, Mumbai - 400 093, India.

3. Kapani, Madhu(2000): *Education in Human Values*, Sterling Publishers (p) Ltd., New Delhi.
4. Mitra Somenath (2003): *3 HV OF EHV-Sri Sathya Sai Education in Human Values*, Omkar Offset Printers, Bangalore.
5. N.C.E.R.T(1987): *A Working Model for the Inculcation of Human Values at the Various Stages of School Education*, Trivandrum.
6. Seetaram, Lekshmi and Seetharam K.E. (2005): *Values Integration for Developing Young Adults*, Institute of Sathya Sai Education, San Pedro, Phase 6, A5, Pacita Complex 1, San Pedro, Laguna, Philippines.
7. Sharma, Kalpana (2008): *An Assault on Dignity*, The Hindu Daily, Sunday Magazine, Dated 13-01-08.
8. Taplin, Margaret (2004): *Education in Human Values Through Mathematics*, Institute of Sathya Sai Education Limited, Suites 1517-1522,Two Pacific Place, 88 Queensway, Hong Kong.
9. Taplin, Margaret and Devi, Anita (2004): *To Teach, Not To Punish—A Practical Human Values Approach to Discipline*, Institute of Sathya Sai Education Limited, Suites 1517-1522, Two Pacific Place, 88 Queensway, Hong Kong.

4

Role of Teachers in Strengthening Values Education in India

Y. Bhaskaracharyulu & D. Pulla Rao

Introduction

Value education refers to a programme of planed educational action aimed at the development of value and character. Every action and thought of ours leaves an impression on our mind. These impressions determine in our behaviour at a given moment and our responses to a given situation. The sum total of all our impressions is what determines our character. The past has determined the present and even so the present i.e., our present thoughts and actions will shape our future. This is a key principle governing personality development. The human values are resolved having lasting impact necessary for bringing about change in thought and conduct, in the 21st century.

Values are socially accepted norms to evaluate object, person and situation that form part and parcel of society. Values system is the backbone of a unified society. Values may change from society to society and also from time to time. For example, every society abides by certain moral values and these values are accepted by all the societies as "Global Values".

Values are the windows of understanding society. It justifies action. Allport (1950) define "anything that yields a satisfaction (or provides a means for such satisfaction) is designated as value". Values are what people like or dislike, need, enjoy, desire or what their culture prescribes for them.

Values are imbibes by an individual through a process of conviction. Values contain the judgemental element in that they carry in an individual's ideas about what is right, good or desirable. Values are necessary not only for individuals but also for organizations, societies and nations for their sustenance and growth. Values are relative in nature. They differ from individual to individual, from organisation to organisation and from country to country.

Values are determined and influenced by the values cherished by the society. Values are not static, but change according to the change in society. There are two types of values.

1. Instrumental values like interests, wealth, prestige, etc.
2. Intrinsic values like health, honour, purity, etc.

Instrumental values cause confrontation, while intrinsic values caused harmony.

What is Value Education?

Value education is education for "becoming". It is an encounter with the total personality of the individual keeping in view all aspects of personality development - the intellectual, social and emotional, will and character. It involves developing sensitivity to and awareness of what is right, what is good, what is beautiful, ability to choose the right values in accordance with one's conception of highest ideals of life and internalising and realising them in thought and action (Seshadri, 1998).

The process of value education calls into play the three domains-knowing, feeling and doing. Not only should the learner be enabled to know the right and the good, but also to feel the appropriate emotions, concern and commitment and exercise the will to do the right thing. It is a process of interacting with the total human being with a view to develop capacities of reflective thinking and independent judgment on issues that are of critical concern to oneself and to humanity. It is a process of helping individuals to think freely and critically, to act responsibly and with courage and conviction. Eventually, it should given place to independent appraisal of a situation after rational deliberation and principled judgment.

Value education is not merely the cultivation of cognitive faculties, but also affective. One cannot merely give a lecture on values. Just as swimming cannot be taught merely by lecturing, but by leading the learner to jump into the water and help him in the practical art of swimming in the midst of water. Similarly, value education requires of the teacher, the ability to inspire the student to enter into the waters of life's situations and give him practical abilities and art of practicing values in concrete situations in life with an attitude:

- to seek honour and act with truth
- for independent thought and action
- towards a strong sense of responsibility
- towards friendship and cooperation
- towards willingness to assume responsibility (Joshi Kireet, 2000).

Relationship Between Education and Values

Education and values are the two sides of the same coin. They are interrelated. Education is the key that opens the doors of life. Education is widely accepted as the essential tool for the attainment of desired goal. It is the principal instrument in awakening the child to cultural heritage. The National Policy on Education (NPE-1986) rightly state that, "education is a unique investment in the present and for the future". Education has an acculturating role. It refines sensitivities and perceptions that contribute to national cohesion, scientific temper and independence of individual spirit – thus furthering the goals of socialism, secularism and democracy enshrined in our Constitution.

Classification of Values in Education

There are different methods of classification of values in education which are intimately associated with man. Some of which are: Biological values, Intrinsic values, Instrumental values, Health values, Recreational values and Spiritual values. Another system of classification of values are: Spiritual values, Material values, Intellectual values, Social values, Moral values, Political values, Economic values and Cultural values.

Whatever the system of classification all the values have inter-relationship with the different scientific systems and the educational implications of these values are best understood in the context of each branch of science which the science educator endeavors to teach.

Importance of Value Education

The present educational system, with all its complexities has proved to be deficient in so far as it neglects or does not give the deserving importance to values in human life. Thus human sufferings and sorrows are for ever on the increase in spite of the phenomenal explosion of knowledge. Values have become the neglected lot in the current educational system and consequently the maxim *"Education changeth man"* ceases to be meaningful or has almost lost its 'value'. "Education without vision is waste; education without value is crime; education without mission is life burden" Education in our life enables us to become comfortable and to look after our family well. But so far as the social progress is concerned, value-based education is an unavoidable necessity. If a nation is to be strong, then the character of the people of that nation needs to be elevated.

Values in Ancient India

In ancient India, the Vedas, the Upanishads, the epics manifested and upheld the values of Indian society. More importance was given to morality, honesty, duty, truth, friendship, brotherhood (Vasudhaika Kutumbam). They were the themes of Indian culture, literacy and Indian society. The pupil could learn the first lessons of duty, devotion, dedication and discipline. The life of Guru used to be the role model for his disciples. Education was closely allied to practical life. Imparting value education and reformation of the society were the solemn aims and objectives for the teachers of the ancient age. Respecting womenhood is the most important cherished value. Value based education was emphasised to promote eternal values among students. This was the type of education we had, till few decades back.

Present Scenario

The population in India has been constantly rising; it has crossed one billion by 2001 and stands at about 110 crores as on date. Due to the explosion of population, advancement in science and technology, knowledge expansion, medical knowledge in curing diseases, industrialisation, urbanisation, mobilisation, IT revolution, globalisation, and flow of western culture – the present society is rapidly changing and the life is centered round the wonders of science. Society is shaped by technical change that is turn, is shaped by society. It is going through modernisation process thereby human life is full of problems, anxiety and struggle and became helpless victim and so he is at the cross roads of modernisaton living in the midst of social, economic, political environmental and value crisis – which are all threatening the humanity in the society. Modernization has led to the change of life styles, thinking processes, traditions and cultural norms. Inequalities persist between rich and poor, men and women, urban and rural. Over consumerism, selfishness, materialistic complex detaching man from real values of life. In a world based on science and technology, it is education that determines the levels of property, welfare and security of the people.

Growing global poverty, pollution, hunger, diseases, unemployment, untouchability, caste system, child Labour, gender inequality, ill-treatment of womenhood, violence, disability, exploitation of natural resources are causing crisis on the globe – all these are making man to loose honesty, sincerity, morality and humanity and as such there is a great transition in human society. To remove the problems of the present era, inculcation of values among individuals and promotion of values in education are essential. For real development we need integrated human personalities. The present educational system has to be reviewed in view of all the above and to meet the challenges in future.

Recommendations of Various Commissions on Value–Oriented Education

It is gratifying to note that all the committees and Commissions on education appointed by the Union Government made a categorical recommendations in favour of value-oriented education. Eminent educationists gave their unstinted support to this worthy cause. A few were referred here for better understanding of importance of values in education.

Central Advisory Board of Education (1943-46) recommended that spiritual and moral education should be provided to children. The University Education Commission otherwise known as Radhakrishnan Commission (1948-49) also emphasized the need for moral and spiritual instruction at University stage. Sri Prakasa Committee (1959) categorically mentioned that there should be allocation of some periods in the school timetable for conscious and intentional teaching of moral education. The committee on emotional integration (1961) insisted on studying the Indian cultural values on compulsory basis. Kothari Commission (1964-66) stressed the instruction in moral, social and spiritual values at all levels of study. UNESCO (1972) suggested that educational system should encourage the promotion of values of world peace, international understanding and unity of mankind. The National Moral Education Conference (1981) in its first session resolved to inculcate moral and human values among students as a core subject and the content should include the common ethical teachings to highest the unity. National Policy on Education (1986) also stated that value education should be content based on heritage, national goals and cultivation of social and moral values. Union Ministry of Human Resource Development urged the educational institutions in 1988-89 to strengthen culture and values. The ministry also decided to review this in 1990 to strengthen the cultural and value education inputs in school education system. Acharya Ramamurthy Committee (1990) set up by Ministry of Human Resource Development to review the New Education Policy 1986 also stressed that review the child needs to be initiated not only with the world of knowledge and skills but also with values. The Parliamentary Standing Committee on Human Resource

Development (1999) observed that it was quite disappointing in the last few decades failed to achieve the results for making education as value-oriented one. But the reports of the above committees and commissions are obvious that there had been consensus of opinion regarding the inclusion of values in education system as a whole. In spite of these, values could not be introduced directly in our educational institutions. Thus it is high time to safeguard the present setup of values from further deterioration and degradation of the society.

Role of Teachers in Strengthening Value Education

The role of teachers is quite significant in the development of social values. Teachers are the real nation builders. It is the teaching community which moulds the future society. Teachers are the section of society who can influence the future generation towards a positive attitude with a healthy value base. The extent of the influence, which a teacher casts upon the students, is well known and understood. The teacher is the role model for the student and what they imbibe gets multiplied subsequently in the society.

A conference was held in Shimla in May 1981 recommended, that value orientation should be the central focus of education and that the teacher should be given the necessary training in the effective methods of development of values among students. The national policy of Education (1986) stated that "The status of the teacher reflects the socio-cultural ethos of a society; it is said that no people can rise above the level of their teachers". A teacher, once he accepts teaching as profession cannot make compromises with life because he has to realise that he is playing with the future of the nation. Through the mastery of his subjects and primary role is to build character. The products of the institutions will be future decision-makers and they can hardly forget the source, which has made them what they are.

Teachers themselves should not be ignorant of basic human values. In fact, they should be the living embodiment of all the human values, both preaching and practicing, more the latter than the former. It is the teacher who can lead us from darkness to light, thereby, from untruth to truth and finally take us from the stages of death to immortality. Guru is an incarnation of God in human form for students. While God is universal, the guru is said personal in relationship. Kalidas, the ancient poet, speaks of the guru as, "He converts darkness into light and makes the invisible God visible".

Gandhiji also highlighted the pivotal role of teachers stating that he always felt that the true textbooks for the pupils were his teacher. Teachers in colleges have themselves to be examples of what they require the students to be. Men in authority who exhort others to follow the path of love and cooperation have themselves to practice those virtues. Teachers should put into practice what they preach to the students. They should guide the students properly, as they are the most important assets of an educational institution. The ultimate factor in education for all times and in all places is the teacher.

The teacher is trusted by the students, parents and the society as a guru with all the hallowed association of that word and this trust must be repaid by honest service. He should discharge his duty of instructing and inspiring the students so that they develop their talents and advance in the perfection of their skills.

Teachers have to be ever inspiring models. In fact they are life long students engaged not in mere study but immersed in practice too. Only a lamp that burns can light another lamp. It may be worth-while here the views of some educationists who have spoken on similar line. The report of the working group for preparing a scheme for Revitalisation of Teacher Education (1986) also says that the teacher should practice values in his own conduct and behaviour. The practice of values by the teacher is more important than their mere inclusion in the syllabus. Likewise Ramji (1973) writes that above all, personal examples of the teacher who endeavours to practice fundamental values such as truth, universal love and service to humanity and who creates loving and healthy atmosphere in the classroom by his gentle and kind behaviour is perhaps the most important factor in any value-oriented education in the education institutions.

There are a large number of studies, which highlight the role of the teacher's expectations in the development of the students. Students achieve what the teacher expects them to achieve, for example Rosenthal and Jacobson (1966) found that teachers' expectations determined pupils I.Q. gain. This phenomenon was termed by them as a 'self-fulfilling prophecy'. Likewise, Nagalakshmi (1987) found that students 'academic achievement' corresponds to their teachers' expectations. The teachers' place in a society is that of a visionary architect whose mission evokes universal respect.

We want our teachers value-oriented because we want them to be rightly equipped as vehicles of values for the benefit of our children and youth. By this very nature, the teacher is a transmitter, a messenger, a carrier. Our determination of what he has to transmit will depend upon what we determine to be valuable for our children and youth.

In our country and culture a teacher is still held in great honour and respect. He is considered as a fountain of all knowledge and a source of great ideals. He is the torchbearer to society. Students look up to him with faith and hope and they seek his counsel in matters temporal or transcendental. Hence if the teacher has a keen sense of values and has faith in the higher purpose of life, he can guide the whole generation through his versatile personality.

Dr. Radhakrishnan and Rabindranath Tagore are examples of great teachers who influenced this country with their philosophy of value-oriented education. Radhakrishnan (1965) states "What the teachers do, the students follow, so they set the example. Teachers by their conduct should be an example to the student".

All knowledge comes from the teacher is the belief of students in the class. Since our children are not turned to independent study from childhood, they believe whatever the teacher says as absolute truth and nothing less than truth. They do not question the authority of the teacher. Hence, if good ideas and values are to be perpetuated and inculcated in the younger generation, they must come from the mouth of teachers in their classes at all the levels of education. Whenever the teacher finds that these values are violated he should point out the dame to the pupils and guide them in changing their behaviour. He should also evaluate the behaviour of the students in relation to the values from time to time, but he should use this evaluation not for grading the pupil but for guiding them for better development of values. The practice of the values by the teacher is more important than mere inclusion in the syllabus.

In the works of Gokak (1985) "Teacher's life-style, manner and substances of his teaching should coincide. The student has a right to expect his teachers, to lead a good life. A teacher-educator may be specialist or a scholar, but these are not central to his personality. The centrality lies in the fact of his being primarily a seeker of truth who is eager to share his passion for truth with the young, and to make them familiar with the mode of living which helps to be in tune with such a pursuit."

Conclusion and Suggestions

Education is becoming day-by-day more or less materialistic and the value traditions are being slowly given up. The modern India is being educated mainly with the bread and butter aim of education and as a result most of our graduates run after money, power, and comforts without caring for any values: moral, religious and spiritual. Education is being deliberately neglected in our educational system. The teacher is the principal agency for implementing educational programmes at various levels. The role of the teacher in this context is not going to be easy and smooth. The teacher has to perform two functions. First, has to play an important role in the transformation of knowledge based on the syllabus and secondly, he should be a key factor in the transformation of our value system.

Teachers may motivate, communicate, illustrate, activate and inculcate the values among the students either by curricular or co-curricular activities.

— Today's youths are worried and depressed about their unemployment. The teacher may guide them to select a right vocation for their future development.

— Good manners verily are likely the oil that helps to keep the machine of the human society running smoothly.

— Cleanliness is next to Goodliness. So, teachers may stress this concept through proper examples.

— The teachers may advise the students to eradicate the social evils like *purdha*, dowry, child marriage, untouchability, begging etc.

— The teacher may give grater emphasis on peace, love, secularism, unity, cooperation, cultural enrichment, national unity and creativity.

— The teacher may allot more time for work experience, music and art and socially useful productive work.

— The teacher may develop leadership skills and responsibilities and promote positive leisure activities.

— Worship and prayer important activities of the daily work of the school. Teaching of moral instruction may be made so interesting and effective that students would be able to accept the subject voluntarily.

— Yoga and meditation programmes may be encouraged by teachers.

— Teachers may develop a sense of self-respect and esteem their pupils by respecting them as individuals of unique abilities.

— Teachers may give opportunities and scope to implement innovations and new ideas.

— Today most of the students follow the hedonistic principle of obtaining maximise pleasure with minimise work. Teachers should create positive work ethics among the students.

— The teachers should emphasise on "man-making" and not "money-making" education.

REFERENCES

1. Gokak, V.K. and Rohedikar. (1982): Teachers Handbook for the Course in Human Values, Sri Satya Sai Bal Vikas Trust, Prasanthi Nilayam.

2. Joshi Kireet. (2000): Education at Crossroads, The Mother's Institute of Research, New Delhi.

3. Kamalakar Mishra. (2003): "Value Education: A Suggested Programme for Teachers and Parents", Journal of Value Education, 3 (1), pp. 27-38.

4. Radhakrishna, S. (1965): The Present Crises of Faith, An Orient Paper Back, New Delhi.

5. Report of the University Education Commission. (1948): Ministry of Education, Government of India, New Delhi.

6. Report of the Secondary Education Commission. (1952-53): Ministry of Education, Government of India, New Delhi.

7. Report of the Kothari Commission. (1964-66): Ministry of Education, Government of India, New Delhi.

8. Report of the Indian Education Commission. (1971): Ministry of Education, Government of India, New Delhi.

9. Rosenthal, R and Jacobson, W. (1966): Teacher's Expectations and Determinants of Pupils IQ Gains, Psychological Reports.

10. Seshadri, C. (1998): "Education in Values-Why and How"? In N. Venkataiah (ed.) Value Education, A.P.H. Publishing Corp., New Delhi.

11. William, R.M. (1968): In Encyclopedia of Social Humanist Ethics.

5

Religious and Moral Education

Problems and Remedies in Imparting at Various Levels of Educational Institutions

V. Chandrasekaran

Introduction

"Religion is one of the necessities of human life and mankind can never do without it"

—Arnold Toynbee

Value is a conception of the desirable and it is in terms of this conception that we make our choices between means and between ends. (Ghose, D.N. -2005) Value means a thing which we appreciate. Each value is uniquely expressible – both by individuals and by groups. All values are cultural products. More specifically speaking, we get our values from our experience with the elements of our culture. Man is always interested in the relative importance of or usefulness of things, of courses, of actions, of principles, of conduct, of ideas etc.

There are several kinds of values, such as physical, economic, social, ethical, utilitarian, religious, intellectual, aesthetic, recreational, instrumental, intrinsic, relative and absolute. Among all these, religious values are controversial. It has been considered as a personal affair. It cannot be and should not be imposed on anyone. Each person should be free to adopt any religion he/she likes. So it is a difficult task to make religious education a part of curriculum in any democratic country like in India which is a secular country. So, it has been considered that introduction of religious study in educational institution would be fraught with grave dangers and consequences. Secularism demands that no religion should be taught in the institution run by the government. This is also a hard fact that diverse forms of religions are practiced in India. Inspite of grave dangers involved in introducing religious study, there is an urgent need for imparting religious and moral education in the country.

Education aims at all round development of an individual-physical, mental, emotional, social, moral, and spiritual. But modern education helps only in physical and intellectual development of man. Physical and intellectual development without moral can bring havoc in the world. (Bhatia, K.K. etal – 1981).

Importance of Religious and Moral Education

Due to influence of various factors and mainly due to materialistic attitude, people are drifting away from religion. Their attitude is becoming more and more materialistic. Human life has become so mechanical that hardly anytime is left for religious chores. Earlier religious and moral education were taught to the children by their parents. But now, in this busy world parents have no time to teach. The secular policy of the government also does not permit the institutions to impart religious and moral education to the children. The lack of religious and moral education has resulted in indiscipline, violence and weakening of social and moral values in the younger generation. The concept of secularism is wrongly understood. A secular state does not imply an irreligious state. In reality, a secular state does not identify itself with any particular religion. It does never mean that a secular state is an anti-religious or irreligious state. In a secular state religious freedom is given to everybody and no discrimination is made in the name of religion. So it is not proper to neglect religious and moral education in educational institutions in the name of secularism and democracy. So secularism, if viewed truly, does not stand in the way of introducing moral and religious education in our schools and colleges.

Modern man thinks that religion has become the thing of the past and they do not feel any need of introducing religion in educational institutions. But it is wrong to think so. No doubt science has given us comforts in abundance; it has broadened our outlook, but at the same time it has starved our soul. Man is not merely a body, he has a soul also. He can't enjoy the material comforts unless his soul feels inner peace and happiness. There is no enmity between science and religion. Educating man on the basis of scientific knowledge alone will be meaningless if it does not fulfill the spiritual needs of him.

It has been also raised that whether morals can be taught effectively without any reference to religion, because religion and morality are two sides of the same coin. There is natural correlation between the moral values and teachings of great religion of the world. Truthfulness, honesty, consideration for others, reverence for old age, kindness to animals and compassion for the needy and the sufferings etc. are some of the morals and these human values are also taught by all the religions of the world.

Religious and moral education plays a prominent role in the formation of character. Character formation is considered to be one of the chief aims of education but this aim stands defeated if moral and religious education is not introduced in schools and colleges. (Bhatia, K.K., etal - 1981).

Recommendations of Moral and Religious Education by Various Committees

Sri Pariahs Committee on Religious and Moral Instruction (1959-60) has made the following recommendations:

1. Need for teaching moral and spiritual values.
2. Removing the defects of home.
3. Silent meditation.

4. Preparation of useful books for all stages – primary to university.
5. Co-curricular activities.
6. Emphasis on good manners.

A.L. Mudaliar Commission on Secondary Education (1952-53) has also recommended the following things to impart value education:

1. Morning assembly with prayer
2. Talks by suitable persons on value education
3. Religious instruction on voluntary basis.

The Kothari Education Commission (1964-66) has recommended the following important suggestions:

1. Central and state governments should take necessary steps to introduce education in moral, social and spiritual values in the institutions under their direct control and privately managed institutions.
2. Suitable teachers should be recruited.
3. Some periods should be allotted for moral education.
4. Periods of moral education should be taken by general teachers not by special teachers. They should be trained by training institutes for this purpose.
5. The commission recommends both direct and indirect methods for moral education. (Dash, D.N. – 2004)

Imparting of Religious and Moral Education

Moral and religious education can be imparted both directly and indirectly. Direct moral education can be provided through books, classroom lessons and preaching of moral and ethical values. Indirect moral education means that the children should be provided with such opportunities as enable them to learn and imbibe moral values incidentally and indirectly.

Primary Level

- School assembly in the morning for prayer and group singing.

- Life-stories of religious leaders should be included in the syllabus for language teaching.
- Use of audio-visual materials showing religions of the world should be used in the teaching of Geography.
- Two periods a week should be allotted to tell stories from the great religions.
- Development of service attitude among the children should be inculcated.
- Team spirit and character building should be inculcated through sports.

Secondary and Higher Secondary Level

- Morning assembly with two minutes silence followed by readings from great literatures or addressing by eminent persons.
- World religions in the curriculum of social studies, languages and general readings.
- An hour a week for moral instruction.
- All important festivals of all religions should be celebrated.
- Social service activities in the extra-curricular activities should teach the students the dignity of manual labour, love of humanity, patriotism and self-discipline.
- Participation in games and sports should be made compulsory for inculcating the sex hygiene.
- Qualities of character and behaviour of students should form an essential part of the over-all assessment of student's performance at school.

Higher Education Level

- Students should be encouraged to meet in groups for silent meditation in the morning.
- A general study of different religions should be an essential part of general education course in degree classes. For this, Dr. Radhakrishnan commission gave the following recommendations:

(a) In the first year of the degree course, lives of the great religious and spiritual leaders like Mahaveera, Buddha, Confucious, Zoroaster, Socrates, Jesus, Sankara, Ramanuja, Madhawa, Mohammad, Kabir, Nanak and Gandhi should be taught.

(b) In the second year, some selections of universal-character from the scriptures of the world should be studied.

(c) In the third year, the central problems of the philosophy of religion should be considered.

- A post graduate course in comparative religion should be introduced. Post graduate courses should be started in the fields of humanities and social sciences.
- A fairly long period of social service should be introduced by all universities.

(Bhatia, K.K. et. al – 1981)

Problems and Remedies in Imparting Religious and Moral Education

At present managements & teachers do not like to involve in the controversial issues. Teachers should be clear about their mission and show right direction to the students in this issue. They feel touching the religion and caste system will be a problematic one. It is not necessary for a teacher to degrade or underestimate any religion or community. They may teach the right things and dogmas in the religions. A teacher should be a majestic person and lover of all faith and religions. Even he may quote the good deeds of the followers of atheism.

If a teacher who belongs to a particular religion or community gives more emphasis for the religion he belongs, may arise certain problems in the institution. Because of this most of the government or government aided institutions do not like to touch any aspect of the religion. Teachers and Management of the institutions feel a spark from the religious controversial side may engulf the whole atmosphere. We do not let out many good things at the cost of petty issues.

A proper guideline should be given to educational institutions for imparting religious and moral education. From the prayer in the morning to the closure of the school many good things, habits, actions should be inculcated among the students. We may notice many students and teachers those who belong to different religion and faith may be thick friends. Why can't we inculcate good things from different religions and make them proud of their own religion? But there should not be any degradation or underestimation of any religion. All faiths should be respected. As recommended by Secondary Education Commission (1952-'53), religious and moral education may be taught on voluntary basis among the teachers and students. (Dash, B.N. -2004). It has also been suggested by Prakasha Committee that qualities of character and behavior of students should form an essential part of the overall assessment of student's performance at school. But in the schools and colleges we are simply giving conduct certificate as good or satisfactory. All the good characters and their good habits and services should be enlisted in the certificate in brief without any bias and prejudices. Small things and petty matters may be neglected but rough behaviours and anti-social activities of a student should be warned severely. Punishments should be mild and make them to change their attitudes in a proper perspective through moral and religious education.

Many students from different religions join in private institutions especially run by different kinds of minorities and appreciate their service. Without any prejudice they move with all the students of different religions. So different faith or different religions among the students are not a barrier for imparting religious education. Some autonomous colleges included Ethics as a part of curriculum. So the moral and religious education should be considered by eminent educationists and the government to include in the syllabus directly or indirectly.

Conclusion

Introduction of moral and religious education in schools and colleges does not mean that principles and practices of a particular religion should be taught. Our present system of education fails to form the character of students because no effort is being made to cultivate moral and spiritual values. So religious and moral education is very much essential for the development of true humanitarianism and improvement of moral, cultural, social and democratic qualities. If character formation is to be the aim of education, provision of moral and religious education must be made in educational institutions.

REFERENCES

1. Aggarwal,J.C., (1977) — *'Introduction of Free India'*, Arya Book Depot, New Delhi.
2. Bhatia,K.K., et. al. (1981) — *"Contemporary Problems of Indian Education'*, Parkash Brothers, Luthiana.
3. Dash, B.N., (2004) — *'A New Approach to Teachers and Education in the Emerging Indian Society,'* Neelkamal Publications Pvt. Ltd., Hyderabad.
4. Dash, B.N., (2004) — *'Trends and Issues in Indian Education'*, Dominant Publishers and Distributors, New Delhi.
5. Ghose,D.N., (2005) — *'A Textbook of Value Education'*, Dominant Publishers and Distributors, New Delhi.

6

The Role of Family Life Education in Impeding the Spread of the Pandemic HIV/AIDS

Mary George & P. G. Thomaskutty

Introduction

HIV/AIDS is prevalent in much of the developing and developed countries. Its spread is more rapid in developing world. It causes the loss of mature population and globally it is the forth most common cause of death. The virus affect mostly the age group of 15-50 years (sexually active), though it affects other groups too. This age group is economically active and under normal circumstances people of this age group is least likely to be ill or die. Cost of antiretroviral therapies (ART) to reverse or slow down the disease progression is so high that it is inaccessible for common man. The cost is estimated to be around US $ 8,000 to 11,000 (approximately Rs. 3,68,000 to Rs. 5,06,000) per annum. Apart from the hardships of getting care and treatment, the tribulations arise from this epidemic is manifold. AIDS is a peculiar disease where there is social stigma and the infected and affected (close relatives) face discrimination.

Unlike many epidemic diseases in the past, HIV/AIDS is not spread by mere casual contact between individuals. As it is now well known, the virus is transmitted only through direct exposure to the body fluids of an infected person, as can occur during sexual intercourse or from sharing needles or during pregnancy from infected mother to her child. In order to prevent transmission of HIV will involve addressing deeply rooted social and cultural values prevailing in a society.

Family Life Education

Non formal family life education is as old as the institution of family itself. The nature and content of family life education varied according to customs and traditions of the society. In these days the term family life education is often ill-understood or miss represented. It is often defined in a narrow sense to represent se education. In fact the term family life education has a deeper meaning and it embrace a comprehensive and elaborate dimension consisting of education embracing the whole of human personality in its successive stages of growth (Oswald Dijkstra 1987 p. 7).

Family life education should focus attention on teaching the target group to acquire knowledge, skill, attitudes and values that go into the making of the right kind of relationship enabling them to pursue a meaningful and productive life in a civilized society. Sex education is an integral part of family life education. We should reconcile with the fear of a large section of the society who have the apprehension that se education means an attempt to teach sexual techniques which may motivate young boys and girls to indulge in immoral activities (CBCI 1992 National Secretariat).

Need and Importance

Researchers and planners are unanimous in the need for combating this menace. ABC- Abstinence, Be Faithful and Condom use are the options discussed widely as measures to control the spread of HIV/AIDS. In this article we try to highlight the merits of the second method- Be faithful (B) and underline the need for proper value education to younger generation. There should be proper instructions in the class room on human sexuality. There is need for well formulated value education in curriculum at all levels of education. Appropriate value inclination will produce positive dividends by generating healthy attitude towards sex and sexuality.

Properly designed sex education classes will help young people to develop a positive attitude towards sex and sexuality at the same time help them cherish on core values and ethos of the community in which they live. Family life education with due emphasis on sex education will play a very positive role in impeding the spread of the killer pandemic HIV/AIDS. Gracious Thomas observes that, although sex is the most universal and powerful drive in human beings that creates curiosity in man from very early infancy, no effort has been made to teach the young about the facts of life. Even if one wants to impart appropriate knowledge on the subject, it is extremely difficult to find reliable information on sex, as whatever is available to us today is only spotty and incomplete (Gracious Thomas 1995 p. 182).

Guiding Principles

The Family Life Education Programme should be respectful of traditions and value system of the society and should be acceptable to all stake holders namely parents, students and teachers. In present day situation parents are highly concerned about the various threats to family system emerging from changes taking place in the society at large and are eager to maintain the closeness, warmth and solidarity of the their traditional family set-up. In order to achieve the goal of healthy family relationship, emphasis should be laid on the importance of human person and his ability to relate. (Oswald Dijikstra 1988) This ability needs to e developed by creating in the students an awareness of the numerous relationships, within and out side the family, which help him/her to grow to maturity and through which he/she can help others to grow. Warmth relationships promote family unity and solidarity. The content of family education should be presenting the role of love (*agape*) in promoting healthy family relation and to humanize sex. Family life education programme should help the target group to develop right kind of values.

Objectives of Family Life Education

Family life education should be comprehensive in nature and should aim at the integrated development of the personality.

- It should empower them to resist any kind of invasion on their sexual autonomy.
- It should help them to acquire deeper insight on the physical, mental, emotional, social, cultural and spiritual aspects of se and sexuality.
- The course content should be comprehensive providing true and factual information about sex and sexuality and should be sufficient enough to remove myth and misinformation which they may have acquired from peer group or from unscientific literature.
- It should help them to acquire and foster healthy and responsible interpersonal relationship.
- It should make young people proud of their sex and to imbibe the spirit of gender equality.
- It should provide an occasion to students to develop ethical, social, cultural and spiritual values which will serve as guide to the individual in personal, family and social relationships.
- It should help them to foster positive values in life and to respect others especially from opposite sex and to maintain healthy interpersonal relationship to the opposite sex.

A Value Loaded View of Human Sexuality

There are various views on human sexuality based on anthropology, biology, sociology, psychology, history and religion. Some prefer to put sex as a mere instinct like any other instinct. Such a view will degrade human beings to the level of animals. A mature view on sexuality may be the one which recognize the fact that sexuality is the gift of God for human beings to strengthen and foster family life. Such an inference will help us to arrive at a conclusion that sexual life outside marital tie is an artifact. This proposition will help us arrive at take more concrete position that is premarital and extramarital sex is unnatural as well as abnormal.

Nature of Family Life Education in the Context of the HIV/AIDS

All family life and sex education programme should start from the above premise ie. Sexual life outside marital tie is an artifact. It should be taught that discussion and practice of any sexual act between any persons other than legally married couple is a taboo and an unethical act. Couples should always remain faithful to their lawful partners. *Be faithful* should be the *mantra* chanted and practiced by couples. In family, being human persons, partners should be tuned to search for something more permanent, more expressive of their personal involvement: lasting communion, love, trust and sympathy. It should be emphasized that human sexuality is designed to be experienced in the context of human relationship. While duly recognizing the psychological aspects of human sexuality the spiritual and moral aspect should not be understated. Emphasis should also e paid on educating the society in preserving and practicing the cherished values pertaining to sex and sexuality. Educating youths on matters related to HIV/AIDS, its spread and consequences will give an opportunity for them take proper decisions in matters like sex.

Conclusion

Properly designed family life education programme will help young people to develop a positive attitude towards sex and sexuality at the same time helps them to cherish on core values and ethos of the community in which they live. Family life education with due emphasis on sex education will play a very positive role in impeding the spread of the killer pandemic HIV/AIDS.

REFERENCES

1. Alan Guttmacher Institute (2001): Teenage Sexual and Reproductive Behaviour in Developed Countries; Can More Progress be Made? New York: The Alan Guttmacher Institute available at: http://www.guttmacher.org
2. CBCI (1992): Family Life Education Programme National Secretariat., Bangalore.
3. Gracious Thomas (1995): AIDS and Family Education, Rawat Publication, New Delhi.

4. Oswald Dijkstra (1988): Family as Church CBCI Commission for Laity, Department of Family, National Family Secretariat, Bangalore.

5. Oswald Dijkstra (1987): A Christian Response to the Gift of Human Sexuality, CBCI Commission for Laity, Department of Family, National Family Secretariat, Bangalore.

7

Proverbs as a Means for Inculcating Values in Students

Smitha. S. Nair

Introduction

"The growing concern over the erosion of values and an increasing cynicism in society has brought to focus the need for adjustment in the curriculum in order to make education a powerful tool for the cultivation of social and moral values".

(National Policy on Education- 1986).

There is a substantial erosion of values in our age. As a result the fabric of society is being torn. Respect is a thing of the past, love is a rare virtue, honesty is a quality of characters in legends, tolerance is a quality of enshrined in our constitution to teach rather than to practice, and patriotism is a quality of men in the past and so on. So there is a great need for value education in modern age to provide direction for personal, emotional, social, cultural, moral and spiritual development of individuals [Sharma -2003].

Values are endlěss beliefs that a specific mode of conduct or state of existence is personally or socially preferable to an opposite or converse mode of conduct. Along with this is the need to focus on what is right and what is wrong. Thus values are beliefs about what is right and wrong and what is important in life [Antony –

2003]. There are moral values, social values, religious values etc. Education which is intended to cultivate values which we need to lead a good and effective life in society as a human being is known as value education.

Values are our subjective reactions to the world around us. They guide and mold our options and behavior. Values have three important characteristics. First, values are developed early in life and are very resistant to change. Values develop out of our direct experiences with people who are important to us, particularly our parents. Values rise not out of what people tell us, but as a result how they behave toward us and others. Second, values define what is right and what is wrong. Notice that values do not involve external, outside standards to tell right or wrong; rather, wrong, good or bad are intrinsic. Third, values themselves cannot be proved correct or incorrect, valid or invalid, right or wrong. If a statement can be proven true or false, then it cannot be a value. Values tell what we should believe, regardless of any evidence or lack thereof [Antony – 2004].

Values Through Proverbs

Proverb (from the Latin proverbium) is a simple and concrete saying popularly known and repeated, which expresses a truth based on common sense or the practical experience of mankind. They are often metaphorical. A proverb that describes a basic rule of conduct may also be known as a maxim. If a proverb is distinguished by particularly good style, it may be known as an aphorism.

Proverbs are often borrowed from different languages and cultures, and sometimes come down to the present through more than one language. Both the Bible and medieval Latin have played a considerable role in distributing proverbs across Western Europe and even further.The study of proverbs is called Paremiology (from Greek 'paremia' = proverb) and can be dated back as far as Aristotle.

Proverbs have become an integral part of peoples' lives. To the most credulous members of society proverbs and proverbial expressions are the accumulated knowledge of the ages, the voice of history etc. [http://www.deccanherald.com]. According to Soklov, proverbs are brief aphorisms, applicable to various aspects of life, which have become turns of colloquial speech.

Proverbs and idioms tell much about people's traditional ways of experiencing reality, about the expected ways of doing things, values and warnings, rules and wisdoms that the elders want to impress on the minds of their young. [http://www.philosophy.su.se/texter /valueofscience.htm].

The word proverb is a sentence which, in time, has become part of the national heritage through widespread or frequent use. Most proverbs express some fundamental truth or describe basic rules of behavior which are often closely related to those values we consider as the basis of our culture, as the "marble pillars" of our personal and common beliefs [http://www.valuesofthewise.com]. Proverbs of cultures living close to each other often happen to present great aspects in common. At the same time, sometimes nuances of meanings and understatements, characterize our countries. As it comes, proverbs happen to represent our unity and our diversity, underlining the richness and uniqueness of our culture [http://www.haworthpress.com].

Applying Proverbs in a Chemistry Class

The application of proverbs in a chemistry class involves two aspects:

1. Pedagogic Aspect

Chemistry is a method and habit of thought and the training on skills and teaching techniques should be selected accordingly. As we view Chemistry teaching for the future, we need to consider students and their goals in a different light than in the past. It should be well closely linked with pupil's emotions and common interests. A thorough and basic knowledge in Chemistry should be provided to students at the specific levels of education. Teaching Chemistry should be well closely linked to the practical aspects of life involving community resources.

Today Chemistry teaching is mainly centered on the verbal presentation of textual material without giving due weightage to innovative approaches and teaching through experience. Teaching Science in general and Chemistry in particular in classrooms is a dull and uninteresting experience for students who lack passion for the subject. Too many facts in the form of reactions, properties, preparation, uses, etc. are presented which make it difficult for the student to grasp and assimilate the right perspective. Over a period of time the teacher also loses interest and enthusiasm, leading to monotony in teaching. Under these circumstances, attracting the attention of the students and engaging their minds needs innovative teaching methods. Any novel approach in classroom teaching, even if its impact is marginal, is to be welcomed.

Teaching Chemistry using Proverbs will impart knowledge in an interesting manner relating to the real life and daily experience of children. Such an approach gives education an outlook of informal education. The familiarity with proverbs and riddles gives them self-confidence and moves them forward to deal with more complex ideas and ideals with more enthusiasm. The judicious selection and use of proverbs in educational process will give pupils chances to express themselves spontaneously through varied kinds of activities and mental operations [http://valuesandproverbs.tripod.com].

2. Imparting Value Education

Spiritual and moral values are learned and caught by the younger generation from parents, teachers, and adults in general in many different ways, some through intentional teaching and some unconsciously. Therefore, we are never able to totally evaluate the impact or effect of the impression left on the young, absorbing mind. Teaching values using proverbs leaves a message in a brief amount of time and space, and often with lasting effect. One unconsciously memorizes the spoken or written proverb, saying, or Scripture text, only to have the lesson retaught many times later in life as well. Proverbs are effective teaching tools. They do not lecture, but rather, convey a concept or value with few words and an easy recall due to their profound simplicity. Each proverb has its own bit of wisdom, and its application in life can often be helpful. Proverbs or sayings are memorized easily, and they teach again and again. This helps a person to adopt that value as one's own. Proverbs helps to unobtrusively enforce; and pictures develop an appreciation for the values parents want to instill in their impressionable children [http://ncert.nic.in].

It is not necessary that separate classes/periods should be there in a school for imparting value education. Teachers can impart value education through their subjects, whether it is Language, Mathematics, Physics or Chemistry. The only thing is that teachers should be efficient enough to incorporate value education through their subjects (hidden-curriculum) without hindering the pedagogic part. The following examples illustrates how an efficient teacher can effectively use proverbs as an important pedagogic tool as well as an effective aid for imparting value education to students in a chemistry class [http://www.ramakrishna.org].

Proverb (1)

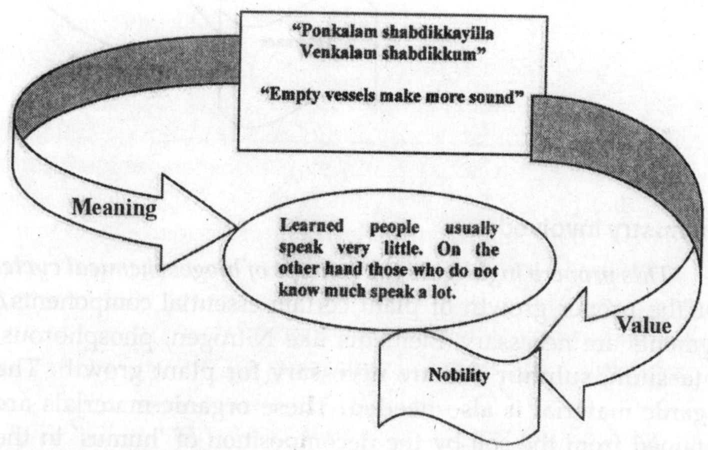

Chemistry Involved

This proverb highlights the chemical inertness of gold as well as the sonorous nature of Bronze.

Chemically, gold is rather an inert metal. It has been valued for its 'nobility', that is, for its resistance to chemical attack of air, moisture, carbon dioxide and even most of the acids (the oxidation potential of gold is extremely low being -1.2 volts). Bronze is obtained by alloying copper with tin. It is a particularly sonorous metal (it makes a ringing sound) as it is used to make bells and cymbals because of the clear ringing sound it produces when it is struck.

Proverb (2)

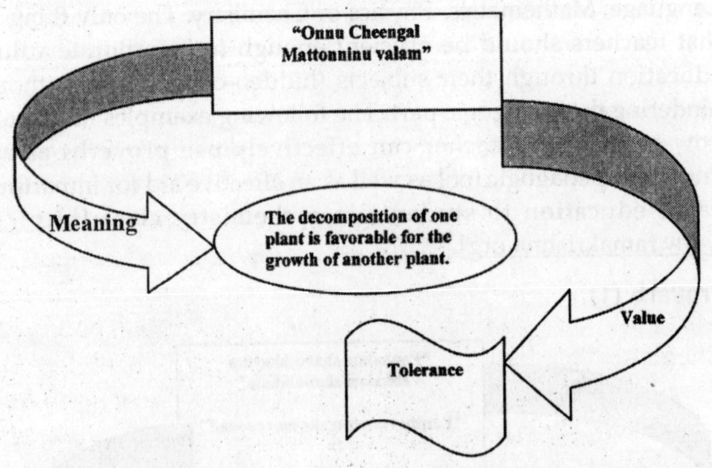

Chemistry Involved

This proverb highlights the concept of biogeochemical cycle. For the proper growth of plant certain essential components/ elements are necessary. Elements like Nitrogen, phosphorous, potassium, sulphur etc. are necessary for plant growth. The organic material is also needed. These organic materials are obtained from the soil by the decomposition of 'humus' in the soil. Humus is obtained by the gradual decomposition of fresh and dried leaves that fall on ground. Decomposition of humus (leaf mould) is a natural fertilizer. It is the most useful medium for raising seedlings and root growth. It makes soil porous by separating clay particles.

Proverb (3)

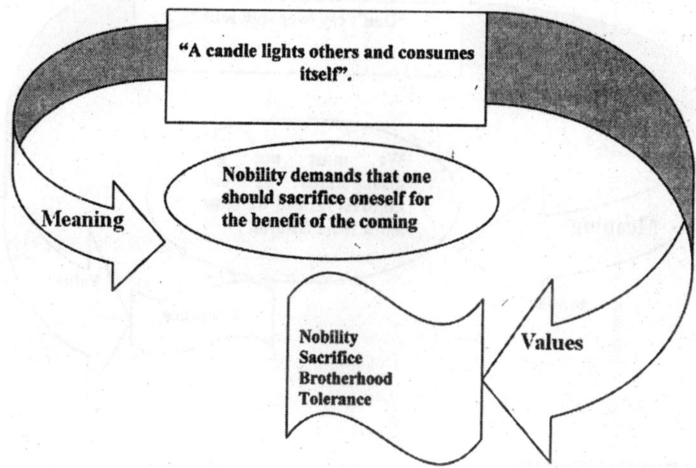

Chemistry Involved

This proverb highlights the Chemistry of candle flame. The candle flame is a small chemistry laboratory. When we light a candle, the wax in and near the wick melts. The wick absorbs the liquid wax and pulls it upward by a process called capillarity. The heat of the flame vaporizes the wax, and it is the wax vapors that burns- a chemical reaction which releases energy in the form of light and heat. The wax is a complex chemical compound of carbon and hydrogen. The process of burning is simply the combination of the wax with the oxygen in the air.

Proverb (4)

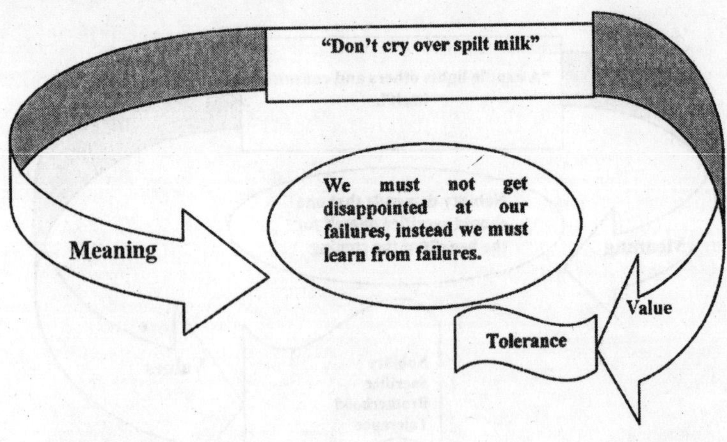

Chemistry Involved

This proverb highlights the chemistry of spilling of milk when it gets boiled. Milk is composed of water, carbohydrate, fat, protein, minerals and vitamins. It is an emulsion in which particles of fat globules are dispersed in water. When milk is boiled water vapor gets trapped in the creamy upper layer and pressure builds up in the boiling milk so that the vapor pressure raises the creamy layer and the milk pushes the creamy layer out and milk spills out.

Likewise, an efficient teacher can judiciously use common proverbs during her classroom teaching as part of her subject and can help a lot to implement values in her students. Such an approach will help the students in retaining what they have learnt and to have familiarity with our rich folk literature also.

Conclusion

One of the very important aims of value education is the ability to make moral judgment based on sound reasoning and has to be deliberately cultivated. Value education cannot be circumscribed by textbook material but should be left to the initiative and inspiration of the teachers in finding the learning resources. There are many ways in which value education can be imparted. Folk literature is one such resource. Folk literature has great importance, since they are true reflections of day-to-day life. Moreover, their transmission from one generation to the next, makes them dynamic effective, and never forgotten. Folk literature is part and parcel of the language and culture of our society. The three models of education-nonformal, formal and informal that go from teaching literacy to literature and other subjects, can make use of folk literature as a powerful educational tool. These may be used to imbibe values, style of language, and many other important learning items in the minds of learners. . A variety of learning resources in folk literature can be used for value education ranging from biographies, scriptures, proverbs, hymns and sayings of great men to current social and political events, stories from religion and mythology, moral dilemmas and schools events.

Educational methods evolved by society play an important role in transforming a biological being into a social being. Given the backdrop of a rich traditional society, there is every reason that our modern Indian educational system takes cue from primitive educational methods. Let us take, for example, folklore and storytelling educational method which revolved around conveying through transformation, information and traditional belief. It highlighted the significance of values and mirrored the informal control these values exercised over people. The natural corollary was dual. One is the awareness of the culture of one's community and the other, preservation of moral order. This method exploited mythical or real heroes from epics like the Mahabharata and Ramayana. The moral each conveyed corroborated the observation and preservation of values that paved the path to harmonious social living [http://www.nehsindia.org].

Proverbs which form an important component of folk literature can be effectively used as a means to impart value education. They are folk literary devices that are statements about the society. Malayalam has a wealth of proverbs which can be effectively used to imbibe values in students. Proverbs and maxims that had a deep impact on character formation of children should be made an essential part of everyday learning. It is the duty of the teacher to include appropriate proverbs in their teaching technique which can be used as a means to impart value education.

REFERENCES

1. Antony, A., (2003) — 'Psychological Base of Education', Hashid Publications, Kollam, pp. 117.
2. Antony, A., (2004) — 'Theoretical Base of Education-Philosophical, Sociological and National', Herbert Publications, Kollam, pp. 260-290.
3. Sharma, R.N., (2003)-'Philosophy and Sociology of Education', Surjeet Publications, New Delhi, pp. 283-284.
4. "Imparting good values", [online], available http: http://www.deccanherald.com
5. "Notes on the Value of Science", [online], Available http: http://www.philosophy.su.se/texter/valueofscience.htm.
6. "The Roles of Grandparents: The Use of Proverbs in Value Transmission", [online], available http: http://www.haworthpress.com.
7. "Values of the Wise", [online], Available http,http://www.valuesofthewise.com.
8. "Value Education", [online], Available http: http://ncert.nic.in.
9. "Values Through Proverbs", [online], Available http: http://valuesandproverbs.tripod.com.
10. "Value Education: Moral Education", [online], Available http: http://www.nehsindia.org.
11. "Value Education", [online], Available http: http://www.ramakrishna.org.

8

Institutional Role in Developing Values Among Students

Baiju K.C & Asha J.V

Education means many things to many people. The very purpose of an educational institution and its existence will be evaluated on the basis of the quality education that it provides. When we consider the factors contributing positively or negatively to the successful functioning of the educational institutions, one major share goes to the morality of the students or the discipline maintained in the campus. If reflected at depth, the task of education is to develop men of character without which it is useless imparting education. Education means an all-round drawing out of the best in child and man – body, mind and spirit (Gandhi, 1949). Character, which refers to appropriate conduct and behaviour, is undoubtedly a very important aim of education. The mind of a child is like a 'clean slate' and the values and education imparted to him/her during the formative years determines not only the career of the student but also the character of the student. Thus, it becomes all the more important for educationists to encourage and incorporate values along with other kinds of instruction.

Significance of Organized School Activities

Development of a moral personality has been a very important aim of education since ancient times. This aim has, during modern times, assumed great importance in view of the sweeping political, economic and social changes brought about by the rapid expansion of science and technology. Human life involves questions of value at each step, in each of its choices and activities. The Kothari Commission (1966) has stressed that the educational system should emphasise on the development of the fundamental social, moral and spiritual values. Secondary Education Commission (1958) has rightly stated: "There is little doubt that the whole purpose of education is not fulfilled unless certain definite principles are inculcated in the minds of the youth of the country". Thus, the development of values and moral character is a recurring theme in the recommendations of major committees.

Value consciousness is the awareness of values in their total implication. It is, however, difficult for an average individual to realise the depth, magnitude and significance of values. In a world dominated by industrial and technological complexes, inculcating a sense of affection and sensitiveness towards higher values of life is a rather different task. Education is a powerful integrating force or a medium, which successfully brings about value changes and nurtures them. Education and values are interwoven.

'Being moral' refers to being able to understand the principles of 'right' and 'wrong' and act in the right way. While all religions essentially have a moral dimension, all morality is not confined to religious faith and practice. Character which refers to appropriate conduct and behaviour is undoubtedly a very important aim of moral education. Actually, moral development denotes the ability to make moral judgements based on sound reasoning. This ability has to be deliberately cultivated. Moral education is also a matter of educating the feelings and emotions (that is 'training of the heart'). Moral development involves both thinking morally and behaving morally. According to research findings of famous psychologists, like intellectual development, moral development also takes in stages and follows a regular sequence.

Moral development will constantly be taking place in the schools whether the teacher is conscious of it or not. Education is a process of bringing about desirable changes of behaviour in the individual in his knowledge status, attitudes and values. The school seeks t achieve this through its curriculum which is nothing but the sum total of all its organised activities. Curriculum thus essentially has a moral basis. Teachers and schools therefore, are engaged in moral development although without explicitly discussing its goals and methods. Apart from the 'hidden curriculum', the schools can adopt direct method and indirect method of moral education.

It is seen that the stress on value education given during the Vedic period was slowly deteriorated during pre independence period from our education system and from our society. Sri Prakash Committee (1956) lamented that all educational institutions are not taking active steps in promoting social, moral and spiritual values. It recommended that a general study of the different religions of the world be included as part of first-degree course and the students should be encouraged to practice silent meditation. A few researches Singh & Singh (1986), Paramesh (1970), Srivastava (1990) Rusnak(1993), Bailey(1999), Linden(1999), Sindhya (2006)etc. were located exploring the different areas of value education and in different angles. The inculcation of desirable values among students in India through value education programmes depends much on the initiative and involvement of the institutions. This inturn depends on the outlook of sincere and dedicated teachers who implement the observance of values and demonstrate themselves as role models.

Perspectives of Teachers on the Role of Institutions in Inculcating Values

Teachers are the role models disseminating the key aspects of values through their interaction with the student community. Teachers are the central stay in the process of value orientation among students and as such they cannot shrug off their responsibility in identifying the hurdles which stand in the way of inculcating values. It is obvious that teachers can very well discuss in unambiguous terms the methods and problems in fostering values among the present generation. Hence an effort was made to list out the perspectives of teachers about the ways of developing values at the behest of institutions. The following objectives were set to prepare a questionnaire and interview schedule for the teachers of secondary schools.

1. To examine the reasons for the decline of values in our society in the view of the teachers of secondary schools.
2. To study the strategies implemented by secondary schools of Thiruvananthapuram district to develop moral values among the students.
3. To examine the direct methods adopted by the secondary schools to develop moral values among the students.
4. To analyse the indirect methods adopted by the secondary schools in developing moral values among the students.

The study intends to probe into the nature of the programmes organised by the secondary schools in developing moral values among adolescents. The scope of the study is to conduct an empirical study using survey method. The study has certain limitations. The study is limited to the secondary schools of Thiruvananthapuram district. Only moral values are proposed to study.

Sample: The sample consists of 78 teachers of secondary schools of Thiruvananthapuram district. The schools were taken at random and included rural, urban, government, aided and unaided schools. All of them responded and gave their perceptions and also suggested a few strategies that could be implemented. Their responses were further analysed and interpreted qualitatively to attain the objectives of the study.

Inculcating Values Among Students—A Discussion Based on the Perspective of Teachers

Values are the central to one's life since they are normative in all of one's actions and understandings. In a plural society, education should foster universal and eternal values, oriented towards the unity and integration of our people. Such value oriented education should help to eliminate obscurantism, religious fanaticism, violence, superstition and fatalism. Value oriented education enable the student to be truly Indian, really modern and deeply human. On discussing, a majority of the teachers (89.7%) expressed strongly that there has been an erosion of values such as honesty, cooperation, social responsibility, spiritualism, patriotism etc. and these values are facing a crisis today in our Indian society. They are also of the view (52.13%) that this is because mostly people have become more and more materialistic due to market based economy and commercialization of products even in the field of education. In this context, the teachers must play an important role in inculcating values among students. They must know that value-oriented education is not a sphere of activity distinct from the professional activities of a teacher. Instead the teacher should see value inculcation as a collective responsibility of the institution as well as the teacher to retain rejected essential values of human aspirations and had make itself a live mechanism imprinted in the young minds. Hence it is the need of the hour to make all possible attempts to inculcate value oriented education in the centre of learning.

Table 8.1

Perception of respondents regarding reasons for decline of values

Reasons for decline of values	% of respondents
Market based economy, commercialization of education, materialistic life	52.13
Exam oriented teaching, not including any weightage to values in the syllabus, throat cut competition	39.3
Media exposure and lack of quality programmes inculcating values	36.24
Lack of role model performance by teachers and parents	32.54
Low SES, poverty, struggle for existence, unemployment	27.27
Corruption witnessed in the society from politicians, govt. officials, other responsible personalities	18.18
Nuclear family and freedom and over pampered kids	11.36

Another major aspect pointed out by the participants (39.3%) was that the exam oriented syllabus followed in our schools and the weightage given to performance in examination for getting jobs and admissions, the throat-cut competition creeping in as a result and these enhanced by the absence of weightage to value education in the syllabus. Other reasons cited by the respondents were: Media exposure and lack of quality programmes inculcating values through the visual media (36.24%), Lack of role model performance by teachers and parents (32.54%), Low SES , poverty, struggle for existence, unemployment (27.27%), Corruption witnessed in the society from politicians, govt. officials, other responsible personalities (18.18%), Nuclear family and freedom and pampering given to kids (11.3%). Every respondent has given more than one suggestion, which were compiled in Table 8.1. It can be seen that the impact of globalised economy has contributed much to speed up the strides of human beings and indirectly this has resulted in the decline of his value system. In fact, we have no time to care and share with our fellow beings, even family members and show concern for them as we are entangled in a rat's alley of competitions today.

The National Curriculum Frame Work for School Education (2000) has stated that it is imperative for the Indian school curriculum to include inculcation of the basic values and an awareness of all the major religions of the country as one of the central components. They have further emphasized that these should be judiciously integrated with all the subjects of study in the scholastic areas and all the activities and programmes in co-scholastic areas that the objectives thereof would be directly or indirectly achieved in the classroom, at the school assembly places, play grounds, cultural centers and such other places. As part of the present study, the teachers were asked to respond to a set of questionnaire which covered the areas described in Table 8.2. This was done with a view to find out how far the schools are taking initiative in inculcating values. As we have moved away from the joint family where it was a responsibility vested upon the elders at home to develop moral values to their heirs. Now this responsibility has been shifted to the institution where the child is studying. The teachers responded well showing that they are ready to take up this added responsibility and they possess clear vision about inculcating these values. Almost all teachers favoured that it is necessary to inculcate values through purposeful activities both direct and indirect in the school. Among the strategies adopted by various schools in developing moral values among its students the direct methods suggested were:

- Conducting value education programme and value education to teachers
- Specifying dos and don'ts to children in school and at home
- Insisting students to observe discipline inside and outside classroom
- Rating Student's participation, leadership, involvement, attitudinal changes, practice of value, reflection on values etc. and noting the same in their progress reports

Table 8.2

Strategies implemented for developing values

Methods adopted for fostering values	% of respodents
Conducting value education programme and value education to teachers	42.83
Specifying dos and don'ts to children in school and at home	54.3
Insisting students to observe discipline inside and outside classroom	46.21
Provide incentives to children exhibiting high moral values such as honesty, social responsibility etc.	41.24
Integrating values through curricular activities in the classroom through stories and highlighting the desirable values persuading students to follow these	28.54
Practicing values through co-curricular activities like assembly programmes, yoga classes, scout and guides, NSS, NCC etc.	47.27
Exposure to invited talks, films, documentaries, inviting NGOs to conduct programmes etc. on values	15.46
Display boards depicting values through proverbs, quotable quotes etc. on values inside the school	25.32
Conducting campaigns in the campus for inculcation of socially acceptable values	13.2
Assigning the responsibility of conducting de-addiction campaign and the like among the public to students	9.24
Teachers & parents demonstrating role models	42.36
Rating Student's participation, leadership, involvement, attitudinal changes, practice of value, reflection on values etc. and noting down in progress reports	43.26

Conclusion

We have seen that the indirect methods for fostering values were:

- Provide incentives to children exhibiting high moral values such as honesty, social responsibility etc.
- Integrating values through curricular activities in the classroom through stories and highlighting the desirable values persuading students to follow these.
- Practicing values through co-curricular activities like assembly programmes, yoga classes, scout and guides, NSS, NCC etc.
- Exposure to invited talks, films, documentaries, inviting NGOs to conduct programmes etc. on values.
- Display boards depicting values through proverbs, quotable quotes etc. on values inside the school.

Apart from this, conducting campaigns protesting social evils and making students take the responsibility to lead such campaigns among the public and the teachers as well as parents performing role models are also helpful in developing moral values among students. The perceptions of teachers regarding the implementation of these strategies are given in Table 8.2. From the discussions and reflections with teachers it has been accepted by all of them that value crisis is mainly due to impoverished moral intelligence among the responsible citizen in the society such as politicians, bureaucrats, teachers etc. While reflecting they gave illustrations like a teacher chewing tobacco before students or involved in sex scandal may cause great damage to the value system. Most of the teachers were in favour of punishing or discouraging such practitioners. Some also opined that not only teachers and parents but also the famous artist or sports person has a social obligation to perform role model in the society. This will surely encourage children and youngsters in favour of desirable values.

In this super industrial society, educational system should not only be geared up to prepare manpower for the industries, but for getting the real meaning of education. ie; all round development of a child. Different committees and commissions had also highlighted similar concern about the decline of values and the need for restructuring the education and societal system for proper value inculcation among children. At this juncture it is the need for the society to streamline its education and the social systems to inculcate proper values among the students and make them fit for the society. Value education should be a part and parcel of our curricular and co-curricular activities. For this purpose the institutions should take up it as an added responsibility to inculcate values among the students.

REFERENCES

Education Commission Report (1958): Government of India, New Delhi: Government of India Press.

Education Commission Report (1966): Government of India, New Delhi: Government of India Press.

Gandhi, M.K. (1949): *To the Student*. Ahmedabad: Navjivan Publishing House.

Paramesh, C.R. (1970): Value Orientations of Creative Persons. *Psychological Studies*, Vol. 15, No. 2., pp. 108-112.

Singh, L.C., & Singh, P. (1986): Effectiveness of Value Clarifying Strategies in Value Orientation of B.Ed. Students. Department of Teacher Education, NCERT, In M.B. Buch (ed.), *Fourth Survey of Research in Education*, pp. 991.

Srivastava, Vinodhini (1990): *A Study of Change Proneness and Job Satisfaction Among Teachers With Reference to Teacher Values*. Ph.D. Thesis, Agra University.

Sindhya.V (2006): *A Study of Value Orientation, Effectiveness and Morale Among Teacher Educators in Kerala* Ph.D. Thesis M.S University, Thirunelveli.

9

Values Inculcating Among Higher Secondary Students

A Learner-Centered Approach

P.N. Faisal

Introduction

Education is the measuring rod of civilization. It is a potent force for social reconstruction. It is concerned not only with social progress but also with moral, political, social and economic development. Gandhiji rightly said, "Education is the preparation for complete living, adjustment to environment, perfection of one's nature, and character–building and harmonious development of personality. It has an implication that education has the responsibility not only to provide training three R's (Reading, Wringing and Arithmetic) but also to develop the qualities of hand, heart and brain. In simple words, the purpose of education is to draw out best of the child by stimulating the spiritual, intellectual and physical facilities of the child.

There is a need to adopt a holistic approach to education in terms of its content. Of late, the focus of education has been towards scientific and economic development. It has also been observed that there has been an erosion of social and moral value system. The Indian psyche is deeply embedded in spiritual value system drawn from thousands of years of common cultural heritage and an educating system devoid of cultural values is not only hollow in its content but unsustainable as well. An education system inter-linked with our cultural heritage on one hand and economic and scientific development on the other is only viable medium to take us successfully ahead towards 21st century.

The values of culture and that of science are to be integrated proportionately with culture acting as a catalyst to sharpen the scientific temperament of our youth. The educational system is to ensure aesthetic and qualitative life of its citizens besides achieving the economic and scientific targets. The invasion of electronic media into our sub-continent has further increased the importance of inculcating, preserving and permeating cultural values in our society.

The National Policy on Education has laid considerable emphasis on value education by highlighting the need to make education a powerful tool for cultivation of social and moral values. Keeping in view the pluralistic base of our society, the education system besides preserving our cultural heritage has also to nurture our youth to be more adaptable to life in the changing environment. An inter-linking of education and culture has also been emphasized in the Programme of Action for implementation of National Policy on Education. As a part of child personality development, particularly in terms of discovering the inherent potential of a child, this needs to be implemented right from the primary stage to the highest level of formal education. And acquisition of modern technical skills along with inculcating sound moralistic character has to be highlighted.

Considering the present scenario, there is a rapid advancement in science and technology, which leads to Globalization, liberalization, and the subsequent development like quick economic growth, Mechanization, Urbanization and craving for Materialistic life. Out of this development, there is marked a remarkable deterioration in values. Therefore Nowadays the role of education to achieve the objectives of values is increasing.

The Concept of Values

Values are closely related to the noble aims of human life. For the achievement of these aims man frames certain philosophical guidelines or notions that direct human behavior along desirable channels. These notions are called values. In the words of John Dewey, "to value means primarily to praise, to esteem, to appraise, to estimate". A value stands for ideals that provide men direction for leading a worthy life. They are part and parcel of the philosophy of a nation, which in turn becomes art of the philosophy of its educational system also. They are the guiding principles of life which are conducive to one's philosophical, mental and social health.

Values are also closely related to the aims of education. It is what is valuable that is transmitted to the younger by the elder generation. The concept of education has to be viewed as nothing but a set of values in essence.

Aims of education are formulated with reference to philosophy of a nation. Values also are integral components of philosophy. Hence, values and education are intertwined and interrelated. According to Harry Schofield, "Value is what a particular society values so highly that it finds it important to pass it on to teach succeeding generation." The guiding social aims and beliefs which are regarded as important aspects of a culture as valued by the people. These ideas which they think worthwhile are called values. Values include all important beliefs, religious teachings, moral attitudes, philosophies of life, etc. which not only help in sustaining the society and its culture, but also bring about corresponding changes in the society and culture. On the whole, values are desirable styles of thought and action that promote individual and social development and well-being.

Adolescence is a period in which many fundamental changes occurred in individual's life, value education in this age has its prime concern. It was at this period many drastic changes have occurred in the life of an individual. It is a pivotal developmental period in which the individual begins to form an enduring sense of personal identity. So that values and the concept of good life must be imparted to the students in this age group with great care and should adopt proper methodology.

Major Objectives of Value Education

The objective of value education should be development of an individual, character building which includes up-holding of human dignity and self respect. In the modern scenario a strong system of value education should have the following objectives:

1. To arouse in children certain elementary sensitivity towards environment.
2. To help in learning through playing freely with natural materials like clay, sand, flowers and plants.
3. To impart the child with basic core of facts about India's cultural heritage through folk songs, local historical monuments, etc.
4. To create a feeling of love for India's natural and cultural heritage.
5. To nurture in children an aesthetic approach based on perception of beauty, emotion and passions.
6. Encouraging the students to inter-act with local artists, writers, cultural organizations.
7. To organize regional or state level competitions.
8. Broad-basing and diversifying of cultural courses like music, fine arts, performing arts, etc.
9. Imparting cultural instructions to students of science and technology.
10. Development of special courses emphasizing India's architectural heritage, maintenance of monuments.

Methods and Techniques of Value Education

The entire curriculum functions as important sources of value education. The democratic practices and activities contribute effectively for value learning. Value education in schools, is effected through direct, indirect, incidental methods. Values get transmitted via both the implicit or hidden and planned curriculum. The entire process of value education is a high comprehensive and complex one that involves a wide range and variety of learning experiences. Learner is the dominant part here he is no longer be an inactive or passive listener. He constructs new ideas, through proactive and divergent thinking and finally finding the ultimate solution. With this analysis and understanding background, the following methods and techniques are suggested for uplifting the methods of educating students towards values

The Concept of Learner-Centeredness

Value education needs to be revitalized for helping the learner acquire knowledge and skills in an interactive environment. The means of value inculcation at school need to adopt methods that promote creativity, aesthetics and critical perspectives and enable children to acquire a well-adjusted life to his environment.

A method of teaching may be adopted so as to enable primarily a scientific way of transferring the curriculum, keeping in mind the psychological and physical requirements of the children. Methods are the means of attaining predetermined goals. In fact it forms the most important link in the total teaching learning cycle. It has on the one hand, the goals and purposes, and on the other hand results, Results can be in terms of cognitive development or the development of desirable habits, interests, attitudes and values and skills related to the various domain of human life. A method connects the objectives with its results.

Methods and strategies of teaching is a dynamic phenomenon. There had been methods suggested by the traditional theories and practices of education. But as a result of recent psychological and technological development many novel tracks have been introduced that are fully learner centered, practical oriented and activity based methods. For inculcating values to the higher secondary schools, it is evidenced that, this method must be adopted so that students can assimilate values in a natural atmosphere. Some effective strategies of value inculcation are discussed below:

Direct and Indirect Approaches to Value Education

Study of values may be given as a separate course like any other subject such as science, mathematics and social studies deliberately after systematic planning. Various strategies can be used here, such as: Story telling, Recreating biographies of great leaders, Proverbs and poems. In indirect approach desired values may be imparted to students as a by-product of teaching some other curricular subject or through any activities in schools, eg: Teaching democratic values through civics.

Curricular and Co-curricular Approaches

In Curricular approach values are imparted through curricular activities either directly or indirectly. If direct approach is followed for the purpose, separate syllabus and time- table have to be provided. If indirect approaches are to be followed it has to be given incidentally in the course of transacting the curriculum. In co-curricular approach learning values either may be purposefully included co-curricular programmes wherever possibly. eg:- Debates, essay competition, story writing, dramas, etc. or incidentally attain by adopting appropriate styles of action.

Cultural and Recreational Activities

Pupil may be encouraged to develop artistic talents and skills. The under mentioned occasions may be utilized for the purpose. They are: Organizing school anniversary, sports day etc, Organizing cultural festivals, art exhibitions, and musical performances literarily displays, etc, Encouraging students to participate in hobbies, games, sports, dramas, folk dances, all depicting ideas like the unity of our heritage, religious toleration. Etc. and organizing inter as well as intra school competitions in different areas.

Citizenship Training Programme

The pupils may be imparted effective training in citizenship and other civic virtues. For which the following measures may be implemented: regularly organizing school assembly, observation of national and international days. Organizing mock parliament and debates on local and national problems and Excursions to places of cultural, religious, and historic importance.

Classroom Learning Activities Methods

A very basic purpose of value education is to develop the moral autonomy of the learner and also sensitivities of value content of school and classroom activities. The methods and activities should be free from attempt to indoctrinate the learner. Capacity for value judgment and internalization are to be achieved by exposing students to a variety of experiences and activities. This may include reading, listening, discussions, narration, direct presentation of ideas by the students and other strategies. These strategies should be used with any of the following sources of value education. (a) Biographies; (b) Stories; (c) Extracts from essays, articles, classics and newspaper; (d) parables, proverbs quotations and poems, (e) Classroom incidents, anecdotes. These sources can be used in any different ways to involve the learner in thinking and reasoning about values.

Practical Activities Method/Approach

Value education merely by cognitive precept is not enough even though it is essential. Children should engage themselves in practical activities which promote the values in daily life. The essence of practical approach is that they provide the learners with suitable opportunities to practice and live according to the principles and values they have perceived and understood. Under this a wide rage of activities may be organized. Practically, all subjects of school curriculum lead to project or practical work and this may be designed as to make it relevant to value education. A sound program of value education may include the activities like: School Campus classroom Maintenance activities, Social forestry community development activities, Work experience - related activities, Organizing campaign or community sanitation, literacy, environmental, awareness, Aids prevention awareness and Eradication of social evils- campaign activities.

Socialized Techniques Approaches

A variety of group of oriented techniques may be used in value education. Learners will get a variety of experiences out of these techniques. It is child-centered sources it will give more opportunity to learn for reflective thinking and taking decision by his own. Socialized techniques is also involved in activities and experiences which best represent for actions and problems of agents of socialization. The experience the learner gets here is not the same type of experience deriving from direct encounters with reality, nor it is completely indirect and abstract as in their case of cognitive area. They are simplified versions of real, social experiences and one necessary and useful when the reality is too abstract and obscured. These include social role playing enacting and modernly.

In social role playing one can understand the interrelationship between the expectations of other and the identification of the self. In the social role playing the learner should be guided property to understand the role behavior and enactment. Negative precepts are to be discussed in role playing. Some indications of the kinds of activities possible under the heads of socialized strategies for value education are: Dramatization activities like staging play, drams, both of traditional, folk and modern on value themes, Problems pertaining to women's role and education, Caring animals, Problems related to environmental protection and Consequences of pollutions. Panel discussions, for meeting working group, conducting minor project weekend awareness developing program are the different activities through which one can impart values related to all these sound relevant issues.

Incidental Learning Methods

An incident is an episode or experience in the life of an individual or group. The incidental approach can be used both inside as well as outside the class room for value education purposes. It consists in identifying the wrong or right actions of individual or group. This approach is psychologically effective since it is like striking in the iron while it is hot. Episodes or incidents central around experience of everyday occurrence in the life can help there identity themselves. And understand theirown thought powers and feelings incidents are to be recorded properly and discussed to promote insight into human problems

Common Approaches of Value Education

Several attempts have been made to evolve methodologies suitable to the development of values in children and youth. There were existed eight approaches. They are commonly used. They are:

1. *Evocation approach.* The students are encouraged to make spontaneously, non-rational choices, without thought or hesitation. It provides an environment which allows maximum freedom for students, and provides a provocative situation for which spontaneous reactions are elicited. For example, the reaction to a picture of starving children.

2. *Inculcation approach:* Students are forced to act according to specific desired values. A positive and negative reinforcement by the teacher helps value inculcation.

3. *Awareness approach:* Here students to become aware and identify their own values. The students are encouraged to recreate their experiences. The teacher presents situations or dilemmas though reading, films, role playing, small group discussions and simulation. Students thus engage themselves in the process of making inferences about values from the thought, feelings etc.

4. *Moral reasoning approach:* This is based upon Kohlberg's theory of six stages of moral developments. It will start from the stage role taking. Through placing themselves in a role and experiencing the process of deciding, students can begin to see moral decisions in a larger frame work than there single point of view. It consists of this student discussing a dilemma and by reasoning they attain a higher level of knowledge.

5. *Analysis Approach:* Here, the students are encouraged to study social value problems. They are asked to clarify value questions, and identified values in conflict.

6. *Value Clarification Approach:* It helps students to use both rational thinking and emotional awareness to examine personnel behavior patters to actualize values.

7. *Commitment Approach:* It enables the students to perceive themselves not merely as passive reactors or free individuals, but as inner relative members of a social group and system.

8. *The Union Approach:* The purpose is to help students to perceive themselves and act not as separate egos but as part of a larger inter related whole - The human race, the world, the cosmos.

Jurisprudential Inquiry Model of Teaching

The Methods given by Donal Oliver and James P Shaver is very useful for clarifying one's own values where a social problem or public issue is largely analyzed. This method is called Jurisprudential Inquiry Model of Teaching (J I M). It is an effective strategy for value inculcation. One notable advantage of this method is that open climate for discussions possible, which is a major feature of learner-centered approach in the classroom. Another Advantage is that teacher also has a pivotal role in this method. This is the reason that the method can be easily incorporate with the climate of Higher Secondary School. Because of its simplicity and application in the Indian classroom settings Jurisprudential Inquiry model of Teaching seems to be quiet useful. The main goal of the model for students is to develop public policy stances and dialogue skills by using three types of competence. That is: Understanding of the values Frame Work of Indian creed, Mastery of the intellectual skills of logical reasoning, And Knowledge of contemporary public issues.

This method involves conception of values through productive dialogue as well as curriculum and pedagogical consideration. During the process of dialogue, students take a position and the teacher challenges the positions with questions.The teachers questions are designed to push students thinking about there stance and to help them learn. The specific features of Jurisprudential Inquiry model of Teaching can be summed up in the following terms; Socratic Dialogue, Public Policy Issue, Conflicting Values, Use of analogies and legal reasoning process, a frame work of Values, Balancing Values and Particular Pattern of Argumentation. Jurisprudential Inquiry model of Teaching is an effective approach for value inculcation among younger generations.

Suggestions

In order to implement this type of right approach in rural schools we must keep in mind the following facts:

(i) To study local cultural resources to be incorporated in the school curriculum.

(ii) Teacher should use various teaching aids like Audio Visual aids etc.

(iii) Teacher should be trained and prepared to understand and recognize the need for change in the field.

(iv) Pre-service Teacher Training should be given for teachers.

(v) Teacher Education should emphasis an integrated cultural component of education.

(vi) Fine arts music, creative writing puppetry and theatre are to be given due place in the curriculum.

Conclusion

It has been accepted that the teachers, the teacher educators the educational workers, and the administrators should try there best to promote value based education. They can play an eminent role in inculcating desirable values among the people through effective organization of different curricular and Co-Curricular activities.

10

Higher Education
Value Free or Value Bound?

Esther Gladiz

Introduction

In an educational system, highly commercialized and vastly de linked from human realities, value–education even runs the danger of turning into academic exercise an essential requirement for grades. What students and youth need today is a tool, a methodology, a help to come face to face with values and counter–values of their society to discuss their own value-patterns and systems, and finally have the courage and conviction to opt for human and just values.

Any academic community placed in the context of many challenges has the obligation to develop in the youth values which can help them become agents of social transformation by taking definite stand against all forces of degradation. There are many thousands of young people proficient in science and technology but shockingly ignorant of moral standards and callously indifferent to their wellbeing. Global and national issues related to environment, nuclear war, genetic technology, sexual perversion, AIDS are some of the challenges the society is facing which in turn threaten to demoralize the future generation.

In a formal educational system education is a dialogue between the teacher and the taught. Undoubtedly the teacher plays a significant role in the promotion of excellence and values in students. In the face of the grim social, economic, ecological and political realities of today, the educationalists should realize that the opportunity before them is tremendous if only they decide to raise leadership from the youth of today with a vision and commitment to serve the society with a philosophy of doing the future now ahead of time with lasting values of faith, hope and love.

The call for values is currently echoing throughout every land, as educators, parents and even children are increasingly concerned about and affected by violence, growing social problems, and the lack of social cohesion. Educators are, once again, asked to address problems which have arisen within their societies.

Traditional Values of Indian Culture

The Upanishads advocated the values hierarchical in nature which have to be developed are *Annamaya* (the materialistic value), *Pranamaya* (The Biological values), *Manomaya* (The psychological values) *Vijanamaya* (the metaphysical value) and the *Anandamaya* (the aesthetical value). Our indigenous culture considered *Sathyam, Shivam* and *Sundaram* or Truth, Beauty and Goodness are the supreme values. They served as the guiding principles for the human kind. They can be equated to the ultimate values of Indian philosophy; that is, *Sat, Chit* and *Ananda.* Sat is truth and goodness, chit means true knowledge and *ananda* is bliss.

Values are internalized through process of conditioning, learning and socialization. Values are basic beliefs that underpin the way we think, feel and respond to things happening in the outer world. Thus the foundation of values rest upon cognitive (thinking), Affective (feeling), and Conation (behaviour) With the giant stride in science based technology, man is coaxed to feel a new power that is strong and dynamic, that it often leads him to feel that he is in any need of values system which could act as a restraining influence . One of the major deficiencies of the higher education system identified is that higher institutions are unduly geared to utilitarian values in their functioning to the almost total neglect to basic human values- social, moral and spiritual.

The educational scenario has undergone a phenomenal change from its primary function of education i.e. building of character or the promotion of moral order, but the emphasis has shifted to the promotion of skill, technical know how and technology for material progress, promotion of careerism, economic good and social prosperity.

Living Values Education (LVE)

Living Values Education (LVE) is a values education programme. The call for values is currently echoing throughout every land, as educators, parents and even children are increasingly concerned about and affected by violence, growing social problems, and the lack of social cohesion. Educators are, once again, asked to address problems which have arisen within their societies.

It offers a variety of experiential values activities and practical methodologies to teachers and facilitators to enable children and young adults to explore and develop 12 key personal and social values: Cooperation, Freedom, Happiness, Honesty, Humility, Love, Peace, Respect, Responsibility, Simplicity, Tolerance, and Unity.

The modern Indian educational thinkers are conscious of this problem. Tagore wants to maintain the unity of values because of his pre-eminently aesthetic reason. Gandhi protests against industrialism on economic grounds, but again ethical and spiritual ideals form the bases of his economics. The whole of education is a process of realizing and assimilating values. Hence every educational system or thought has to have a clear picture of the hierarchy of values. Even though certain values are basic, all of them can't be treated on the same par and their interdependence must also be shown clearly. All the significant thinkers of modern India have received their inspiration from ancient Indian religion in its purest spirit and this spirit and this guided their thoughts.

Values are a set of attitudes, unique in each individual, which govern our behavior and guide the way we look at the world. Each individual seeks to achieve certain goals in life, and his or her values are in tune with these goals. For instance, some individuals may see their family life as most important to them. They thus hold values that illustrate this- they believe that spending time with their family is more important then working long hours, and they may disagree with individuals whom they perceive as holding a more work-oriented value system. Looking back at their life, they hope to see that their family was always their top priority. Clarifying our values now can help us prioritize our lives in order to avoid disappointment and unhappiness later in life. Living a life in tune with our values is important because they are what determine what means most to us.

Value Education: A Vital Component of Higher Education

The aim of higher education is the harmonious development of all the domains of the student. It is common knowledge that higher education aims in general to make a systematic effort on the development of cognitive domain only. Not much is done towards the development of the affective and psychomotor domains. A brain developed without the simultaneous development of the affective side will naturally tend to produce dangerous consequences.

Courses on value education/ethical education/moral education/Gandhian thought are offered on full-time or part time-time basis. Only few students join these courses and get benefited. Various co curricular activities like NCC, NSS etc and students services like orientation seminars go a long way in instilling certain values in the students. When subjects are taught in the class rooms values become integral part of them.

In spite of the many achievements in quantity and quality, education stands at crossroads and our political and social life is threatened with erosion of the long-accepted values. Our goals of secularism, democracy and professional ethics have come under enormous strain. The youth of today and tomorrow should be imbued with "a strong commitment to human values and to social justice" Higher education should provide ample scope to study critically the social ,economic, cultural, moral, and spiritual issues facing the people today. It should lay primary emphasis on eliminating 'obscurantism, religious fanaticism, violence, superstition and fatalism.'

- *Obscurantism* refers to a class of philosophies that favour limits on the extension and dissemination of scientific knowledge, believing it to be the enemy of faith.
- *Fanaticism* is an unwillingness to tolerate beliefs or opinions contrary to ones own. It is notable that followers of a religion and not the religion itself are the target of accusations of religious fanaticism.
- *Violence* is the aggressive tendency to act out destructive behaviours. Violence can also be divided into two forms—random violence, which includes unpremeditated or small-scale violence, and coordinated violence, which includes actions carried out by sanctioned or unsanctioned violent groups —such as war (i.e. *inter-societal violence*), in some cases certain types of revolution, or terrorism.
- *Superstition* is the irrational belief that future events are influenced by specific behaviours, without having a causal relationship. Superstitions are based on general, culturally variable beliefs in a supernatural 'reality'.It may relate to things that are not fully understood or known.
- *Fatalism* is the view that human deliberation and actions are pointless and ineffectual in determining events, because whatever will be will be.

Values are not born in nature. They are shaped, nurtured and developed at home and educational institutions. The value orientation must begin at the grass root level so as to have lasting effect on the conduct and way of life of the adult. There can be direct and indirect approach to value education. Direct as interdisciplinary subject, prepare curricula, teaching-learning materials and methodologies for effective value education, moral science, ethics ,Value clarification approaches such as discussions, seminars, round tables, news paper cuttings, writings on bulletin boards, wall magazines etc. Indirect approaches is to high lighting values at various occasions on an act of bravery, meetings, sports day, arts day, informal gatherings, Global and national issues related to environment, nuclear war, genetic technology, sexual perversion, AIDS etc.

Some of the identified areas of focus in higher education should include the nature of values, Nationalism, the concept of man and the aim of education, aesthetic values in education, truth, moral, spiritual education etc. Every interaction with children provides an opportunity to teach values. In order to live up to these values in individual and collective life, desire, greed, malice and anger have to be transmitted into noble aspirations. Our religious tolerance and love of peace have been the legacies of these values, upheld generation after generation.

Conclusion

Educational programmes for ethical values and character formation should neither be conceived as a way of transmitting the values of the societies of the past, nor as a means of salvaging whatever is good in existing societies against the onslaught of modern technology and of fast-spreading pragmatism. Rather educators must make a concerted, deliberate and broad-based effort: To preserve and make available to modern generations what is humanly relevant and inspiring in one's own cultural tradition and to search and help others discover the new values to be found in the emerging societies. Let our youngsters learn about our values through daily interactions, learn through our examples, learn through the values we strive towards, learn values and beliefs through their exposure to the larger world and learn values through our explanations of the world. We have to reinforce our traditional values while at the same time we learn to cope with the requirements of modern society. Our institutions of higher education must bring about a blend between traditional and modern knowledge. Theoretical knowledge of values are of no use unless it is put into practice.

REFERENCES

1. Daniel J.T.K and Nirmal Selvamony (1990), *Value Education Today* AIACHE, New Delhi.
2. Eric James (1954), *Education and the Moral Basis of Citizenship*, William Heinmann Publishers, UK.
3. Hema Malini (2206), *Values Sustainability in the Tradition of Indigenous Knowledge and Their Implications*, University News 44 (05): 1.

4. Mahesh Puri (2005), *Value Orientation in Higher Education—An Overview*, University News 43 (47): 11.
5. *Report on the Public Forum Presented on the 4th Anniversary of the Gujarat Massacre*, by the South Asian Network for Secularism and Democracy (SANSAD) on Febr. 26, 2006 in West Hastings, Canada.
6. Thomas G Bergui and Max Fisch (1961), *The New Science of Giambattisita*, Cormell Univ. Press.
7. http://dir.123india.com/education/colleges_and_universities/ January 7th2007.
8. http://www.physicsforums.com/archive/index.php/t-85845.html, January 7th2007.
9. http://en.wikipedia.org/wiki A policy of withholding information from the public, January 7th 2007.

11

Ethical Aspects and Its Implications in Education
With Special Reference to Different Schools of Philosophy

Sajna Jaleel

Introduction

"Education is the process of making desirable changes in pupil's behaviour". In the above definition the term 'desirable' is determined by the judgment of whether the 'changes' are good or bad. The discipline which deals with the 'judgment of something is good or bad' is Ethics; it is a branch of philosophy and deals with the value concept. Thus, Education depends on Philosophy for its action and the direction for Education is given by the values. What is 'desirable' in the 'desirable changes' is determined by Ethics and ethics directly determines educational aims?

According to Dr. S. Radhakrishnan, Philosophy is the logical enquiry in to the nature of reality. A Philosopher tries to have a synoptic view of the universe, of the discrete events of the human life. Plato defined a philosopher as "He who has a taste for every sort of knowledge and who is curious to learn and is never satisfied may justly termed philosopher". Philosophers according to their beliefs, point of view, and methods of approach, group themselves under many schools of Philosophy. Through this study, the investigator aimed to analyse the value concept (ethical aspects) of different schools of thought.

DETAILS OF THE RESEARCH

Statement of the Problem

The problem is stated as Ethical Aspects and its Implications in Education with special reference to different Schools of Philosophy.

Definition of Key Terms

Ethical Aspects: Aspect of or relating to ethics (the discipline dealing with what is good and bad with moral duty and obligation) (Webster's Ninth New Collegiate Dictionary 1987).

Schools of Philosophy: Group of thoughts which demonstrate some common influence or unifying belief.

Objectives of the Study

1. To analyse the ethical aspects and its implications of different Schools of Philosophy.
2. Comparison of the ethical aspects and its implications of different Schools of Philosophy.

Method Adopted for the Study

Qualitative method was employed for the study. According to Hittleman and Simon (1997), qualitative research is characterised not by the use of numerical values but by the use of text-written words – to document variables and the inductive analysis of the collected information.

Values and Kinds of Values

"To value" in the words of John Dewey (1916), "means primarily to prize, to esteem, to appraise, to estimate. It means the act of cherishing something, holding it dear and also the act of passing judgement upon nature and amount of its value as compared with something else. Lindsay (1964) "value" as "a person's idea of what is desirable, what he and others want, not necessarily what he actually wants." Value or significance of things depends upon how they satisfy our desires, wants, cravings and urges. According to Thorndike and Gates, a thing or a condition or an act is more valuable or more worthy or better than another because it satisfies wants more fully, or satisfies more wants, or causes less deprivation of wants.

Values may be classified from several points of view. Plato considered them in terms of universal thought as *Truth*, universal feeling as *Beauty* and universal will as *Goodness*. Ralph Barton Perry viewed values in terms of interests: positive and negative interests, potential and actual interests, subjective and objective interests and immediate and mediate interests. If a value helps in the achievement of certain end, purpose or objective that value is called instrumental value. Against this there are inherent values lying in the excellence of a thing itself. They are called intrinsic values, which instead of leading to any further consequences are good in them and good for their own sake. When our immediate likings or instinctive hungers are satisfied by some values, these values are called consummatory values. There are contextual values such as economic values, social values, cultural values, moral values, religious values, educational values and aesthetic values. The primary values are those which help to sustain life. According to J.S Mill, happiness is the prime value.

Kant developed the hierarchy of values based on the sanctity of man, who is always an end and never the means. Anything that debases or injures man is immoral. He, therefore, advises men to live "as though you yourself are member of an ideal society". The highest values are spiritual and intellectual; the lowest values are material and physical. Among the values, intrinsic value takes precedence over instrumental values. Similarly eternal values are superior to temporal values. In the like manner all inclusive values should claim priority values over exclusive values. The values that have greater productivity or creativity are naturally preferable to the values that have less productivity or creativity. This hierarchy of values is very helpful in making a choice between alternative courses of action. When we prefer one course of action over the other, we feel that course serves a value more desirable than the other.

Findings of the Study

Ethical aspects and its educational implications suggested by different Schools of Philosophy

In this study, the investigator selected four schools – idealism, naturalism, pragmatism and realism. Following sessions describe in detail the ethical aspects and its implications of different Schools of Philosophy.

Ross (1942) has rightly remarked, "most educational systems draw their substance from more than one school of philosophical thought: like the ordinary man in his philosophy they are, to a greater or less degree, eclectic."

Although Adams called Rousseau as "the most prominent naturalist who ever wrote on education", Rusk (1929) has seen him as an idealist who opposed nature "not to spirit, but social convention" and Ross felt his "methods especially in the earlier stages of education were decidedly naturalistic, his aims were idealistic". Similarly no educational theory can be labelled as idealist, naturalist, pragmatist or realist as it must be overlapping and all embracing in nature. Each educational trend either in the filed of curriculum or methodology or aims and objectives is not so clear cut and rigidly compartmentalized. In spite of this, there are peculiar features in every "ism" which influence educational doctrines, especially aims and ideology accordingly. With this understanding we will discuss the values and aims of education with special reference to idealism, naturalism, pragmatism and realism.

Idealism

Idealism is a school of philosophy and takes various forms. Socrates, Plato, Descartes, Berkeley, Fitche, Hegel, Hume, Kant, Schelling, Schopenhauer, Spinoza and Gentile may be said to be some of the chief representatives of idealism. Idealism does not regard the word as a natural phenomenon. It regards it as the creation of mind. Only that is real which exists in the absolute mind of which our finite minds are a part, that is, reality is that which the mind projects into the world. To idealism, the human personality is the union of ideas and purposes, and it is the ultimate reality. Idealism conceived man as a free personality. There fore function of education is to cultivate the free personality. Horne (1928) sounds this idea in this way: "education is the awakening of life to the sublime realities and meanings of existence. Education is the awakening to the life of God in the soul of man, involving praise, prayer and worship". The true reality according to idealism can be understood by our mental and spiritual vision. The mind can discover its own laws and can dwell upon itself. Idealism thinks that the mind is not physical, but spiritual. Idealism regards the world of experience as more important than the material universe. Man, spiritual in nature and he expresses himself in the forms of culture, art, morality and religion. To idealism, the "spiritual or cultural environment of man's own making; it is product of man's creative activity" (Rusk, 1929). The aim of man should be to enter into his cultural heritage, acquire the necessary from it for his self fulfilment and ultimately adding to the common stock. Again, Rusk (1929) says that, "education must enable mankind through its culture to enter more and more fully into the spiritual realm".

Idealists believe in immortal and unchanging values. They believe in eternal values or absolute values such as truth, beauty and goodness which has no physical comparison. According to idealists, exploration of these values and ultimately self realization is the main aim of education.

Idealism regards education as self development. Therefore, the biological and social emotions of the pupil should be so developed as to make him a well developed self. Bagley (1913), "the main aim of education is to instil ideals that will function as judgments...the subject matter of instruction must be totally subservient to this aim...it is the subjective attitude of the pupil that is important". The child has to capitalize on his experience towards the development of his creative self. Nunn (1930) says that, the school should give place to those human activities "that are of greatest and most prominent significance in the wider world, the grandest expressions of the human spirit".

Naturalism

In the 18th century, Rousseau (1712-1778) gave a new impetus and inspiration for naturalistic ideas in his famous work "Emile".

He described naturalism as a philosophy of education. Rousseau as a man of emotional nature, exalted natural instincts and desired over rational behaviour. He was against all inhibitions and restrictions in education. His imaginary child Emile was to be educated in contact with nature in pursuance of its laws, away from the society. Emile would be given negative education which aimed at perfecting the organs that are the instruments of knowledge. Joyce (1924) defines naturalism as "a system whose salient characteristic is the exclusion of whatever is spiritual or indeed, whatever is transcendental of experience from our philosophy of nature and man". It is a type of philosophy to which nature is the whole reality. That which is hidden and is not known is only a part of nature itself; and science has to find it out. According to Ward (1899), naturalism is the "doctrine that separates nature from God, subordinates spirit to matter, and sets of unchangeable laws as supreme". Naturalists believe in living according to nature as the best type of life. "Follow nature" is their slogan. In the words of Rousseau, "education by nature will restore the natural unsophisticated man, whose sole function is to be a man. In the natural order of things, all men being equal, their common occasion is manhood: and whoever is well trained for that, cannot fail to perform any occasion connected with it".

According to naturalists, 'pleasure' is the highest good. They have no belief spiritual values, belief in relative values. Values are identified by the needs of human beings. Aim of education according to them is self expression. In other words, aim of education is to give full opportunity for the development of the natural endowments of the child.

According to naturalism, the world moves in consonance with natural laws and matter is the only reality. Man is of the higher species in nature's creation. Naturalism has mainly three forms which are distinct from each other: (i) the naturalism of physical sciences endeavour to explain the experiences in the light of natural laws which are external in nature; (ii) another form is mechanicalism which regards man as a machine only; (iii) the third form is called biological naturalism which tries to explain man as a product of evolution and as the highest creative who inherits the racial past consisting of natural instincts and emotions. Aristotle, Conte, Bacon, Hobbes, Lamark, Rousseau, Huxley, Herbert Spencer and Bernard Shaw are some of the supporters' naturalism.

Pragmatism

Pragmatism as a school of philosophy has not only been developed in America, but also has reflected the American life styles, thoughts and ideology. This philosophy was originated from America as a result of the peculiar problems and situations prevalent there. The people who emigrated from England and other European countries had individual liberty, religious freedom and a new pattern of living. They were active and adventurous people. They had to face problems continually and found solutions through experiments and reasoning. Consequently, a philosophy of life was developed there through experiences and not through set theories and established values or traditions. No absolute values and no fixed pattern of life were held by them. They had strong optimism and confidence in shaping environment according to their own needs and convenience. William James, John Dewey, Schiller and Kilpatric are the chief exponents of this philosophy.

The term pragmatism is derived from the Greek work *"pragma"* which means action or practice. The important doctrines of this philosophy are: man creates his own values and there are no eternal truths. Truths are man made and a judgement in the process of making is never complete. There is not established system of ideas that will be true for all times to come. All such systems are relative to the situations in which they develop and the persons they satisfy. All the facts are always subject to continuous verification by consequences. And values of life change in different times and climes. The old values, therefore, cannot be accepted as they are. Human life and the world is a laboratory in which values are developed. Everyone should seek values according to his tendencies and abilities. Pragmatism does not believe in predetermined aims of education, its exponents do not start with any aim "in the sense of a priori scheme of values". As Dewey (1916) has stated it, "the educational process has no end beyond itself; it is its own end". Pragmatists hold that goals are to be arrive at by learners themselves in the light of their won experiences. Their approach to the problem of aims is general, not specific. The child would be placed in such a position in the process of education that he would be able to create values for himself.

A follower of Dewey, Kilpatrick (1933) suggest aim of education as exaltation of intelligence. For pragmatists educational aims are as personal as one's values. Although they seem to hold to an ultimate aim of education like education itself, they interpret that aim in such a way as to indicate that aims are never fixed but always experimental.

Realism

Realism regards the world of physical reality as the truly fundamental thing in experience. The cardinal principle of realism is that which we see alone is real and which we don not seeing is unreal. It thinks that the physical world alone is objective and the factual world is something which can be easily accepted as it is. Realism is not prepared to accept the existence of any infinite or absolute mind as the first cause of universe. Realism believes that mind has originated in the course of evolution as anything else in the world. It is as much or less real as any other thing in the universe.

Realism starts with undeniable certainties and tries to build up a body of systematised knowledge which is certain and objective and agrees with the stand points of physical sciences. Realism disregards everything subjective personal and emotional, except in the study of psychology from the behaviourist point of view. Realism tries to see things as they are, and to understand reality in its won colour without any fear or favour.

Realism believes that the regularities of the material environment are the chief source of all human experience. So the problem of values should be approached more or less in the same was as we approach knowledge. That is by objective understanding of facts and events for which people express desire, admiration, dislike and disapproval. Also, realist school of philosophy gives considerable emphasis to aesthetic values and feels that aesthetic feelings are aroused by more than objects of beauty.

All men share certain common traits which determine vague tendencies in every child. These tendencies must be realised together in an orderly way if human life is to be really fulfilled. Man has not been endowed with an exhaustive array of inflexible instincts which automatically propel him to the proper acts, instead, he has been given very flexible tendencies together with the power of cognition by which he may rationally understand his essential needs and freely determine his conduct in accordance therewith. The invariable universal pattern of action, individual as well as social, required for the completion of human nature is called the 'moral law' or 'natural law'. By self observation, every individual has some minimal knowledge of it. By disciplined study of human nature and events of this history, this knowledge may be increased and clarified. So knowledge is the only trustworthy guide for human action.

"In its more materialistic phases, realism reduces mind itself to an aspect of matter. Possibly, excepting this, realism seems a very common sense point of view" (Brubacher J S - 1950)

The aim of education according to realism is to give to the pupil a complete knowledge and understanding human society, human nature, motives and institutions. To Milton, education should prepare for actual living in a real world when he writes: "I call, therefore, a complete and generous education that which fits a man to perform skilfully, justly and magnanimously all the offices, both private and public, of peace and war".

Realism aims to gain practical knowledge of life in general and of professional functions in particular as can be theoretically grounded and justified and to transmit this in a coherent and convincing way both to the young and to old and through out human community. In other words, aim is to prepare practical man for the practical world.

Comparison of the Ethical Aspects and its Implications of Different Schools of Philosophy

The following table shows the comparison between the four different Schools of Philosophy based on the ethical aspects and their implications.

Table 11.1

Comparison of the ethical aspects and its implications of different schools of philosophy

Aspects	Schools of Philosophy			
	Idealism	Naturalism	Pragmatism	Realism
Value concept	Immortal and unchanging values. Belief in eternal values or absolute values	No belief in spiritual values, belief in relative values. Values are identified by needs of human beings	No fixed values	Knowledge is the only trustworthy guide for human action
	Self realisation	Self expression, enable		To gain practical knowledge of life
Aims of Education	exploration of universal values, God realization or spiritual realization	the individual to adjust himself to the environment	No fixed aims	in general, and of profession functions in particular as can be theoretically grounded and justified

On the question of values, different schools of philosophy are at variance. The idealists believe that "the objective of living and learning is to develop the natural man into the ideal man." According to them, the values substantially exist "and man values them because they are realities and part of the fabric of the cosmos." They, however, add that while the values exist in themselves, "the act of valuing them is an individual experience." According to them every object, idea or act has intrinsic value. The valour has to discover it. They believe that the student realizes values and value has existence in his interests and desires. God or the ultimate reality or the universal mind also exists and re-embodies perfect values, perfectly realised.

Unlike the idealists, the pragmatists hold that values are not pre-existent, fixed or eternal. Pragmatic values are not absolute in them selves but are valuable in a relative way to the situation requiring a choice and also to the future situation that might hypothetically exist as the result of immediate alternatives of action. Man creates values according to circumstances and environments. According to them, "truth holds good if it works out well as judged from consequences. They are instrumentalists and hold that values are not intrinsically good but are good for them in a particular situation. The pragmatists have propounded a theory of values as they come into being within the individuals. As a primary requirement of this theory a person should have language symbols in order to communicate with others. This will enable the individual to listen to the thoughts of another and thus finally to develop the capacity to think thoughts of his own. In this way he becomes self conscious. This is the second pre-requisite. The third step is that the person should fully grasp his individual and social relationship to society as an initiator of events with future consequences for himself, in order to be an agent in the making and realising of values. They believe that all values are relative and subjective. A value may be acceptable to one person, but may not suit another. Education should help in creating values, in discriminating them, in shifting them. Knowledge and more knowledge about men and things help in the process of building a philosophy of values.

The naturalists and their first cousins realists believe that values are found in nature and are discovered by man who is a rational being. A naturalist has no purpose other than self expression, while a realist educates for some vocation. Though they believe in sense (as foundation of knowledge) a realist will plead for direct knowledge while a naturalist for indirect experience and discipline by natural consequences. Pragmatism is only an expression of a realist approach to life. But, pragmatism deny the past and realises the importance of cultural values, but realist doesn't. A realist would accept the so called absolute values in terms of material and economic property while pragmatism believes in relative values. A realist has individualistic conception of education; that of a pragmatist has social bias.

Realism expresses itself in vocational aims, psychological methods and scientific and practical contents. Extreme form of realism is based on an erroneous assumption that things alone and, not words are real. But Ross (1942) says, "Words are symbols of things and are as real as things; there is no inherent antithesis between words and things".

Quite contrary to idealism, realism regards the worldly realities of every day life as true. Realism is not prepared to accept the existence of any infinite or absolute mind as the first cause of universe. It stands for a scientific outlook of life.

Since the aims of education are originated from the value concepts of various philosophies or are determined in the context of different "isms", they take different forms. When sources are different, the products also naturally vary. This has been evident from the above discussion. In spite of all the differences and diversities, all these four philosophies are interrelated and sometimes overlapping. That is why education takes an eclectic approach and a conciliatory view about its various aspects including aims of Education.

Implications of the Study

1. As the aims of Education are determined by Ethics, the study of ethical aspects in various Schools of Thought help to develop aims of Education for our self and modifying the value concepts.
2. The values educational, economic, health, recreational, associational, aesthetic, moral and religious can be obtained through the study of various Schools of Philosophy and this will enable the individual to develop his aims of education.
3. Teachers can develop the value system if they are aware of the ethical aspects of different schools among their students.

REFERENCES

1. Baglay, W. C. (1913). *The Educative Process*. London: Mac Millan.
2. Best, J.W. and Kahn, J.V. (1996). *Research in Education* (7th Ed.) New Delhi: Prentice-Hall.

3. Broudy,H.S.(1965). *Building a Philosophy of Education* (2nd ed). NewDelhi: Prentice-Hall.
4. Brubacher,J.S.(1950). *Modern Philosophies of Education*. NewYork: Mac Graw Hill Book Company. INC.
5. *Chambers 21st Century Dictionary* (1999). New Delhi: Allied Chambers (India) Ltd.
6. Chaube, S.P and Chaube, A. (1996). *Foundations of Education*. New Delhi: Vikas Publishing House Pvt. Ltd.
7. Dewey, J. (1916). *Democracy and Education*. New York: Macmillan Co.
8. Hittleman, D.R and Simon, A. J. (1997). *Interpreting Educational Research*. New Jersey: Merrill.
9. Joyce, G.H. (1924). *Principles of Natural Theology* (2nd Ed). London: Longmans Green and Company.
10. Kilpatrick, W.H. (1933). (ed). *The Educational Frontier. New York*: Appleton- century crofts, Inc.
11. Lindzay, G.A.(1964). *Handbook of Social Psychology*. Vol. II. New York: Addison Wesley Publishing Co.
12. Nunn, T.P (1930). *Education: Its Data and First Principles*. London: Edward and Co.
13. Ross, J.S. (1942). Groundwork of Educational Theory. London. Harrap & Co.
14. Rousseau, J. J. Emile, Quoted by Davidson, T. (1898) in Rousseau and Education According to Nature. Charies Scribner's Son.
15. Rusk, R.R. (1929). *The Philosophical Bases of Education*. London: University of London Press.
16. Thorndike, E.L and Gates, A.I. Elementary Principles of Education. New York: The Macmillan Co.
17. Ward, J. (1899). Naturalism and Agnosticism. New York: The Macmillan Co.

12

Women and Human Rights

Aleyamma Vijayan

My observations are based on my work as a social activist and as a feminist for the past 30 years with the marginalized communities like fish workers, women in the informal sector and with the women's movement in Kerala.

The language of Human Rights(HR) occupies a very important position in the various discourses of political philosophies today. The Rights discourse has a certain power and recognition and a degree of immunity from challenges. But we should not forget that the rights discourse has grown out of the liberal tradition of the 18th century and enacted and upheld within an institutional legal framework which is not always conducive to social change. There are several arguments about the HR positions which presupposed a certain *non existent* equality between people's conditions. In our society there is an inter-sectionality of racial, caste and gender discriminations and such discriminations are perpetuated as a strategy and a process of social and political control which functions to exclude opportunities and benefits to certain groups in the society. Hence the discourses on human rights should be based on a socio-political analysis of the conditions of the lives of the deprived, the poor and the marginalized in our societies. We need to ask why after decades of the declaration of the UDHR and various other conventions, substantive equality is not experienced by a large section of population.

We must also keep in mind the shift in the language of rights and the shift in focus from civil and political rights which focused largely on the rights of the individual, in the mid-'70s a new human rights discourse, based on economic and social rights, collective rights and people's rights. These began to be articulated within the framework of social and political empowerment.

The Human Right discourse becomes meaningful only if we emphasize the ethics and values out of which the HR discourse arises. The heart of the rights discourse is the value that is the essence of all ethical systems (not just western as many would argue). As we all know the code of ethics is based on the universal principle of equity and justice, respect for people and personal and professional responsibility. Ethics is not just the study of values but also the shaping of the character of individuals, of peoples and organizations. Education is the process through which this shaping of character takes place and value based education should receive utmost priority in a civilized society.

Colleges and universities are custodians of knowledge. Knowledge is the source of power; it gives the ability to influence decisions in contemporary society. Hence these institutions are also the gateway to power, significantly affecting the quality of economic and social life. Thus, insofar as colleges and universities create and disseminate knowledge within a particular society, they are institutions with moral responsibilities to maintain the well-being of that society.

What we need to ponder in workshops like this whether the institutions of higher learnings fulfill that role and contribute to the well being of the society in which it is located? If there are several signs of erosion of such values within campuses (ragging, violence, etc.,) and in the society a round like corruption, conflict etc, isn't it assign for educationists to rethink the content and processes of education? I just want to elaborate on one or two issues to place the context of today's topic as I understand it.

We are living in an era of globalization and Knowledge revolution. Globalization as we all know is more than the simple increase in flows of trade, finance or communication between countries. Globalization in fact is a process that is asymmetrical, unequal and market dominated and controlled. While it is shrinking the world into a global village and brings about integration we must also remember that it is fragmenting communities, nations and regions. Social tensions and conflicts are ignited when there are extremes of inequality between the marginalised and the powerful, as it has happened and is happening in many countries. The fast changing world presents many risks of sudden disruptions in patterns of daily life in jobs and livelihoods, in health and personal safety, in the social and cultural cohesion of communities. Threats to human security can now speed their way around the world- the collapse of financial markets, HIV/AIDS, global warming, global crime. Jobs and incomes have become more precarious. The growing levels of income concentration and social exclusion of large masses of people is leading to increasing conflicts. Violences of all forms are on the increase.

What is relevant in this context is to examine what are the values that are propagated by this neo liberal process. The characteristic of the global ideology is dominance of the market as the very expression of efficiency. What is expected of individuals is spirit of competition, consumerism, and the ability to perform. The great disease studies by psychiatry today are those which "performance" fails-depression and panic syndromes! The IT capital of India Bangalore has a proliferation of psychiatrist and psychologists. This helplessness is managed with the help of drugs!

Let us also look at Kerala, which is globalised much earlier than other states in India. The contradiction is that the most literate society in India has the highest number of suicides in India, the highest per capita consumption of alcohol, the highest rate of road accidents, increasing rate of violence against women and one can go on...We are a people who have no faith in each other. We are suspicious of everything and float so many theories of conspiracy. About foreigners coming and stealing our data, attributing some ulterior motive to anyone attempting to do some good in society!

What is education doing to our society, if it is not equipping the citizens to cope with challenges of life? Do our educational institutions perceive their role as preparing the youth to be the global citizens, who can compete in the globalised world, who can migrate to anywhere in the world, be competitive and be able to perform?

The value formation of students cannot happen in classrooms but in interaction with the communities around them. Student should have opportunities to undertake socio-political analysis of the realities around them and get involved in the lives of people. And this community involvement should not be in a 'welfare mode' as doling out charity or doing some service and making people dependents. If human dignity is valued, it is important to help people to help themselves. There several examples that comes to my mind.

Another most important issue I want to raise is that of the HRs of women. Women's equal dignity and human rights as full human beings are enshrined in the basic instruments of today's international community. From the Charter of the United Nations' endorsement of the equal rights of men and women, to the Universal Declaration of Human Rights and the subsequent international treaties and declarations like CEDAW- (Convention on the Elimination of Discrimination Against Women), the rights of women are central to our vision of a democratic society. CEDAW was adopted by the UN in 1979 and became a treaty in 1981. Althought it is listed as a major HR instrument no other convention has been subject to so many reservations and the convention continues to be largely ignored by the political scientist and judiciary.

But the fine words of these documents and of the Vienna Declaration in 1993 and the declaration of Beijing in 1995 stand in sharp contrast to the daily reality of life for millions of women. Millions of women throughout the world live in conditions of abject deprivation of, and attacks against, their fundamental human rights for no other reason than that they are women. Of the 1.3 billion people living in poverty, 70 per cent are women; the majority of the world's refugees are women; female illiteracy is invariably higher than male illiteracy. Women and girl-children are treated as commodities in cross-border prostitution rackets and the pornography industry. In many countries, women lack access to reproductive health care and every day women are targeted in armed conflicts. Women's economic, social and cultural rights continue to be neglected.

We live in a world in which women do not have basic control over what happens to their bodies. Millions of women and girls are forced to marry and have sex with men they do not desire. Women are unable to depend on the government to protect them from physical violence in the home, with sometimes fatal consequences, including increased risk of HIV/AIDS infection. Women in state custody face sexual assault by their jailers. Women are punished for having sex with a person of their choosing (rather than of their family's choosing). Husbands and other male family members obstruct or dictate women's access to reproductive health care. Doctors and government officials disproportionately target women from disadvantaged or marginalized communities for coercive family planning policies.

Ideas like appropriate feminine behaviour are culturally constructed and the entire society and social institutions have deeply absorbed such values. Patriarchy, like class and caste is a system of hierarch of oppression and discrimination. Its values are so deeply ingrained that nay violations of HRs of women are considered as natural and normal!

The paradox is that as long as gender equality remains an abstract principle, there is unanimous acceptance. But spelling out the terms of such equality and its realization of it is fraught with conflict and opposition. The clear example is the continued existence of personal laws governing marriage and its dissolution, adoption, inheritance etc. There is a gap between the formal guarantee of gender equality and the substantive inequality experienced by women. There can be no peace, security or sustainable economic development in societies which deny human rights, including the human rights of women.

If human rights are to have real meaning, they must be linked to public participation. And participation must be preceded by empowerment of the people. A sense of empowerment requires a sense of dignity, self-worth and the ability to ask questions. The sense of empowerment along with a sense of legal entitlements and constitutional guarantees gives rise to a political consciousness based on rights. A process of political empowerment and a sense of rights empower citizens to participate in the public sphere.

Human rights are legtimised claims and the State has an obligation to respect, protect and fulfill these rights. However, rights become real only when people begin to realize their full potential as human beings and assert their rights in the private and public sphere. The role of education is bringing out the full potential of human beings, so that they can assert their rights and respect the rights of others.

13

Islamic Studies

Protector of Women Rights

Umid Abidhodjaev

Pure Islam

World society appreciates social place of religion and it's cultural position in human world. Cultures should be judged not merely by the heights of achievement to which they have ascended but by the depth of brutality to which they have descended. The measure of cultures is not only their virtues but also their vices.

Speaking about Islamic culture I must point out that it has not been hospitable to Nazism, fascism or communism. Muslims are criticized for not producing the best, but they are seldom congratulated for an ethic that has averted the worst. For example: The Republic of Senegal in West Africa, which is nearly 95 percent Muslim, had a Roman Catholic president for two decades (1960-80). In his years of residing over the that relatively open society , Leopold Sedar Senghar never once had to deal with anti-Christians disturbances in the streets of Dahar. His political opponents called him a wide range of derogatory names – hypocrite, stooge of the French, dictator, political prostitute – but virtually never accused him of being KAFIR (infidel)

When Senghar became the first African head of State to retire voluntary from office, Abdou Diof , a Muslim , succeeded him. But the ecumenical story of Senegal didn't end there; the first lady is Catholic.

Women and History

Westerns regard Muslim societies as unenlightened when it comes to the status of women, and it is true that the gender question is still trouble some in some Muslim countries. Islamic rules on sexual modesty have often resulted in excessive segregation of the sexes in public places, sometimes bringing about the marginalization of women in public affairs more generally. British women, however, were granted the right to own property independent of their husbands only in 1870, while Muslim women have always had that right. Indeed, Islam is the only world religion founded by a businessman in commercial partnership with his wife. While in many western cultures daughters could not inherit anything if there were sons in family, Islamic law has always allocated shares from every inheritance to both daughters and sons. Primogeniture has been illegal under sharia for 14 centuries.

The historical distances between the west and Islam in the treatment of women may be a matter of decades rather than centuries. Recall that in almost all Western counties except for New Zealand, women did not gain the right to vote until the twentieth century. Great Britain extended the vote to women in two stages, in 1918 and 1928, and the United States enfranchised them by constitutional amendment in 1920.france followed as recently as 1944. Switzerland did not permit women to vote in national elections until 1971–decades after Muslim women in Afghanistan, Iran, Iraq and Pakistan had been casting ballots.

Two of the most populous Muslim countries, Pakistan and Bangladesh, have had women prime Ministers – Benazir Bhuto headed two governments in Pakistan and Khaleda Zia and Hasina Wajed served consecutively in Bangladesh.

Feminism

Whether living in the Middle East or Africa, in Central Asia, in Pakistan, in the Southeast Asia, or in Europe and the Americas,

Muslim women tend to view the feminist movement with some apprehension. Although there are some features of the feminist cause with which we as Muslims would wish to join hands, other features generate our disappointment and even opposition.

Men may fear or distrust "feminism" if they think it means nothing more than women gaining control over them. But genuine women's liberation would be liberation for all people., men and women alike. Not an issue of who wields power over whom, but transcending that whole issue of power, lifting our consciousness to a higher plane. A woman who is truly liberated would not be stuck in that old power struggle; she would not seek to control men any more than she would accept being controlled by men. Rather both men and women would rejoice at being freed to relate to one another as loving, spiritual beings. This is real , and most of all the Sufis have actualized it. This is what Prophet (peace be upon him) brought , if only that original liberating spirit could be released from under the dead weight of centuries of cultural repression like *"purdah"*, which came not from Islam, but from the ancient Greeks and Romans, where women had no rights and were property owned by their fathers , husbands , and slave masters, so it is nothing but JAHILIYA pretending to be Islam, while Islam established the independent, equal status of women for the first time in civilization.

At the beginning Islam was the most revolutionary liberalization of women's rights the civilized world has ever seen. Women's rights were established by the Qur'an and the Prophet (p.b.u.h.) who after all loved women; we need to filter out the spurious anti-women hadiths that were added later. Although the term feminism has developed a some what poisonous connotation in today's discourse, it really just means the promotion of women's God-given rights liberties, which is to the good of everyone.

Equality and Identity

There are a lot of references from the Qur'an and Hadith about the rights of women guaranteed by Islam. Attitudes towards women: "O you who believe! You are forbidden to inherit women against there will. Nor should you treat them with harshness, that you may take away part of the dower you have given them, - except where they have been guilty of open lewdness; On the contrary live with them on a footing of kindness and equity. If you take a dislike to them it may be that you dislike a thing, and Allah brings about through it great deal of good (An-Nisa 4:19).

It's only in relation to each other and society that a difference is made – a difference of role or function. The rights and responsibilities of a woman are equal to those of man, but they are not necessarily identical with them. Equality and Identity are two different things, Islamic traditions maintain – the former desirable, the latter not. Men and women should therefore be complementary to each other in a multi-function organization rather than competitive with each other in a uni-function society.

The equality demanded by Islamic traditions must, however, be seen in its larger context if it is to be understood properly. Since Muslims regard a differentiation of sexual roles to be natural and desirable in the majority of cases, the economic responsibilities of male and female differ to provide balance for the physical differences between man and woman and for the grater responsibility which women carry in the reproductive and rearing activities so necessary to the well-being of the society. To maintain, therefore that the men of the family are responsible for providing economically for the women or that women are not equally responsible, is not a dislocation or denial of sexual equity. It is instead a duty to be fulfilled by men as compensation for another responsibility which involves special ability of women. Likewise the different inheritance rates for males and females, which is so often sited as an example of discrimination against women, must not be seen as an isolated prescription. It is but one part of a comprehensive system in which women carry no legal responsibility to support other embers of the family, but in which men are bound by a law as well as custom to provide for all their female relatives.

Form of an Islamic Feminism

The advent of Islam brought profound changes to the Arabian society in general and to women in particularly. Islam reversed or abolished the repressive and cruel practices committed against women such as female infanticide:

"When news is brought to one of them, of (the birth of) a female (child), his face darkens, and he is filled with inward grief! With shame does he hide himself form people, because of the bad news he has received! Shall he keep this (child), despite the contempt (which he fills for it) or shall he bury it in the dust? Oh, evil is indeed whatever they decide." (Qur'an 16: 58-59). Where women's rights were taken away or ignored, Islam restored them, and where women enjoyed any degree of freedom, Islam reinforced and enhanced it.

As profound as the women's rights advocated by Islam may be, however, by no means are they exhaustive the message of Islam is a universal message intended to guide all of mankind for eternity. But in order to survive and thrive, the Qur'an had to be addressed to, understood and accepted by the Arabs of 6-th century. This concept is crucial to understanding the status of women in Islam and extent of their rights as well as their obligations. The rights of women established in the Qur'an, although progressive in their essence and content, were limited in their scope and implementation in order to suit the human society which received the divine message at the time. As we approach the end of the 20-th century and taking into account the enormous socio-economic changes that have taken place since the time of the Prophet, women's rights must be extended to the best of what they can mean in our modern time. Based on the Quranic teachings of what is fair (al-adl) and what is generous and perfect (al-ihsan), we must go beyond the literal or interpretative limitations and examine the Quran's underlying principles which promote the equality of men and women – morally, spiritually, intellectually, socially and politically. It is this general principle that should serve as our guiding light in defining women's rights.

Adam and Eve

"Man is not made in the image of God. Neither is a flawed female helpmate extracted from him as an afterthought or utility. Dualism is the primordial design for all creation; from all (created) things are pairs." (Qur'an 51:49). Islam brought radical changes regarding women and society, despite the deeply entrenched patriarchy of seventh-century Arabia. It's clear, that the Qur'an aimed to erase all notions of women as subhuman. There are more passages that address issues relating to women – as individuals, in the family, as members of the community – than all other social issues combined.

The Qur'an provides women with explicit rights to inheritance, independent property, divorce and right to testify in a court of law. It prohibits wanton violence towards women and girls and is against duress in marriage and community affairs. Women and men are equally required to fulfill all religious duties, and are equally eligible for punishment for misdemeanors. Finally, women are offered the ultimate boon: paradise and proximity to Allah: "Whoever does an atom's weight of good, whether male or female, and is a believer, all such shall enter into Paradise" (Qur'an 40:40).

Spiritual equality, responsibility and accountability for both men and women is a well-developed theme in the Qur'an. Spiritual equality between men and women in the sight of God is not limited to purely spiritual, religious issues, but is the basis for equality in all temporal aspects of human endeavor.

The concept of Gender Equality is best exemplified in the Qur'anic rendition of Adam and Eve. The Qur'an states that both sexes were deliberate and independent. The Qur'an describes how Adam and Eve were told to avoid a specific tree, which they both approached. For this act of disobedience to God, they were consequently banished from the garden; however, later both repented and were forgiven by God.

The Role of Woman in Society from an Islamic Perspective

1. Spiritual Aspect

(a) *According to the Qur'an, men and women have the same spiritual human nature:*

"O mankind; Reverence your Guardian Lord Who created you from a single person created of like nature of his mate and from them twain scattered(like seeds) countless men and women; reverence *Allaah* through Whom you demand your mutual (rights) and (reverence) the wombs (that bore you); for Allah ever watches you" (Qur'an 4:1).

"(He is) the Creator of the heavens and the earth: He has made for you pairs from among yourselves and pairs among cattle: by this means does He multiply you; there is nothing whatever like unto Him and Her is one that hears and sees (all things)" (Qur'an 42:11).

(b) *Both genders are dignified and are trustees of Allah on earth*:

"We have honored the children of Adam, provided them with transport on land and sea; given them for sustenance things good and pure; and conferred on them special favors above a great part of our Creation" (Qur'an 17:70).

(c) *According to the Qur'an, woman is not blamed for the "fall of man"*:

Pregnancy and childbirth are not seen as punishments for "eating from the forbidden tree". On the contrary, the Qur'an considers them to be grounds for love and respect due to mothers. In narrating the story of Adam and Eve, the Qur'an frequently refers to both of them, never singling out Eve for the blame:

"O Adam! Dwell you and your wife in the garden and enjoy (its good things) as you (both) wish; but approach not this tree or you (both) run into harm and transgression. Then began Satan to whisper suggestions to them bringing openly before their minds all their shame that was hidden from them (before); he said " Your Lord only forbade you this tree lest you (both) should become angels such beings as live for ever". And he swore to them both that he was their sincere adviser. So by deceit he brought about their fall; when they tested of the tree shame became manifest to them and began to sew together leaves of the garden over their bodies. And their Lord called unto them: "Did I not forbid you that tree and tell you that Satan was an avowed enemy unto you?" They said: "Our Lord! We have wronged our own souls; if you forgive us not bestow not upon as Your mercy we shall certainly be lost." Allah said:" Get you (both) down with enmity between yourselves. On earth will be your dwelling place and your means of livelihood for a time." He said: "There in shall you (both) and there in shall you (both) die; and from it shall you (both) be taken out (at last). O you children of Adam! We have bestowed raiment upon you to cover your shame as well as to be an adornment to you but the raiment of righteousness that is the best. Such are among the signs of Allah that they may receive admonition! O you children of Adam! Let not Satan seduce you in the same manner as he got your parents out of the garden stripping them of their raiment to expose their shame: for he and his tribe watch you from a position where you cannot see them: We made the evil ones friends (only) to those without faith." (Qur'an 7:19-27).

On the question of pregnancy and childbirth the Qur'an states:

"And we have enjoyed on the person (to be good, to his/her parents; in pain did his/her mother bear him/her and in pain did she give him/her birth. The carrying of the (child) to his/her weaning is (a period of) thirty months. At length when he/she reaches the age of full strength and attains forty year he/she says: "O my Lord! Grant me that I may work righteousness such as You may approve; and be gracious to me in my issue. Truly have I turned to You and truly do I bow (to You) in Islam (submission)"(Qur'an 46:15).

(d) *Men and women have the same religious and moral duties and responsibilities*:

They both face the consequences of their deeds. And their Lord has accepted of them and answered them:

"Never will I suffer to be los the work of any of you be it male or female: you are member of one another…" (Qur'an 3:195).

"If any do deeds of righteousness be they male or female and have faith they will enter paradise and not the least injustice will be done to them." (Qur'an 4: 124).

"For Muslim men and women, and for believing men and

women, for devout men and women, for true men and women, for men and women who are patient and constant, for men and women who humble themselves, for men and women who give in charity, for men and women who engage much in Allah's praise, for them has Allah prepared forgiveness and great reward." (Qur'an 33:35).

2. Economic Aspect

(a) The Islamic Shariah recognizes the full property rights of women before and after marriage. A married woman may keep her maiden name.

(b) Greater financial security is assured for women. They area entitled to receive marital gifts, to keep present and future properties and income for their own security. No married woman is required to spend a coin from her property and income on household. She is entitled to full financial support during marriage and during the waiting period (iaddah) in case of divorce. She is also entitled to child support. Generally, a Muslim woman is guaranteed support in all stages of her life, as a daughter, wife, mother, or sister. These additional advantages of woman over men are somewhat balanced by the provisions of the inheritance which allow the male, in most cases to inherit twice as much as the female. This means that the male inherits more but it's responsible financially for other females: daughters, wives, mother and sister. While the female (i.e., a wife) inherits less but can keep it all for investment and finance security without any legal obligation so spend any part of it even for her own sustenance (food, clothing, housing, medication, etc).

3. The Social Aspect

(a) *As a Daughter*

(i) The Qur'an effectively ended the cruel pre Islamic practice of female infanticide: "When the female (infant) buried alive is questioned for what crime she was killed" (Qur'an 81-89).

(ii) The Qur'an went further to rebuke the unwelcoming

attitudes among some parents upon hearing the news of birth a baby girl, instead of a baby boy: "When news is brought to one of them, of (the birth of) a female (child), his face darkens, and he is filled with inward grief! With shame does he hide himself form people, because of the bad news he has received! Shall he keep this (child), despite the contempt (which he fills for it) or shall he bury it in the dust? Oh, evil is indeed whatever they decide." (Qur'an 16: 58-59)

(iii) Parents are duty bound to support and show kindness and justice to their daughters. Prophet Muhammad (peace be upon him) said: "Whosoever has a daughter and he does not bury her alive, does not insult her, and does not favor his son over her, Allah will enter him into Paradise." (Ahmad)

(iv) Education is not only a right but also a responsibility of all males and females. Prophet Muhammad (peace be upon him) said: "Seeking knowledge is mandatory for every Muslim ("Muslim" is used here in the generic meaning which includes both males and females)."

(b) *As a Wife*

Marriage in Islam is based on mutual peace, love and compassion, not just satisfaction of man's needs: "And Among his Signs is that He created for your mates from among yourselves that you may well in tranquility with them and He has put life and mercy between your (hearts); verily in that are signs for those who reflect." (Qur'an 30:21)

"He is the Creator of the heavens and the earth ; He has made for you pairs from among yourselves and pairs among castle; by this means does he multiply you; there is nothing whatever like unto him and He is the One that hears and sees (all things)"(Qur'an 42:11). The Qur'an urges husbands to be kind and considerate to their wives even if they do not inherit women against their will. Nor should you treat them with harshness that you may take away part of the marital gift you have given them except where they have been guilty of open lewdness; on the contrary live with them on a footing of kindness and equity. If you take a dislike to them it may be that you dislike a thing and Allah brings about a though it a great deal of good (Qur'an 4:19).

Prophet Muhammad (p.b.u.h.) taught: "I command you to be kind to women. The best of you is the best to his family (wife)...)..."

Question of Polygamy: Like many people and religions, however, Islam did not out law polygamy but regulated it and restricted it. It's neither required nor encouraged but simply permitted and not outlawed. The only passage in the Qur'an (4:3) which explicitly mentioned polygamy and restricted its practice in terms of the number of wives permitted and the requirement of justice between them was revealed after the Battle of Uhud in which dozens of Muslims were martyred leaving behind widows and orphans. This seems to indicate that the intent of its continued permissibility is to deal with individual and collective contingencies that may arise from time to time (i.e. imbalances between the number of males and females created by wars) This provides a moral, practical and humane solution to the problems of widows and orphans who are likely to be more vulnerable in the absence of a husband/father figure to look after their needs: financial, companions, proper rearing, and other needs.

"If you fear that you shall not be able to deal justly with the orphans marry women of your choice, two or three or four; but if you fear that you shall not be able to deal justly (with them) then only one." (Qur'an 4:3).

(c) *As a Mother*

Kindness to parents (especially mothers) is next to worship pf Allah: "Your Lord has decreed that you worship none but him and that you be kind to parents. Whether one or both of them attain old age in your life say not to a word of contempt nor repel them but address them in terms of honor" (Qur'an 17:23).

REFERENCES

1. John L. Esposito, Women in Muslim Family Law, Syracuse University Press, 1982.

2. Leila Ahmed, Women and Gender in Islam. New Haven, Yale University Press, 1992.
3. Qur'an Translations by Muhammad Asad, 1980.
4. Qur'an Translations by Abdulaziz Mansur, Tahskent Islamic University Press.
5. Zeenat Shaukat Ali, Marriage and Divorce in Islam: A Appraisal. Bombay, Jaico Publishing House.
6. "Gender Equity in Islam" Jamal A.Badawi , Ph.D., World Assembly of Youth Studies on Islam.

14

Human Rights Violation on Dalit Women

Sajeena Beevi

Introduction

Most of the South Asian countries, like India, Nepal, Pakistan, Bangladesh and Sri Lanka, Dalits have endured discrimination based on work and descent for centuries, and this discrimination continues today. The Dalits – known as 'untouchables' or outcastes – number around two hundred and sixty million people in South Asia. On account of their caste, they experience discrimination, social exclusion and violence on a daily basis. Although economic growth in the region has been strong over the past decade, caste disparities remain and are in fact increasing. The situation of Dalit women in these countries needs urgent and special attention. They constitute one of the largest socially segregated groups anywhere in the world and face systemic and structural discrimination thrice over: *as Dalits, as women*, and as poor.

Violence and Discrimination: India

Women in India are subject to discrimination not just on the basis of gender but on the basis of numerous other factors such as caste, community, religious affiliation and class. India's caste system involves a social hierarchy and is a feature of Hinduism. People are born into a caste where they remain throughout their lives. Broad caste categories (varnas) separate caste groups according to occupation. Outside these categories are the "untouchables" or dalits whose occupations were viewed as "polluting" and who are subject to segregation. Many of those belonging to dalit communities are expected to stay in the profession they are born into, and overall, members of dalit and adivasi communities are less well educated than their non-dalit counterparts. Adivasis ("tribal" peoples outside the caste system) are also subject to forms of untouchability in Uttar Pradesh and Rajasthan where they are often indistinguishable from dalits, making them vulnerable to similar abuse and exploitation. Literacy levels among dalit women are lowest in the country.

The problems of Dalit women, however, have not received the attention it deserves. There are specific reasons for this neglect. The mainstream view on this issue is that the problems confronting Dalit women are identical with that of general women. So there is no necessity to make special efforts for them.

This paper intends to examine the secondary sources of data for the following objectives:

1. To highlight the specific problems of Dalit women concerning human rights violation;
2. To Understand the reasons behind the violation of human rights; and
3. To pose some issues for the Human Rights Commission.

Dalit Women in India

The situation of Dalit women in India needs special attention. They are one of the largest socially segregated groups anywhere in the world, and make up 2% of the world's total population. Dalit women in India constitute 80 million or 48% of the total Dalit population, 16.3% of the total female population in India. 81.5% of Dalit women live in rural areas. They, along with their male counterparts, constitute a sizeable social group that continues to suffer work and descent based discrimination and untouchability arising out of the caste system. Dalit women in India suffer from three oppressions: gender, as a result of patriarchy; class, from being from the poorest and most marginalized communities; and caste, from coming from the lowest caste, the 'untouchables'. Although discrimination on the basis of caste is against the Indian constitution and prohibited by many laws, its practice is still widespread, especially in rural India.

Human Rights of Dalit Women

Article 14 of India's constitution ensures equality by providing that: "The State shall not deny to any person equality before the law or the equal protection of the laws within the territory of India." Article 15(1) provides that the "State shall not discriminate against any citizen on grounds only of religion, race, caste, sex, place of birth or any of them," while articles 16(1) and 16(2) prohibit discrimination in general, and gender discrimination in matters of public employment. To promote equality, Article 15(3) provides that the state is free to make "any special provision for Women and children". Part IV of the constitution lists the Directive Principles of State Policy, including Article 39(b) of the constitution which provides that the state direct its policy toward ensuring equal pay for equal work for men and women.

India is a democracy and is a Party to most of the major human rights treaties. These treaties provide the same rights for men and women. Because India is also a Party to the Convention on the Elimination of All Forms of Discrimination Against Women (CEDAW), the Government has an extra obligation to make sure that women can realize their rights. It is generally accepted in international law that governments have to do more than just pass legislation to protect human rights. The Government of India has an obligation to take all measures, including policy and budgetary measures, to make sure that women can fulfill their rights. It also has an obligation to punish those who engage in caste-based violence and discrimination.

India is a Party to the International Covenant on Civil and Political Rights. Based on this treaty, the Government of India has an obligation to make sure that Dalit women can enjoy a whole range of human rights, such as the right to life, freedom from torture or cruel, inhuman or degrading treatment or punishment, freedom from slavery, the right to be equal before the court, the right to recognition as a person before the law, the right to privacy, the right to marry only with free and full consent, and the right to take part in public affairs. The life and dignity of Dalit women depends on the realization of these human rights. However, they are breached systematically.

An essential precondition for the realization of civil and political rights of Dalit women is registration. Article 24 (2) of the Covenant provides that every child shall be registered immediately after birth. In India, 46 % of all children are not registered. There is also no system of registration of marriages. This is not only a barrier for the realization of civil and political rights; it also prevents the protection of Dalit girls from sexual exploitation and trafficking, child labour and forced and early marriages. Dalit women hardly enjoy any of these human rights.

Violence Against Dalit Women

Certain kinds of violence are traditionally reserved for Dalit women. Singularly positioned at the bottom of India's caste, class, and gender hierarchies, largely uneducated and consistently paid less than their male counterparts, Dalit women make up the majority of landless laborers and scavengers, as well as a significant percentage of the women forced into prostitution in rural areas or sold into urban brothels. As such, they come into greater contact with landlords and enforcement agencies than their upper-caste counterparts. Their subordinate position is exploited by those in power who carry out their attacks with impunity.

Throughout the report, Human Rights Watch has documented the use of sexual abuse and other forms of violence against Dalit women as tools by landlords and the police to inflict political "lessons" and crush dissent and labor movements within Dalit communities. In Laxmanpur-Bathe, Bihar, women were raped and mutilated before being massacred by members of the Ranvir Sena in 1997; in Bihar and Tamil Nadu, women have been beaten, arrested, and sometimes tortured during violent search and raid operations on Dalit villages in recent years. Like other Indian women whose relatives are sought by the police, Dalit women have also been arrested and raped in custody as a means of punishing their male relatives who are hiding from the police. As very young women, they are forced into prostitution in temples under the *devadasi* system.

Cases documented by India's National Commission for Women, by local and national nongovernmental women's rights organizations, and by the press, reveal a pattern of impunity in attacks on women consistent with our findings. In all cases of attacks on women documented in this report, the accused state and private actors escaped punishment; in most cases, attacks were neither investigated nor prosecuted. Until recently, the plight of Dalit women has also been neglected by various political movements. As explained by Ruth Manorama, head of the newly constituted National Federation for Dalit Women: Dalit women are at the bottom in our community. Within the women's movement, Dalit issues have not been taken seriously. Within the Dalit movement, women have been ignored. Caste, class, and gender need to be looked at together.

Dalit Women As Victims of Caste Hierarchy and Atrocities

Descent based discrimination based on caste imposes social exclusion on persons belonging to Dalit communities and their physical separation from the dominant castes in housing patterns, strict enforcement of the prohibition of inter dining at public places, seating arrangements in education institutions, particularly schools, and the forces the performance of degrading occupations like manual scavenging and carrying of night soil by Dalit women. Caste discrimination results in the violent appropriation and sexual control over Dalit women by men of the dominant castes, evident in the systematic rape of Dalit women and perpetuation of forced prostitution in the name of religion through the Devadasi system.

In a reported incident, four Dalits in Khairlanji village in Maharashtra were killed in the broad day light on 29 September 2006. Four members of a Dalit family, specifically the mother and the daughter had been brutally murdered, raped and their bodies thrown into the canal by a crowd of non-Dalits as an off shoot of their resistance to the forceful grabbing the land from the family. Earlier the family appealed to the local police and various authorities to intervene in the case and the total silence led to this gruesome atrocity. Even in this incident, the police would not register the case immediately, only after a massive protest by the Dalit community the authorities moved into register the case more than two months after it took place. In the name of maintaining law and order the state police arrested hundreds of Dalit demonstrators and charged them under various sections and put them in prison.

The Annual Report of University Grant Commission for 1999-2000, shows that Dalits in general have very low participation rates in higher education (*Annual Reports of U.G.C*).The main reasons for the very low literacy rate among Dalit women could be some or all of the following:

- The Lack of educational resources especially in rural areas.
- Privatization of schools and colleges.
- Humiliation and bullying by the high caste students and teachers. (Thind, G.S-1999).

According to India's Ministry of Labour, 85% of the Dalit women have the most formidable occupations and work as agricultural laborers, scavengers, sweepers, and disposers of human waste. Many of these women work for minimal wages under the upper caste landlords. When the Dalit women refuse to work for ridiculously low wages or fail to follow their harsh orders of their employers it results into open violence, humiliation, beating, rape, and jail. There are also a number of cases where the houses of Dalit women have been burnt down (Agarwal- 1999). In one particular case, a four months pregnant agricultural labourer, from the southern part of India, was stripped naked and beaten, in front of the whole village and her family, by the upper caste landlord. Later, she was retained in jail, where the police tortured her. This resulted in the miscarriage of her baby. In another case, a school student in Gujarat made a mistake of joining the dancing in the main square of her village, in which most of the participants were of the upper caste. The upper caste boys pulled her out and threatened to rape her. For interfering, her mother was slapped. In the hope for justice, she forced her parents to file a complaint to the police against her assailants. Her mother was constantly threatened by the upper caste families for complaining to the police. Feeling deeply humiliated by no justice and rumors of rape, the girl committed suicide (*News Archives*).There are many similar cases like the one above.

The worst exploitation of dalit women involves a lifetime of suffering, torture, and rape (Thind, G.S-1999). Justified by the Vedic scriptures, the *Devdasi system* (also known as temple prostitution) was introduced by the High caste Hindus, and it still exists in some parts of India (Thind; Agarwal; Narula). According to the *Human Right Watch Report* in 1992, an estimated 50,000 girls were sold every year to Hindu organizations that are involved in the Devdasi system These girls are called the "female servants of god" and are sexually exploited (Thind,G.S-1999).After a lifetime of living as a prostitute and servant, the women in their later years are sold to brothels, where they are further tortured and often die of neglect or AIDS (Thind; *News Archives*). The Devdasi system and Child marriage are also justified by Hindu Scriptures (Thind; Agarwal; *News Archives*).The 1992-93 Annual report from the Ministry of Welfare shows 1,236reported cases of rape on Dalit women. The National Commission for SC/ST reports that approximately 10,000 cases of human right violations on Dalits are reported every month. But what is even more disturbing, is that only one out of ten of the cases are reported annually whilst, nine go unreported. After fifty-five years of India's independence and despite the excellent laws in place to protect Dalit women, they are still suffering unimaginable atrocities from the high caste Hindus. It is believed that thousands of these cases go unreported and unpublicized because the poor Dalits that live in rural areas, who are the worst victims, have no control on power, wealth, justice, police and the media (Thind, G.S-1999).

Systemic Discrimination, Violence and Impunity

The hardships of Dalit women are not simply due to their poverty, economical status, or lack of education, but are a direct result of the severe exploitation and suppression by the upper classes, which is legitimized by Hindu religious scriptures (Thind; Agarwal). We see many examples of brave Dalit women who being quite aware of the horrifying truth and despite the heavy odds still strive to put an end to their suffering (Thind; Agarwal; *News Archives*). In doing so, they most certainly ensure a brighter future for the generations to come. Ruth Manorama, once stated that in a male dominated society, "Dalit women face a triple burden of caste, class and gender" in which she sums up the plight of Dalit women, highlighting the fact that Dalit women are a distinct social group and cannot be masked under the general categories of "Women" or "Dalits".

In Ancient India (3200-2500 B.C.), the caste system was non-existent since even the most learned men were good householders and had varied occupations. The women of ancient India were just as superior as men in learning, education, and intellect. The choice for her mate was according to her own wishes and marriage was practiced after the coming of age. She attended parties, competitions, and religious functions as she wished. The remarriage of young widows was also a common practice (Thind, G.S—1999).The creation of a number of Hindu religious books including the *Manusmriti, Atharva Vedas, Vishnu smriti*, and many others like these and their strict compliance by the Brahmans , led to a society in which equality between men and women was far from existent (Agarwal-1999). Dr. B.R. Ambedkar, the architect of the Indian Constitution, also makes it very clear in his article titled "The rise and fall of Hindu woman" that the root cause of suffering for women in India are these so called Hindu religious books (Thind; Agarwal). Books like the Manusmriti divide people into a stratified caste system and promote inequality between men and women (Thind; Agarwal). According to the *Manusmriti*, women have no right to education, independence, or wealth. It not only justifies the treatment of dalit women as a sex object and promotes child marriage, but also justifies a number of violent atrocities on women as can be seen in the verses (Agarwal; *Manusmriti*):A man, aged thirty years, shall marry a maiden of twelve who pleases him. If his duties would otherwise be impeded, he must marry sooner. Be a girl, be a young woman, or even be an aged one, nothing must be done independently, even in her own house. Her father protects (her) in childhood, her husband protects (her) in youth, and her sons protect (her) in old age; a woman is never fit for independence

A Brahman, Kshatriya, or Vaishya Man can sexually exploit any herds of woman. Even the killing of a dalit woman is explicitly justified as a minor offence for the Brahmins: equal to the killing of an animal. If the killing of an untouchable was justified as a minor offence, you can imagine the treatment they received throughout their lives.

In a male dominated society, Dalit women suffered unimaginable oppression, not only through caste, but gender too, from which there was no escape. The laws in the *Manusmriti* and other Vedic scriptures close all economic, political, social, educational, and personal channels through which Dalit women could be uplifted (Thind,G.S-1999). The horrendous Laws in the *Manusmriti* were incorporated into Hinduism because they were favorable only to the Upper-castes, which form the majority of India. Even today, we see the severe oppression and exploitation of Dalit women. The Laws of the Manusmriti have a devastating effect on the level of education reached by Dalit women (Thind,G.S-1999).

Assertion by Dalit Women

Dalit women today are not simply passive victims; the current mood is not one of mere acceptance, but one of determination to 'transform their pain into power'. In fact, they have been active throughout history, though often this has not been recognized and recorded. They have been actively involved in the anti-caste and anti-untouchability movements. Today they are the strongholds of the Dali movements in thousands of South Asian villages, and are often at the forefront of struggles for basic human rights. They continue to play a critical role in the movements for land and livelihood rights and against unsociability, pointing to the potential for their self-emancipation, given adequate support. They are making their mark as independent thinkers and writers in the literary world by critiquing dominant caste ideologies. They participate today as visionary leaders in the local governance institution by asserting their rights. While they continue to struggle against structural discrimination and exclusion, violence and impunity are systematically unleashed by dominant castes to keep them in their place. While recognizing the gendered nature of caste discrimination for Dalit women, these women have turned their 'suffering' into one of 'resistance', actively participating shoulder to shoulder with men in their communities in the anti-caste and anti-untouchability movements. In this regard, Dalit women build their identities on a culture of resistance against the hegemonic culture of the caste system, expressing their defiance and revolt against the caste, class and gender discrimination that oppresses them. This assertion of distinct identity and simultaneous forging of a collective identity in multiple struggles marks the Dalit women's movement in various ways.

The question of Human Rights of Dalit women poses a challenge to the Human Rights Commission. At the moment the NHRC has no agenda for Dalit women. So NHRC (National Human Rights Commission) should make a beginning in this respect on the following lines:

1. The NHRC should bring out periodical reports on the human rights situation of Dalit women in India.
2. It should bring out reports on the social and religious institutions perpetuating socially sanctioned prostitutions such as Devadasis and Joginis in Andhra Pradesh and Maharashtra and also in other states and make efforts to stop this system both legally and other measures.
3. Bringing out reports on the social and economic situation of Dalit women which leads to the violation of human rights and suggests social and economic measures to promote the atmosphere in which Dalit women could enjoy human rights.
4. Give representation and participation to Dalit women in NHRC and other Commissions for women.

Conclusion

The courage, struggle, and persistence of today's Dalit women against suppression, exploitation and torture has the power to ensure that the future generations will not have to face the bleak reality Dalits have faced for the past two thousand years.

The caste system is truly a crippling disease to approximately 250 million Dalits in India today. Since its roots are embedded in the Hindu religious scriptures, it seems this disease has no cure, but every voice rose against caste-based discrimination and suppression through Dalit Organizations will turn this from a losing battle to one of victory in which every Dalit woman will have equal rights, access to education, and a chance to succeed and prosper. Many of the Dalit NGO's are involved in establishing schools, scholarships, and basic supplements to Dalits in the rural parts of India. NGO's such as the Ambedkar Centre for Peace and Justice and the National Campaign on Dalit Human Rights are involved in bringing the plight of the Dalit people to the attention of the international community and to document and publicize human rights abuse. The long term objectives are to enfranchise Dalits as full citizens of their society and eliminate caste-based discriminations.

In this regard we can quote Dr. Ambedkar, who championed for Dalit rights: Our struggle is not for wealth or for power, our struggle is for freedom. Ours is a struggle for the reclamation of human personality."Our struggle is to be free of segregation, exploitation and violence on the rights of the Dalits".

REFERENCES

1. Katare P.M, Barik B.C (2002) Development, Deprivation and Human rights Violation. New Delhi: Rawat Publications.
2. Subhash Chandra Singh (2006) Social Justice and Human Rights in India. New Delhi: Serials Publications.
3. Mehartaj B (2000)Human Rights in India-Issues and Perspectives. A.P.H. Publishing Cor.
4. Agarwal. S. (1999) Genocide of Women in Hinduism. Jabalpur: Sudarsan Books.
5. Thind G.S (1999) Our Indian Sub-Continent Heritage. Canada: Crosstown Press.
6. Narula.S. (1999) Broken People: Caste Violence Against Indias Untouchables. London: Human Rights Watch.
7. The Annual Reports of University Grants Commission, Govt. of India, 1999.
8. The National Commission for SC/ST, Govt. of India.

15

Human Rights and Gender Equality

Dhanya M.B

Introduction

A right may be defined as something to which an individual has a just claim (Hand book of human rights-2006). It is clearly pointed that all human beings are born free and equal in dignity and rights. Universal declaration of human rights contains a long list of Civil, social, political, economic and cultural rights as equality before law, protection against arbitrary arrest and detention, right to vote, right to social security, right to own property, right to free education and free participation in cultural life. These human rights are granted as fundamental rights by the constitution of India. No one shall be subjected to torture and cruel or inhuman treatment and punishment .The declaration had both genders in mind, but for over three billion of the world's women human rights are seen as mainly linked to one gender alone.

Gender equality is an important issue of human rights and social justice. Violence is seen as the most shocking yet most common manifestation of gender inequality in society. Among many types of violence, the United Nations General assembly has emphasized on violence which includes " any act on gender based violence that results in, or likely to result in physical, sexual or psychological harm or suffering to women, including threat of such acts, coercion or arbitrary deprivations of liberty whether accruing in public or private life". Crime against women takes place in a planned, systematic and sustained way. Even if it happens at the heat of the moment, it reflects deep-seated discrimination and disrespect for women as a human being.

Obstacles in Achieving Equal Rights of Women

India has ratified various international conventions and human rights instruments committing to secure equal rights of women. Key among them is the ratification of the convention on elimination of all forms of discrimination against women [CEDAW] in 1993.The Mexico plan of action [1975],the Nairobi forward looking strategies (1985),the Beijing declaration as well as the platform for action (1995) and the outcome document adopted by the UNGA Session on gender equality and development & Peace for the 21st century, titled "Further actions and initiatives to implement the Beijing Declaration and the platform for action" have been unreservedly endorsed by India for appropriate follow up. The Nairobi conference has analyzed the following factors causes the major obstacles in the realization of equal right of women (Sen.A.N-2005):

1. *Physiological difference:* The discriminations and inequality against women is generally on the basis of physiological difference between men and women .The fact is that there is no physiological basis to regard the house hold and family affairs as specification of the women, or to devalue the domestic work. Similarly there is no physiological basis to regard the capacities of women as inferior to those of men and thus to perpetuate inequalities against them. There is need for attitudinal and structural change in order to eliminate inequality.

2. *Gender inequalities:* Women, by virtue of their gender are denied of equal access to the power structure that controls society and determines development issues and peace initiatives. In addition the practices of discriminations on the basis of race, labour, colour, prevalent in some country cause further inequality in the status of women.

3. *Fundamental resistance:* any effect to raise the status of women and to eliminate discrimination against them is

resisted. As a matter of fact it results in to uneconomic use of women's talent and waste of valuable human resources necessary for the development and for strengthening of peace. Ultimately, society is the loser if the talents of women's are underutilized as a result of discrimination.

4. *The sharp contrast between legislative changes and effective implementation of these changes:* Generally legislative changes are introduced to promote marital or family status for women but in the absence of effective implementation, the indirect discrimination often persists. The law as a resource does not automatically benefit all women equally because of the socio economic inequalities, which in turn affects women's knowledge of, and access to the law and their ability to exercise their full legal rights without fear of incrimination or intimidation. Thus the lack of information of women's right has hampered the promotion of women's right to equality.

Above all, there is still a deep rooted resistance on the part of conservative elements in society to being change in attitude necessary for a total ban on discriminatory practices against women at the family, local, national, and international level.

Status of Women—Bewildering Contrasts

As per the 2001 census, the total female population of India is estimated at 495.74 million. This is 48.3% of the country's total population. The figure shows that women and children are vital human resources of the country. Thus they are considered to be the most critical determinant for its over all socio economic development. But there is no doubt ours is a male's world dominated by the males .The women rightly feel that they have been exploited and sidelined for centuries together .For a very longtime the right place of a women has been considered to be the home where she should attend to the kitchen work. She has also been considered fit only for producing and bringing up children.

Women have now raised their voice against their oppression and they want their due rights and privileges in all walks of life.

The women of today want a change in their status in the society. But a few patches of achievements here and there cannot hide the yawning hiatus between precept and practice in our glib talk on women's emancipation. Here is a picture of bewildering contrasts. We have had an illustrious galaxy of women governors and chief ministers, judges of the high courts, Supreme courts, IPS officers and also women working in Army, Navy and Air force .In the unorganized sector, too, women have been playing a cardinal role. Most of them have climbed up the ladder of success on their own despite several impediments in a largely man's world. From small post to high position women have successfully broken the male monopoly and have stormed the predominantly male bastion. They have proved beyond the shadow of doubt that, given an opportunity, they could be successful in any field. The forgoing account indicates that we have a proud record of women, who have securely a place of merit alongside men.

These shining achievements cannot hide the bitter truth that gender equality is yet to become a reality to the mass of female population in the country. Where there is a large-scale discrimination against women there is no gender equality. And this discrimination starts even before a girl child is born and is sustained right up to widowhood. In other words it is a monumental shame and outrage that we practice gender inequality right from the cradle up to the grave! We know the running scourges stalking womanhood in India are female foeticide, female infanticide, child marriage, adverse sex ratio against the female, neglect of female education, sexual harassment, molestation and rape, and to crown it all, the total neglect of widows.

The greatest curse that perpetuates gender inequality is dowry, which persists despite law and education. And let us not forget that dowry is interconnected with such other evils like female foeticide, female infanticide and child marriage. Families just refuse to welcome the birth of girl child just because they cannot afford the huge dowry they have to pay for their daughters as they grow up and get married. So the easy and clandestine way is: better kill them before they are born or kill them even after thy are born. Early marriage especially without the consent of the girl is another form of the human rights violation, as it prohibits them from making their future bright. Domestic violence may be seen in the form of mental and physical torture, murder, rape etc.A fatal consequence of the violence is to inducing the victim to suicidal behaviour.Several studies also show the link between domestic violence and suicide. Rape can occur anywhere, even in family, where it can take the form of marital rape or incest. According to WHO, every 54 minutes a women is raped. Kidnapped or abducted women are usually sold for prostitution or marriage. Trafficking in girl has been frequently reported both at inter state and international level. Sexual harassment in the workplace is a growing concern for women. Supreme Court has defined sexual harassment at workplace as follows [Namrata Prasad-2003].

1. Physical contact and advances.
2. A demand or request for sexual favours.
3. Showing pornography material.
4. Any other unwelcome physical, verbal or non-verbal conduct of sexual nature.

Employers abuse their authority to seek sexual favours from their female co-workers from subordinates by sometimes promising promotions or other career advancement or simply creating an untenable and hostile work environment. Women who refuse to give in to such unwanted sexual advances often run the risk of anything form demotion to dismissal. Women are victims of violence; in every five minutes one woman is victimised. Table 15.1 ascertains the level of atrocities committed on women in India. It is to be noted that growth rate of crime against women is higher than population growth!

Table 15.1

Level of atrocities committed on women in India

1	1.	One woman get tortured in every 20 minutes
2	2.	One molestation in every 22 minutes
3	3.	One Kidnapping in every 40 minutes
4	4.	One rape in every 43 minutes
5	5.	One sexual harassment in every 15 minutes
6	6.	One connected with prostitution in every 70 minutes

Source: Proceedings on 'Vertical interaction course on Gender justice and Role of Police' by NIPCCD, Banglore on November, 2004.

Extend of Rights and Status of Women

The constitution of India adopted in 1950 not only grants equality to women, but also empowers the state to adopt measures of affirmative discrimination in favor of women. It further imposes a fundamental duty on every citizen to renounce practices derogatory to the dignity of women. The right to share property and the right to divorce are available to women. There have been a number of legislations, usually called legislations relating to dowry prohibition, sati prevention, child marriage restraint, guardianship and maintenance, sale of minors, equal remuneration, minimum wages, maternity benefits and industrial disputes and special marriage. However the benefit of these institutions did not accrue to women as each community prefers to keep alive ritual and discriminatory practices. Education, employment, opportunities and economic independence are still largely male prerogative. A majority of the women remain poor, illiterate subject and invisible.

In many countries, women fall victim to traditional practices that violate their human rights .The persistence of the problem has much to do with the fact that the most of these physically and psychologically harmful customs are deeply rooted in the tradition and culture of society. It also shows the traditional male dominance in the society. Again it reveals the violation of human rights of women. Today the Indian women is far from equal to the Indian man there is a negative female sex ratio at the national level [929:1000 in 1991] which has been steadily falling from [972:1000] in 1901.There are noticeable differences in literacy rates among adults and enrolment and dropout rates in schools.

One might ask why legislation has failed to curb the evil. The answer is simple. No law can change social or human behavior totally. We have law against child marriage, female foeticide, rape, immoral trafficking, dowry prohibition etc. but has the incidence of any of these evils come down because of the law? Dowry will go only if the man changes or only if society treats man and woman as equal partners in life. The tragic part of the story is that even education has not made any difference to the evil practice. The result is for all to see. Bridegrooms are for sale in the matrimonial market and the highest bidder can get hold of them. And the price tags of the bridegroom vary depending upon their qualification, employment and family status. So the would–be-father in law knows that he has to pay a dear price in order to get highly qualified boys with such labels as IAS, IPS, MBA, CA, Engineer, Doctor and the like. The more the educated, the higher the Price tag of the would-be-son in law, the higher would be the dowry.

The status of and the attitude to the widows have not changed through we claim to live in cyber age and space age. If one wants to see the real degradation of widows, one must see the real plight in the pilgrim center of Mathura, Brindavan and Varanasi in Uttar Pradesh. Widows from west Bengal and elsewhere are dumped here and they survive here on alms given by pilgrims and a few young are sexually exploited too. Widows are still looked down upon as if they are responsible for their husband's death. In the economic field and the world of work, barriers of discrimination have started crumbling down in a limited way with the enactment of such legislation as equal pay for equal work. But in the unorganized sector where bulks of women are employed, they are an exploited lot with lower wages and denial of basic amenities.

Five Year Plans and Women

Since independence, significant efforts have been made to strengthen the legal, constitutional and institutional framework to protect and promote human rights. The formation of the national human rights commission in 1993 & the creation of various state human rights commissions are initiated for protecting the human rights for all citizens. The plan documents over the years have reflected the evolving trend in gender matters.

From the very beginning of independent India's development planning process, one of the main issues has been that of providing equal status to women. While the thrust of the first four plans was on organizing various welfare activities and giving priority to women's education, the fifth and sixth plan witnessed a shift from welfare to overall development women with thrust on health, education and employment of women. The sixth five-year plan was a milestone in women's development .It made a review of the status and situation of women and reached the conclusion that despite legal and constitutional guarantees; women had lagged behind in almost all sectors. The document pointed out the declining sex ratio and the lower life expectancy of women as the basic indicators of their low status. Setting up of cells at a district level for improving women's participation through self employment, was suggested in the document .It mention that the government should review the adequacy of the implementing machinery of various special legislations passed for the protection of women's right .The stress of the seventh plan was on identifying and promoting beneficiary oriented programmes with a view to extending the direct benefits to women. Eighth five year plan stressed the need to give additional attention to women and on the prime and important need for employment were mentioned and it urged for a changing societal attitude towards women through awareness creation.

Ninth five year plan focused on empowering women as a catalyst of social change and development, a 'National Policy for Empowerment of women 'would be formulated .The plan proposed the setting up of a 'Development bank for women entrepreneurs'. The most important resolve of the plan was to have a special women's component in the plan to ensure 30% flow of funds to women development sectors. Tenth plan reinforces commitment to gender budgeting to establish its gender differential impact and to translate gender commitments into budgetary commitments.

Gender Inequality

Table 15.2 shows India's global position in gender development. India is ranked 127th in Human Development Index (HDI) out of 177 countries and 98th for gender development index (GDI) out of 140 countries in 2003 as reported in the Human Development Report, 2005. The Gender development Index of around .5 for India along with Pakistan, Bangladesh etc showed that women suffers the double deprivation of overall achievement in human development .The Maternal Mortality Ratio in India 540 per one lakh births compared to only 16-17 developed country's points to the structural deficiencies in access to healthcare and nutritional disadvantage. Adult female literacy rate shows half of Indian women are still illiterate .The Female Economic Activity Rate is only 42.5 percent as compared to 72.45 in China & 60.3% in Norway.

Table 15.2

India's Global Position in Gender Development

Countries	Human Development Index	Gender Development Index	Maternal Mortality Ratio	Adult Female Literacy Rate	Female Economic activity Rate
Norway	0.963	0.960	16	–	60.3
United States	0.944	0.942	17	–	59.6
China	0.755	0.754	56	86.5	72.4
Srilanka	0.751	0.747	92	88.6	43.5
India	0.602	0.586	540	47.8	42.5
Pakistan	0.527	0.508	500	35.2	36.7
Nepal	0.526	0.511	740	34.9	56.9
Bangladesh	0.520	0.514	380	31.4	66.5

Source: UNDP, Human Development Report, 2005.

The Gender Inequalities inhibit the social and economic progress of the country. Inspite of the progress achieved reducing gender disparities in India during last few decades there are still widespread discrimination against the girls and women. Their number is relatively much larger regarding undernourishment in the country. Their representation in different spheres of life is much lower. The recent report of the world food programme, the United Nations food agency that 18000 children die of hunger and malnutrition every day underscores the urgent need for all governments to respond to poverty in all its manifestations. Poverty is probably the most serious human rights and development challenge both advanced and developing countries. The recognition of poverty as a human rights issue is a recent development. The World Bank Report (1997) notes that 20% of the world's poor live in India & 80 % of them are women. Feminization of poverty is a tragic consequence of women's unequal access to economic opportunities.

Conclusion

There are Gender inequalities in the country whether it is social, political, economic or cultural participation undermining the importance of females in national Development. Therefore government both in the central, state as well as at regional levels should implement effectively the ongoing projects for eliminating all sorts of social and economic discrimination against females for improving their capacities and enabling them to contribute to the national level. Mass campaigns should be carried out at the local levels by involving local people for removing gender inequalities. We have made Adequate Provisions for gender equality, but in the societal mindset the female is still looked down upon as inferior to the male. Unless this mindset is changed totally all other steps taken in other fields to achieve gender equality will come to naught. In conclusion there is a need for changing the mindset towards women so as to give equal rights as enshrined in the constitution. Gender equalities also allow the people to meet their other choice such as freedom of thought, guaranteed human rights and dignity of labour. Dr. A.S.Anand, the former Chief justice of India has focused on the vital need for change in social attitudes towards women. In a speech delivered at the India Habitat center in New Delhi on December 2, 2000, he said: " Let me caution...that the cry for gender equality should not be treated as if it is a fight against men. It is a fight against traditions that have chained women- a fight against attitudes that are ingrained in society-it is the fight against the proverbial Lakshman Rekha, which is different for men and different for women. Therefore men must rise to the occasion. They must recognize and accept the fact that women are equal partners in life. They are individuals who have their own identity...society needs to change its attitudes. It is high time that human rights of women are given proper priority."

REFERENCES

1. Govt. of India., Plan Documents.
2. Handbook of human Rights and Criminal Justice in India-The System and Procedure, (2006): South Asia Human Rights Documentation Center, New Delhi.
3. Monro Surya, (2005), 'Gender Politics—Citizenship, Activism and Sexual Diversity', Pluto Press Publications, London.
4. Namrata Prasad(2003): 'Human Rights-Gender Based Violence', Yojana, (December).
5. Sen. A.N (2005): "Human Rights", Sri Sai Law Publications, Faridabad.
6. Umadevi. K. (2005), 'Violence Against Women: Human Rights Perspective (ed.)', Serial Publications, New Delhi.
7. UNDP, (2005): Human Development Report.
8. Zainab M Khuram (2006): 'Bridging the Gap-Gender Budgeting', Yojana (October).

16

Rights for the Rightless

Human Rights Scenario in Indian Prisons

Sanjoy Kumar Mukherjee

Western Concept of Human Rights

The essential features of human rights are derived from a number of documents and declarations, which grew out of some epoch-making political events. More prominent among these documents and declarations are: the Magna Carta (1215), the Bill of Rights (1689), the American Declaration of Rights (1774), the US Declaration of Independence (1776), the French Declaration of Rights of Man and Citizen (1789). One common theme in all these documents is that some rights are natural and, therefore, inalienable and universal. Its most notable articulation can be found in the Lockean concept of 'reserved rights'. According to Locke, human rights are to be enjoyed by all individuals irrespective of their position in the society. Human rights are, therefore, as applicable to the people incarcerated in prison as to those in the open society.

Increased Global Concern for Human Rights of Prisoners

An ever-increasing concern for the preservation of human rights even for the prisoners can be noticed particularly since the end of the Second World War. For example, the UN Declaration of Human Rights (1948) and, more prominently, the

International Covenant on Civil and Political Rights (1966) talked about the human rights of all persons including the prisoners. However a comparison between the above two documents shows that the latter not only contained more rights; it made more specific reference to prison rights as well. Article 10 of Part III of the Covenant would testify to it. It lays down that all detained persons shall be treated humanly and with respect for his inherent dignity. This is a positive obligation instead of mere prohibition of inhuman treatment found in other texts. It further provides for separate standard for accused persons and juveniles who should be treated distinctly from convicted persons. Paragraph 3 of the same article stipulates that the aim of the penitentiary system shall be the reformation and social rehabilitation of the prisoners. Thus we find an ever-increasing concern on the part of the international community for the prevention of any violation of the human rights of the prisoners. Apart from this Covenant there are a number of other important international conventions with a bearing on the criminal justice system and human rights.

Relevance of Human Rights in Prisons

Should human rights be granted to the prisoners? This apparently simple question has found the concerned scholars sharply divided among themselves. One group argues that as the convicted prisoners have violated the rights of others in some form or other, they have forfeited their rights to be treated as human beings. This debars them from any entitlement to human rights. This argument actually questions the essential human traits of the convicts. To them, to be human one must have rationality and respect for others' rights. The alternative view argues that a human being is always a human being irrespective of rationality or respect for others. No person, this group would suggest, ever becomes a non-person by committing a crime and, therefore, each person is entitled to human rights. Otherwise a retarded person or a person committing violence on others out of momentary passion has to be considered a non-person and must be deprived of his or her human rights. The argument and the counter-argument have their own merits. But if human rights are viewed as inalienable and universal natural rights, then the state cannot deny him these rights even if he takes away the natural, inalienable rights of another person or body of persons – no matter whether out of momentary passion or cold calculation. In other words, man-made laws are not entitled to take away the natural right of the individual.

It is rightly observed by the Supreme Court of India that a person coming to prison does not become a non-person. A prisoner remains a human being with all his/her human rights except those that are specifically taken away by the law of the land for his or her offence. Hence, prisoners do have their human rights, which are enjoyed by others as natural. So human rights are relevant for the prisoners too. Secondly, prisoners, unlike the ordinary free persons in the society, are under the direct care of the state. So the state has the direct obligation to maintain not only the safety and security of their persons but also their dignity as human being. Thirdly, the judiciary has the moral obligation to protect the human rights of the prisoners because prisoners are inside the high walls because of the judgements passed on them by the judiciary. Imprisonment, by itself, is the punishment for the offence committed. Additional punishments and torture, therefore, cannot be inflicted on him inside the prison. So the preservation of the human rights of the prisoners is a relevant issue for the judiciary also. Fourthly, prisoners remain in prison for some years and shall be released after the completion of the term of their sentence. So eventually they return to the mainstream society with their prison experiences. If they are meted with inhuman treatment within the walls, they may be tempted to take reprisals by meting the same treatment to the society at large. Their incarcerations are not meant to further downgrade them as human being. Preservation of human rights in prison is, therefore, a relevant concern for the larger society also. Fifthly, prisoners are more vulnerable to human rights violation because they live beyond the eyes of the people in general. It is a world beyond our world. In case of violation of human rights they hardly get any opportunity to substantiate their complaints against the violators. Neither the officials nor the fellow inmates are likely to come forward to give witness for any violation of human rights against the powerful violators. Again, prisoners, in general, have little scope to bring the facts of human rights violation to the civil society including the mass media. Moreover, most of the Indian prisoners are poor and ignorant of their human rights, majority of them being, therefore, subdued and passive. Hence preservation of human rights in prisons is important and relevant.

Areas of Human Rights Violation in Prison—the Indian Scenario

The major areas of human right violation inside most of the Indian prisons are as follows:

(a) *Accommodation:* Prison population fluctuates; prison space does not. Generally, Indian prisons are over-crowded due to unusual delay in the release of Under Trial (UT) prisoners. Moreover, any major outbreak of law and order abruptly increases their number. There are instances when prisoners do not get even a minimum space for sleeping and, therefore, remain standing for over 24 hours. This paucity of space causes a number of problems amounting to human rights violation. They become victims of contagious diseases and suffer from acute shortage of drinking water and sanitation facilities. It also arouses the temptation for homosexuality.

(b) *Corruption in Prison:* Indian prisons are marked by rampant corruption by a section of prison officials in collusion with some 'convict officers'. Quite common among the corrupt practices are stealing of food meant for the inmates – including the special diet allotted to the sick prisoners, extorting money for allowing even their officially sanctioned quota of food and other amenities and taking bribe from the visitors for mulaquat (interview). Weak and subdued prisoners are often forced to act as sex partners of the seasoned convicts. This degrading practice is not absent even in the female wards. Inflicting physical torture for non-compliance of any demand of the convicts with right connections is also quite common.

(c) *Health rights:* Officially, there must be a hospital attached to all the prisons irrespective of their categories. In reality, in most states only central prisons provide this facility. But there too the doctor-prisoner ratio is absolutely inadequate for proper health care services to the prisoners. Especially pitiable is the number of female doctors in most of the Indian prisons. Round-the-clock medical officers are rarely found even in majority of the central prisons in India. As a result, semi-literate convicts often act as not only health assistants – at odd hours, they even work as doctors. Most prison hospitals are absolutely ill-equipped necessitating medicare from outside government hospitals. To send sick prisoners to such hospitals is, however, no easy task. It requires police protection and availability of bed in government hospitals. Neither of these is readily available even for critical patients. The result is treatment delay and, in worst cases, custodial death. Prison hospitals perpetually suffer from lack of medicines. The problem is often compounded by the rackets supplying expired or fake medicine. This makes the prisoners unwilling for health check-up till their conditions turn serious. Convict officers engaged in hospital duties sometimes help medically fit persons to have medical diet while the deserving ones often remain deprived. All these omissions and commissions rob the prisoners of their human rights by denying them their basic right to health.

(d) *Female Inmates and Their Human Rights:* In India female prisoners are comparatively very small in number. At present they constitute only 3% of the total Indian prison population. But they are not free from the violation of human rights. In a male dominated society, female prisoners are more stigmatized than the males. As a result of their incarceration female prisoners generally lose all their family and social connections, and therefore, they suffer from additional mental depression. To add fire to fuel, some female prisoners are coming to prisons along with their children and if the children are below six years of age, they are supposed to stay with their mothers in an environment not at all congenial for healthy development of their psychology. These children for no fault of their own suffer the psychological and physical pain of imprisonment. Post-release rehabilitation of the female prisoners is more difficult than the males. Sometimes, they are forced to sacrifice their dignity and human rights to rehabilitate themselves. Nevertheless, their chances to return to the mainstream society are very slim. Most of the state governments do not have with any plan whatsoever to rehabilitate these prisoners of weaker sex.

(e) *Human Rights and Sex in Prison*: Sexual abuse is very common in most of the Indian prisons. Its extent, however, varies from state to state. My own study done in four of the six central correctional homes in West Bengal shows that over 50% of the prisoners belong to the age group of 24 to 34. Condemned to a unisex environment at their prime youth some prisoners naturally get lured to satisfying their carnal desire through homosexual relationship with multiple partners depending on accessibility. Such sexual relationship often occurs forcibly against the will of the weaker prisoners. Moreover, indiscriminate homosexual relations has come out to be a major source of different venereal diseases and, more alarmingly, of HIV. Under Trial (UT) prisoners are often susceptible to sexual harassment by the more powerful convicts. Moving like waves in a sea, many of the UT prisoners before their incarceration get used to dangerous practices like frequenting to brothels and consumption of drugs. When such persons become sex partners of the convicts the risk of STD naturally increases. One NGO working on the problem of HIV/STD/AIDS inside the prisons in West Bengal has estimated that at least 4% of the UT prisoners are HIV positive. It is no wonder that they would be a potent source of HIV infection inside the prison.

(f) *Human Rights of the Children inside the Indian Prison:* Part III, Article 24 of the UN Covenant on Civil and Political Rights calls for the protection of the rights of children. In this regard, however, one finds sort of a dilemma in the administration of Indian prisons. According to the jail manuals obtaining in most states in India, children below six years of age are supposed to stay in the prison with their convict mothers. One cannot miss the humane urge behind such a system. But, Indian prisons are no ideal place for the children to live and grow up. In prisons the children not only get deprived of their basic rights to play, to have education and to flourish their inherent faculties. They become forced to grow up amidst a lot of vices, which are harmful not just for their own future. The larger society also runs the risk of accommodating adult people with unwarranted traits.

(g) *Human Rights and the Prison Staff:* Prison staff has a crucial role in the preservation/violation of human rights of the prisoners. However, their work condition is not at all sensitive to such important responsibility. In fact, they themselves are often deprived of their basic rights. Almost all the prisons have acute shortage of manpower which means the workers are perennially overburdened. What is often demanded of them is humanly impossible to meet. This cannot but erode the quality of their service. Its adverse effects on the prisoners are simply awful. The warders have three-shift duty of three-hour duration per day. In other words, they are notionally on duty for 24 hours and they are supposed to remain ever alert. They cannot leave the compound without the prior of permission of superintendent and it is often not easy to obtain such permission. It is widely held by the prison staff that their salary is not at all commensurate with the burden they are to bear. In other words, like the prison inmates, they also have, as if, a prison life without committing any offence to the law of the land. It is not difficult to guess that the tolerance and humane attitude that the preservation of the human rights of the prisoner entails can hardly be fulfilled by a set of people groaning and grumbling in adverse conditions.

(h) *Public Perception and the Human Rights Agenda of the Prisoners in India:* If the state is insensitive to the human rights of the prisoners the civil society and the public in general contribute to that. In general perception, convicts are incorrigible criminals and, hence, they are social outcasts no inhuman treatment to whom registers in public psyche and, therefore, does not evoke any sympathetic response. Even in this age of media activism both print and electronic media maintain curious silence in taking up the stories within the walls. Prisons being projected as high-risk zones the government is almost allergic to any public gaze on the happenings in the prisons. Thus even if someone is willing to take up the cudgel he is invariably debarred on security ground. This unbridgeable distance between the prison population and the larger society in which the prisons are located helps perpetuate the arbitrary rule of the authority in the prisons. A prison is a society of its own where rules of civility are yet to gain ground.

Official Steps for Securing Human Rights Inside the Prisons in India

Even during colonial rule some concerns to meet some of the basic needs of the prisoners were occasionally expressed. Many jail conferences were held and committees were formed, the first being the Prison Discipline Committee in 1838. The first Jail Manual was published in Punjab in 1858, which was written by Mr. C. Hathaway, the then Inspector of Prisons, Punjab. Very shortly, in 1864, the Jail Manual of the Lower Provinces of Bengal was published. These early documents mainly talked about accommodation, food, clothing, classification of the prisoners and the works to be assigned to them. They also included some provisions for the prevention of torture, inhuman punishment like keeping prisoners without food and whimsical punishment for even trivial lapses. The documents also emphasized the need to preserve the dignity of the female prisoners by keeping them separated from their male counterpart, not cutting their hair unless otherwise required as a punishment measure. At least officially, some human consideration was shown by the British-administration to the prisoners. After independence, the first All India Jail Manual Committee was set up in 1957. The All India Committee of Jail Reform was set up in 1980. Its report was published in 1983. As the prison administration in India is in the

State List, so each state government has its own jail manual to govern its own prisons. In both the reports of 1957 and 1983, the approach to prisoners appears more humane. The National Human Rights Commission set up in 1995 is also concerned with the preservations of human rights of the prisoners. There does not seem to be much confusion as to the post-colonial Indian State's adherence to the principle of securing the human rights of the prisoners. In practice, however, incidents of violation of their human rights are plenty. These incidents generally take place for reasons we have cited above.

Remedial Measures

The main problem in the prison management is to strike a proper balance between the security and preservation of human rights of the prisoners. Our prisons are suffused with security concern than human treatment or correction of the prisoners. If gunti (counting of heads) is all right, then every thing in prison is presumed to be fine – this is the general mindset of prison administration in India. Since high-risk prisoners are dumped with the less-risk or no-risk prisoners within the same boundary walls such orientation is comprehensible. Human rights of the prisoners thus become an automatic prey. Rational segregation of prisoners according security risks is, therefore, necessary both to ensure the rights of the less-risk prisoners and to facilitate civil society's scrutiny of prison conditions. Such transparency has two distinct advantages. It can at least partially do away with popular misconception about the prisoners. They may realize that most of the prisoners are the victims of social circumstances, disturbed upbringing or momentary loss of temper. They are not born criminals. They too are human beings. They need and deserve care, sympathy and correct guidance. Secondly, an opportunity to have interactions with the free population is likely to enhance the self-confidence and also the self-esteem of the prisoners. They may possibly be motivated to view themselves as a part of the mainstream society. Last but not the least; continuous vigilance by the judicial authority inside the prison is also desirable. In sum, an impartial third-party intervention is required for the maintenance of human rights in the Indian prisons.

17

Human Rights Violation

Health Rights of Prisoners

D. Sivankutty & Shan Eugene Palakkal

Introduction

Human rights are rights to which all human beings are entitled, simply because we are human. Our human rights are inalienable and they belong to all of us, whatever our caste, class, race, age, gender, religion or belief and should not be taken away from us under any circumstances. The term human rights cover a broad range of rights, from the rights to freedom of religion to the right to food and shelter. All are important as each other and are owed to us in equal measure. The voice of the prisoners for vindication of their rights was heard throughout the years after India became independent and full-fledged democracy with a written constitution guaranteeing certain fundamental rights. All prisoners and detained persons have the right to the highest attainable standards of physical and mental health and they should have free access to the health services available in the country.

Moreover, a thorough study of academic journals, conference proceedings, government reports, etc has been made and finally arrived to a conclusion that reforms are to be implemented in due course. Though the human rights violation of the prisoners is a vast topic, I felt the need to take up the study to the aspect of health rights of the prisoners. The scope of the study is immense, but paucity of time has forced me to restrict the study.

Present Scenario

Literature on the rights of prisoners is innumerable but the health/medical rights of prisoners are scarce. Therefore the purpose of this study is to highlight the health rights violation of the prisoners. For the completion of my study the data has been collected from the Welfare officer, Prison Head Quarters, Poojapura Trivandrum ; Police Training college, Trivandrum. This article also provides information on prison conditions, prison abuses, human rights protections for prisoners, and related issues.

Details of the Study

The conditions in which the accused are held in prisons are very poor in general and they vary greatly depending on the circumstances of detention. On this basis, the objectives of the study were:

- to direct the focus on the health rights of prisoners and to study the problems faced by them in the prison and also to promote the awareness of their rights to the common mass.
- to emphasise that proper health care is a basic right which applies to all human beings and that the conditions of health care in prisons affect public health.
- to find, whether the prison conditions are decent and human, and that they meet proper health requirements.
- to underline the primary responsibility of doctors, nurses and all other health care personnel, working in prisons and other places of detention, to look after the health of the prisoners.
- to chalk out suggestions, that would facilitate the improvement of the conditions of prisoners and their prison environment.

The prison inmates – the most disillusioned victims or beneficiaries of our prison reform efforts, even today, are incessantly begging for human treatment, better food, adequate medical services and improved recreation facilities. In the light of the above circumstances, Supreme Court has increasingly come into action in the recent past to make the government machinery work. The judicial activism has instilled a ray of hope that prisoners will be treated in a human way. But unfortunately, most of the provisions have remained paper-tigers without teeth and claws because there has been woeful lack of implementation of these protections and safeguards of the prisoner's rights.

Treatment of women prisoners is often badly neglected. They suffer from unhealthy living conditions, exploitation and separation from their families, which is a sheer violation of human rights. Many of them are totally ignorant of the jail rules and procedures. Rights of the persons behind the prison walls are least known to the public. People in general are not concerned about prisoners, their rights and the treatment meted out to them in prisons which provide fertile ground for persistent and all pervasive violation of human rights. Therefore, I hope the study will make a useful contribution towards raising the awareness of the people and sensitizing the police, prison officials to the medico-legal rights of prisoners and instilling in them respect for the prisoners, so that they may treat them with dignity.

Thus, it can always be remembered that one of the significant post-independence developments in the field of prisons has been, the emergence of the prisoner's right touchstone, which has been responsible both for the demystification of prisons, as well as the movement towards standardization.

Health is a crucial determinant of the quality of life and the productivity of the vast human resource in India. Health can mean different things to different people. The World Health Organisation has attempted to construct a positive definition of health and has described health as 'a state of complete physical, mental and social well being and not merely the absence of disease of infirmity'. The right to food, education and health are important because they are complementary to the non-deniable right to life which is the foundation of all rights. Notwithstanding the impressive spread of the human rights culture, many marginalized sections do not have access to human rights. Prisoners do form an important segment of the deprived groups.

This paper focuses its attention on some of the basic rights to which the prisoners are entitled to, penologically speaking persons, kept inside the prison shall not be termed as prisoner, but they have to be called as inmates of the custodial institutions or correctional institutions. Proper health care is a basic of any person and so too a prisoner also. The health care conditions in prisons are also concerns of public health in many ways. The inadequacy of medical services in prisons, often resulting in the death of prisoners has been much in evidence. Jailed for petty crimes, they find themselves being put through a rigorous daily routine not provided proper, timely treatment and the food is either stale or rotten. There seems to be an evil nexus between the jail involving the staff and the hard core criminals.

People in general are not concerned about prisoner, their rights and treatment meted out to them in prisons, which provide a fertile ground for persistent and all pervasive violation of human rights and the reason is the invisibility surrounding these violations.

Every prisoner must be provided health care equivalent to health care standards of the state. Prisoners should have medical check-up and screening on admission and periodically. A medical officer should regularly inspect, advice and direct prison authority upon the quality of food, hygiene, cleanliness, sanitation, heating, lighting work, clothing, and availability of other basic facilities and conditions of punishment imposed to the prisoners which he thinks fit. (Dr. Shah, Giriraj.-2002)

The occasions for judicial intervention in prison matters is so varied and the range of interest covered so vast that, at times, the outcome is rhetorically described as the 'prisoner's rights jurisprudence'. Lack of prisoner's right orientation has been one of the notorious features of the pre-reform prison legislations like the Prisons act 1894 and so on, which conceived prisons as classical control institutions that conceded very limited obligations towards the prison inmates. The courts have extended the compensatory remedy for physical harms suffered while inside prison (*Smt Kevalpati* 1995). Violations in many cases occur because of the lack of awareness on the part of the prisoners about what they are entitled to. Educating them about the rights and obligations, procedure for lodging complaint, the conduct that is expected for jail administration etc. should be prepared in simple language for the prisoners' benefit. In Ranchod v State of Madhya Pradesh (1988,16 reports (MP) 147), the Madhya Pradesh High court highlighted the callous behaviour of doctors, maltreatment by prison staff in a jail in that state. Prisoners die in custody and often the death may be due to suicide or negligence of health conditions. The following below gives an idea of certain rights that apply to the prisoners, some of which are violated:

Rights during Incarceration – (Prison Stage)

1. *Right to live with basic human dignity:* A court sentence of imprisonment does not deprive a prisoner of all his fundamental rights except those that are inherent in the very nature of imprisonment (*Charles Shobraj* 1978). Other than those taken away by the very fact of imprisonment, every prisoner has the right to read and write, and recreation, to comforts like protection from extreme cold and heat, to freedom from indignities such as compulsory nudity, forced sodomy and other such unbearable vulgarity, to minimal joys of self expression (*Sunil Batra* 1980)

2. *Right to equal treatment amongst fellow prisoners:* Inequality and discrimination on the basis of social and financial status of prisoners is prohibited. Affluent criminals cannot be treated with luxury and lowly indigents as pariahs (*Ramesh Kaushik* 1980)

3. *Right to get Compensation:* Any person, whose fundamental right to life and liberty is violated, is entitled to claim monetary compensation from the state (*Rudal Shah* 1983)

4. *Right to information about prison rules etc.:* Copies of jail rules should be exhibited both in English and vernacular to which all prisoners have access (Section 61, *Prisons Act 1894*)

Prisons Act of 1894 – this act is the first legislation regarding the prisons regulation in India. This act is more concerned with the prison working than with the treatment of prisoners (Chapter 2, *Prisons Act 1894*) This section conferred the right to physical protection of the prisoners and imposes duties upon the state to provide accommodation at least under a roof and in some room typed habitat. Therefore minimum human condition of life is to be provided to the prisoners which are prerequisite any reformatory programme. Section 24 (2) of the act prescribes that every individual prisoner shall be examined under the general or special orders of the medical officer, who shall enter or cause to be entered in a book, to be kept by the jailor, a record of the state of health of the prisoner and of any wounds on his person, and any further observations which the medical officer thinks fit to add. Another section of this act lays laid down that in every prison a hospital or proper place for the reception of sick prisoners shall be provided (Section 39 of *Prison Act 1894*).

International instruments protect everyone, including prisoners, against gross violations of their health and the integrity of their person. The Universal Declaration of Human rights guarantees to everyone include to prisoners the right to a standard living adequate for health and well being including medical care and necessary social services (Article 25, paragraph 1, *International Covenant on Economic, Social and Cultural Rights*). International covenant on Economic, Social and cultural rights recognizes the right of health to everyone, including prisoners (Article 12, para 1, GA Resolution 2200A (XXI), 21 UN GAOR Supp (no.16), UN Doc A/6316 1966). The Body of Principles for the Protection of All Persons under any form of Detention or Imprisonment provides that detained or imprisoned persons shall be offered a proper medical examination as soon as possible after admission and that medical care and treatment shall be provided free of charge (Principle 24, *GA Resolution 43/173, annex, 43 GAOR supp (No.49); UN Doc A/43/49*, 1988). The prisoners' right to proper healthcare begins at the point of admission to custody. The purpose of screening new prisoners on admission is for the sake of the prisoners' health and not for the benefit of prisoner authorities. Having deprived a person of his/her liberty, there is an obligation on the state to care for that person. The obligation extends to health care. Prison staff should be able to respond to the results of the medical screening by identifying prisoners' problems both physical and mental and dealing with them in a confidential manner.

The need for continuing medical supervision and treatment for prisoners is confirmed in Rule 24 of the Standard Minimum Rules for the treatment of prisoners (Rule 23 of the Standard Minimum Rules for the treatment of prisoners deals with the special medical needs of women and nursing infants, Adopted on 30 August 1955, by the first United Nations Congress on the Prevention of Crime and the Treatment of Offenders). Rule 10 provides that all accommodation shall meet the requirements of health due regard being paid to climatic conditions, lightings, etc. Basic principles for the treatment of Prisoners provide that prisoners shall have access to the health services available in the country without discrimination on the grounds of their legal situation (Principle 9, *Basic Principles for the Treatment of Prisoners*). The best examples of prison healthcare often occur when it is under the control of community healthcare authorities. All prisoners are entitled to be held in conditions which are decent and humane. Standard Minimum Rules for the treatment of prisoners requires: (1) the medical officer shall regularly inspect an advise the director upon: (a) the quantity, quality, preparation and service of food; (b) the hygiene and cleanliness of the institution and the prisoners; (c) the sanitation, heating, lighting and ventilation of the institution; (d) the suitability and cleanliness of the prisoners' clothing and bedding (Rule 26 of *Standard Minimum Rules for the Treatment of Prisoners*).

All prison staffs need to have an understanding of basic health matters. In many prison systems, a significant proportion of prisoners suffer from some form of mental illness. There should be a close relationship between the Prison Medical Officer and the Healthcare Specialist in the community so that use can be made of community expertise. There are no specific provisions of the prisoners' right in the Constitution of India, yet certain rights which have been guaranteed in Part III of our Constitution are also available to the prisoners because a prisoner should be treated as a 'person' in the prison. There were many instances which showed that the health aspects of prisoners were not given much attention. In the ancient period, the captives were chained like dogs and humiliated by the warders. Food and water were denied when asked for (Balambal, V.- 1998). But the Arthasastra deals in detail about the prisoners and their treatment by officials (Kangle, R.P.- 1963). Prisoners were treated according to their station in life and the nature of crime they had committed. The allowance of food was regulated by weight and not by price. Due consideration was given to the prisoners' health and if required, they were release (Datir, R.N.- 1978).

Law enforcement officials shall ensure the full protection of the health of prisoners in their custody and, in particular shall take immediate steps to secure medical attention whenever required (Article 6, Code of Conduct for Law Enforcement Officials).

The Supreme Court in its landmark judgement ruled that Article 21 of the Constitution casts an obligation on the state to preserve life. The patient whether he be an innocent person or a criminal liable to punishment under the laws of the society, it is the obligation of those who are in charge of the health of the community to preserve life so that the innocent may be protected and the guilty may be punished. Apart from the long list of conventions and declarations protecting the human rights of people in general and health rights of people in particular the UN has adopted the following principles for adoption and follow-up by the member nations. The Principle of Medical Ethics are relevant to the role of health personnel, particular physicians, in the protection of prisoners and detainees against torture and other cruel, inhuman or degrading treatment or punishment (Principal 1-6, GA.Res. 37/194 annex, 37 UN GAOR Supp (No.51) at 211, UN Doc. A/37/51, 1982).

As far as the prisoners were concerned, until 1800 their condition was miserable. The shocking conditions in the jails, the terrible sufferings of the prisoners, the cruel treatment metered out to them, disease ad malnutrition were all without parallel. Even after the introduction of the system of 1802, the conditions did not improve much. But the Charter Act of 1833 marked the end of the haphazard and incoherent process by providing for a definite body of law. From the administrative report of 1862-63, it was noticed that the remuneration paid to the prisons was exceedingly scanty and there were no sanitary arrangements to keep the jails clean and to ensure the health of the inmates. The result was that there was considerable mortality (Velupillai, T.K.-1940). Later the medical charge was transferred to the Durbar physician and each jail was provided with a medical subordinate. Regarding dietary conditions, prisoners undergoing rigorous punishments were allowed 26¾ oz of rice and a rupee weight of salt, besides 8 cash for condiments and the same were allowed for prisoners under simple imprisonment except for 21¼ oz of rice Velupillai, T.K.-1940). Brahmin convicts were fed with rice. A hospital attached to the central prison was located in a separate building and prisoners who fell ill were removed to it. During periods of epidemics all those infected were removed to the jail hospital, while the rest were treated in the jail building itself. A surgeon was required to attend daily and one of the apothecaries was to be always on duty. Thus the treatment and the rights of prisoners were taken much care and were not violated. Further the Indian Jail Committee report appointed in 1864 was presided by Mr A A Roberts and it looked into the causes of deaths in jails which was at that time 7% and it concluded the reason to be poor health of prisoners, poor dietary conditions and jail discipline (Chishti, Anees -2001).

Later in 1919, the Rules for the Superintendence and Management of the Central Prison was adopted for the betterment of the prisoners. The medical officers were to carefully examine the prisoner and record the weight, age and state of health. It was found that the penal diet of the prisoners during that period was restricted to:

Europeans and Eurasians – 1½ lbs bread/diem with water

Indians – 16 oz rice with ½ oz salt diem with water

The effect of penal diet on a prisoner's health was carefully watched by the superintendent and the medical officer and if the health of the prisoner was injuriously affected to a material extent by the penal diet, the prisoner was restored to the ordinary diet (Chapter XIII, *Rules for the Superintendence and Management of the Central Prison*, Trivandrum, 1919, p. 41).

During the pre-independence period, the conditions of the prisons and the prisoners in Kerala were obnoxiously repulsive. Ventilation was nil. Accommodation was very limited. Sometimes, in places where 2-5 prisoners were put, 20-30 were accommodated leading to prisoners fainting and falling sick, thereby leading the government to spend upon them to take care of their health (*Cochin Legislative Council Proceedings*, 1942). Overcrowding certainly affects the health and hygiene of prisoners and if no steps are taken by the state government then it would amount to violation of right to life of the inmates of the prison.

In 1950, the Travancore Cochin prisons act was enacted to check on the health rights of the prisoners. The duties of the medical officers in protecting the health of the prisoners who were ill have been depicted in the act. Food, clothing, bedding of civil, non-convicted criminal prisoners were also enumerated (Act XVIII of 1950, *The Travancore Cochin Prisons Act*). Thus the health rights of the prisoners were taken note of and were under check, thanks to the set of rules.

During a parade held at the Central Prison, Trivandrum in November 1977, some prisoners complained about the improper and unsatisfactory distribution of diet articles and the issue of lesser quantities. Some complained about medical attention. But no proper action was taken. A magisterial inquiry described the conditions thus: 'all the toilets were in a deplorable condition. There was inadequate supply of safe drinking water, water samples of the tube wells, deep bore hand-pumps were found to be contaminated. It found the poor conditions to be because of neglect of the departments concerned and lack of foresight'. Also the estimate committee of the 9th Kerala legislature made some valuable suggestions with regard to the rights of prisoners in the state of Kerala, but all in vain (The Committee submitted its report on 28 January 1993, P M Aboobecker –Chairman, 9th Kerala Legislature Estimate Committee, 1991-1993, p. 5).

Analysis by the NHRC, of the deaths of prisoners reported from the state revealed that, many lives could have been saved if proper medical examinations had been carried out at the time of the admission of a person and if this had been followed-up with periodical medical checks. Because of the distressing conditions and the often inhuman treatment of inmates in various remand homes in the country, the commission had issued instructions to the secretary of the welfare department of the state to undertake measures to improve the maintenance and upkeep of these homes and to ensure the better treatment of their inmates (*National Human Rights Commission - Annual Report 1998-1999*, p. 23).

In 2002, the Kerala State Human Rights Commission member T K Wilson had visited the central jail following a complaint about the conditions of the prisoners. It was found that there was acute shortage of drinking water and lack of basic necessities. The health care facilities in the Central Prison also were left much to be desired (*Kerala State Human Rights Commission- Annual Report 2002*, Thiruvananthapuram, p.29) The cause of a remand prisoner's death had created a controversy about the health care of the prisoners in the central prison (*The Hindu*, 12 August 2004, Thursday, Vol. 127, No. 192, Thiruvananthapuram, p. 3). The prisoners had later jointly represented to the jail authorities regarding the ill treatment but no action was taken against the delinquent officials. This was indeed a violation of the health rights of the prisoners. Mr. M G A Raman, DGP (prisons) had remarked that the overcrowding of the prison was another pressing problem.

In 2005, in the Central Prison, the authorized strength was 1000, but 1612 prisoners including 38 females were lodged. Added to this was the fact that the prisoners were not evenly distributed owing to administrative and technical reasons. Overcrowding worsened when jails were closed for repairs (An Interview with K.A. Kumaran, Chief Welfare officer, 20 December 2006, Prison Headquarters, Poojapura, Trivandrum). The daily diet of prisoners that year consisted of:

Rice	–	(250 gm with *sambar*) – 2 days
Bengal gram curry	–	1 day
Dhal	–	1 day
Fish	–	2 days
Mutton curry	–	1 day

Later the revised menu was introduced which was as follows: rice (250 gm) to be supplemented with popular Keralite curries such as *theeyal, thoran, mezhukkupuratty, sambar, kichadi,* vegetable coconut curry, *erissery, moru curry, pulissery,* butter milk, curd and pickle. The evening meal comprised of rice (200 gm) and *puzhukku* made of large vegetables or dry tapioca and green gram curry. Thus the dietary conditions were improved which lead to reduction of prisoners falling ill (the Interview with K.A. Kumaran, Chief Welfare officer, 20 December 2006, Prison Headquarters, Poojapura, Trivandrum).

The Kerala State Human Rights Commission during its visit to the Poojapura Central Prison on 7 April 2005 received complaints of lack of medical attention, overcrowded cells and unclean toilets. There was only one doctor and the sick prisoners were being housed in a room that had beds and facilities only for three. About 1600 prisoners including those in judicial remand were housed in crammed conditions. The toilets in the cells were unclean and lacked proper lighting (the Interview with K.A. Kumaran, Chief Welfare officer, 20 December 2006, Prison Headquarters, Poojapura, Trivandrum).

As of September 2005, about 6950 prisoners excluding those on parole were housed against the total sanctioned capacity of 5415 prisoners in the state (*The Hindu*, 8 November 2005, Thursday, Thiruvananthapuram., p. 2). The Kozhikode district jail at Puthiyara was reportedly extremely overcrowded. The district sub jail also lacked modern facilities and alleged interference of politicians in the administration of the jail was a problem. Some of the jail staff were allegedly involved in corruption. Liquor and drugs were given, special treatment such as use of mobile phones inside the prison and getting food supplied from hotels in connivance of the jail authorities (*The Hindu*, 14 January 2006, Tuesday, Thiruvananthapuram, p.10).

The tragic stories, revealed by the press and other agencies of public relations, on the brutal savage of actions of the prison authorities on the helpless human beings within the prison walls inspired many attempts for vindication of prisoner's rights against arbitrariness.

This study's main thrust is to investigate into the health conditions of the prisoners in the Trivandrum Central prison and on that basis suggest relevant changes.

The old system of mass treatment, rigid repression and regimentation, severe punishment, poor and insufficient food, confinement in small, unsanitary and poorly lighted cell were being replaced by individualized training and treatment of offenders within a well-equipped and well-staffed institution with due regard for human dignity. And the present situation of the prisoners has been improved to some extend.

Dietary Conditions of the Prisoners

During the visit of the then State Human Rights Commission Chairman V.P. Mohankumar at the Kozhikode District jail at Puthiyara on 16 February 2006, the prisoners complained of the poor quality of good provided to them. Doctors visited the jail only once in a week. Mr. Mohankumar found that many of the undertrial prisoners were not being produced before the court owing to the non-availability of police personnel to escort them. Yet according to Mr. Mohankumar, Kozhikode district jail was better than those in other parts of the state he had visited earlier (An Interview with V.P. Mohankumar, Chairman, Kerala State Human Rights Commission on 15 March 2006, Thiruvananthapuram). At present in Poojapura Central Prison, the prisoners are classified into II class and III class prisoners. II class prisoners consist of political people and III class consists of people registered under criminal cases. The dietary of prisoners is entirely under the control of the Chief Medical officer. These have a separate restricted penal diet.

The diet given to the class III prisoners is as follows:

Articles	Mon.	Tue.	Wed.	Thu.	Fri.	Sat.	Sun.
Wheat	200gm	200gm	200gm	200gm	200gm	200gm	200gm
Rice*	450gm	450gm	450gm	450gm	450gm	450gm	450gm
Mutton	–	–	–	–	–	87gm	–
Fresh fish	170gm	–	170gm	–	–	–	–
Cherupayar	–	–	–	–	157gm	–	85gm
Sambar	–	–	–	–	–	–	2 cup
Parippu	14gm	14gm	14gm	14gm	14gm	14gm	–
Leafy Vegetables	–	–	–	140gm	–	–	–
Curd	55ml	55ml	55ml	55ml	55ml	55ml	55ml
Tea**	120ml	120ml	120ml	120ml	120ml	120ml	120ml

* Rice can be substituted with wheat if the prisoner desires. Rice is given in noon and night time scheduled respectively at 12:30 pm and 7 pm.

** Tea is served in the morning and evenings respectively at 6 am and 4 pm.

Source: An Interview with Dr. Anil, Chief Medical Officer, Central Prison, Thiruvananthapuram, 13 January 2007.

But in the case of class II prisoners which consists of political persons the diet changes. They are given the hospital diet daily which consists of:

Egg	–	1
Milk	–	400ml
Banana (*ethakka*)	–	200gm
Mutton/fish	–	200gm (alternate days)
Cuppa and *Cherupayar*	–	170gm (dry) and 85gm (on Sundays only)

Thus still the segregation regarding dietary conditions persists even now. There are also special diet given to those who are sick and laid up with diseases.

The Tuberculosis affected prisoners; the weak lethargic prisoners' diet consists of:

Milk	–	300ml
Banana	–	200gm
Mutton	–	100gm
Egg	–	2
Bread	–	100gm

The distribution of the diet quantity is detailed in the Kerala Prisons Rules, 1958. At times the food which are supplied to the prisoners are practically not in accordance with the quality and quantum of the prescribed diet. The problem could be the corrupt practice, in supplying adulterated as well as less quantity of foods by the persons entrusted for the same. Food shortages in some prisons, combined with extreme overcrowding, create ideal conditions for the spread of communicable diseases. It is the right of the prisoners to get substantial food and adequate clothing from the prison administration. Scale diet of prisoners should be strictly according to medical norms and special extra diet should be given if medically prescribed. Prison manual must be physically available for easy reference by inmates and staff and accredited visitors.

Health Personnel

A prison should have proper health care facilities and medical staff to provide for a range of health needs. Regarding the staff in the central prison, the following are deputed in the prison hospital:

Medical officers	–	2
Hospital head warder	–	1
Pharmacist	–	1
Laboratory technician	–	1
ECG technician	–	1
Male attendants	–	2
Psychiatrist	–	1

The medical staff allotted to the prison is therefore inadequate. For other complicated treatments, the prisoners are sent to Medical College hospital, SUT and Cancer Institute all at Trivandrum (An Interview with Mr. Vikraman, Hospital Head Warder on 13 January 2007, Poojapura Central Prison). The beds allotted in the prison hospital are only 120 which is too less to accommodate sick prisoners. Most prisoners are worried about how they will face the society once they are released. At times they suffer from depressive disorders and need constant reassurance about their self-worth. Therefore a clinical psychologist or counsellor should be made available at the prison on a regular basis which is not availed presently. If it is not possible to transfer prisoners to outside facilities, they must be transferred to a prison with equivalent facilities. Screening and monitoring of mental health prisoners helps to identify those who should not be in prison. Special provision may have to be made for prisoners who are drug-dependents and are in the process of withdrawal. Health personnel shall not commit or give their permission for any acts, which may adversely affect the health of prisoners. The medical staff must be particularly careful not to be involved in any way in the disciplining or punishment or restraining a prisoner for any reason other than a medical one. There should be more allotment of nursing staff to reduce negligence of the health care of prisoners. A district medical officer should also be deputed to inspect that, proper records are maintained, to hear the grievances of the health of prisoners and thereby take prompt action.

Hygiene and Health Conditions of Prisoners

The present accommodations provided to the prisoners are not according to the standard of modern prisons. Such conditions make the mind of the prisoners to be more hardened criminals and antagonistic to the society and the political authority. So, the architectural changes possible in the existing building, are to be considered so that the cells designed for keeping the prisoners be more healthy and hygienic congenial for improving the mental condition and attitude of the prisoners. Present arrangement for sanitation inside is not at par with the number of prisoners.

Due to non-supply of mosquito curtains to the prisoners, there remains every possibility of spreading infectious diseases like malaria, filariasis etc amongst them. Prisoner death rates are often far higher than corresponding rates among the populations outside prisons.

The number of sick prisoners as on 17th January 2007 is:

Sick prisoners	Number
Diabetic prisoners	186
Cancer prisoners	6
AIDS/HIV prisoners	4 (including 1 female)
Tuberculosis prisoners	6
Prisoners undergoing dialysis	1

Source: An Interview with Dr. Anil, Chief Medical Officer Central Prison Hospital, on 13 January 2007.

Proper diet and treatment are provided for these patients. While violence is a factor in some penal facilities, disease - often the predictable result of overcrowding, malnutrition, unhygienic conditions, and lack of medical care - remains the most common cause of death. Efforts are on to improve the medical facilities for the prisoners. Totally there are 12 blocks incorporating the prisoners of which 2 blocks are for undertrial prisoners, 1 hospital block, 1 block for female prisoners. Each block has 5-6 cells each which accommodate nearly 50 prisoners; and a maximum of 983 prisoners can be accommodated. Whereas at present till 17th January 2007, a total of 1821 male and 26 female undertrial prisoners adding up to a total of 1847, make the cells over crowded (An Interview with the Mr. K J Varghese, Jail Welfare Officer on 17 January 2007, Poojapura Central Prison). Each prisoner is provided with a mat, a rug and 1 bedsheet whereas, for class II prisoners an extra cot, a pillow, a mat, a rug and 2 bedsheets are provided. Recreation facilities are also available with a television which is open for view from 8 am to 5.30 pm daily and 1 newspaper for every 25 prisoners. The sleeping wards and cells are thoroughly ventilated, and opened during the day. Hard Labour is given to prisoners who undergo rigorous imprisonment only, for which they were paid Rs. 13/- per day. Cooking, gardening, cleaning etc. were done by the prisoners themselves. The jail area was found to be clean, free from refuse and stagnant water, cesspools and drains. Thus there is no report of infectious diseases. All prisoners are entitled to be held in conditions, which are decent and humane.

It is deeply disturbing that some prisoners of Kerala have been languishing in mental hospitals for over three decades when they should have been freed many years earlier. About 500 lifetimes including a lot of aged ailing and women prisoners are thus kept illegally in Kerala jails (*The Hindu*, 14 November, 2007, Wednesday, Thiruvananthapuram, p. 2). While the Supreme Court has struck a blow for prisoners' rights, it is for the government to review the functioning of the prison health system in its totality.

Kerala was the first state to order a ban on smoking in all public areas. But the Law Department is still sceptical about how the Kerala High Court would view the decision to allow prisoners to smoke. *Beedis* and cigarettes were liberally available to prisoners in jail canteens till the then Congress-led government of Oommen Chandy ordered a ban on smoking in prisons in 2004. The Left government had been deluged by pleas from convicts aching for a smoke and therefore they lifted the ban on smoking (*The New Indian Express*, 22 June 2007, Friday, Thiruvananthapuram, p. 3). That *beedis* pose a health hazard to prisoners were neglected.

All prison staffs need to have an understanding of basic health facilities. Additional training and education are necessary periodically to keep the staff and prisoners up to date on the latest health problems such as drug abuse, HIV/AIDS, Tuberculosis and other transmittable diseases. Women in prison should have access to reproductive health care maintained by a lady doctor which is not present. Regarding the overcrowding of the cells, alternative facilities should be provided outside the cell blocks. Prisoners carrying out work which makes them dirty and those preparing or serving food should be given the opportunity to wash more regularly and take extra care. Sufficient beds and clothes may be provided which are neat and clean with facility for washing. Care should be taken that the requirements of hygiene are not used as a cloak for imposing discipline. Young prisoners tend to be more volatile and impulsive. They may need more organized exercise, possible in the form of physical exercise, possibly in the form of physical exercise or competitive games to channel their surplus energy into constructive activity.

Corrupt prison officials also arrange preferential treatment for prisoners with connection to crime bosses. Such treatment may be the provision of entertainment – including sexual pleasures, often at the expense of another inmate's liberty and body – unrestricted movement inside the jail and uninterrupted visitor sessions. Meanwhile, common convicts in the same jail were denied even basic facilities. In Viyyur Central Prison, affluent prisoners were allowed to bring food from the best hotels in town, a share of which goes to the prison officials and other designated inmates. During inspections, however, inmates are not in position to make complaints, since jail officials accompany the visitors. Anyone daring to make a complaint faces the consequence once the inspection is over.

Maltreatment of prisoners is common throughout India. In Kerala for example, every male convict entering prisons must face the ordeal of 'jail call'. Immediately on arrival, the prisoner is told to bend down, after which a few heavy blows are delivered, causing pain along the length of the victim's spine. While the female inmates do not get this treatment, they suffer continuous ill-treatment throughout the custody, often including sexual harassment and rape (Written statements submitted by the Asian Legal Resource Centre (ALRC) a non-governmental organization in general consultative status- 17 July 2006, 61st Session of the Commission on Human Rights, Thiruvananthapuram).

Most detainees are housed in conditions amounting to cruel, inhuman or degrading treatment. Most spend 22 hours a day in total isolation and suffer other forms of sensory deprivation. A majority of them have been held for nearly six hears with no prospect of a fair trial, no direct access to their families and no access to a lawyer. These conditions have had a shattering impact on their psychological and physical health.

Prisoners have unalienable rights conferred upon them by international treaties and covenants; they have a right to health care, and most certainly have a right not to contract diseases in prison. Prison jurisprudence recognizes that prisoners should not lose all their rights because of imprisonment. Yet, there is a loss of rights within custodial institutions, which continue to occur. The Jalandhar Central jail, in which about 1500 prisoners went on the rampage in protest against the intolerable behaviour of jail authorities, draws painful attention to the uncivilised state of most Indian prisons. The locking of some prisoners in dark cells, the denial basic facilities and the forcible shaving of a Sikh prisoner's head suggests that for much of the prison establishment, the scope of human rights excludes the jail population. The Jalandhar blow-up was not very different from what happened last in Bihar's Beur jail; agitated inmates, mainly left wing extremists, temporarily took control of the prison complex, after staging a protest against alleged maltreatment that drove a fellow prison to suicide. In 1983, the All India Committee on Jail Reforms, chaired by Justice A.N. Mulla, spotlighted the "overcrowded prisons...unsatisfactory living conditions, lack of treatment programmes and allegations of an indifferent and even inhuman approach of prison staff." Little seems to have changed in 25 years.

Public health policies are meant to ensure the best possible living conditions for all members of society, so that everyone can be healthy. Prisoners are often forgotten in this equation. They are in constant contact with all kinds of people who come in and out of prison every day. This constant movement in and out of prison makes it all the more important to control any contagious disease within the prison, so that, it does not spread into the outside community. Violence in prison settings has many causes. Clashes may have ethnic causes, or rivalries between clans or gangs. The closed, often vastly overcrowded, living conditions also lead to hostilities between inmates. The tedious prison environment, lack of occupation of mind and body and just plain boredom, lead to accumulated frustration and tension. This environment leads the way to high-risk activities, such as use of drugs and sex between men. Others, however, are forced to engage in them, in a coercive play for power or monetary gain. Risky lifestyles can lead to the transmission of diseases from one prisoner to other prisoners, and pose a serious public health risk if unchecked. Prisoners are more likely to already be in a bad state of health when they enter prison, and the unfavourable conditions therein worsen the health situation. Hence the need for health care and treatments will often be greater in a prison than in an outside community. However, providing even basic health care to prisoners has proved extremely difficult in India, especially Kerala as the health system is chronically insufficient. Prisoners have a right to live in conditions where their individual safety is guaranteed. The living conditions in prison breeds indiscipline, degeneration and devaluation of human spirit. This constitutes the violation of prisoner's rights. Thus it can always be remembered that one of the significant post-independence developments in the field of prisons has been, the emergence of the prisoner's right touchstone, which has been responsible both for the demystification of prisons, as well as the movement towards standardization

REFERENCES & NOTES

1. Dr. Shah, Giriraj. et al. – 2002: 'Human Rights: Perspective Plan for the 21st Century', Diamond Pocket Books Pvt. Ltd., New Delhi, p. 91.
2. Smt. Kevalpati v State, 1995 Cr. LJ 2920 (SC); Murti Devi v State (1998) 9 SCC 604; Watchdogs. International v Union of India (1988) 8 SCC 338.
3. 1988,16 reports (MP) 147.

4. Charles Shobraj v Superintendent, Central Jail Tihar, (1978) 4 SCC 107.
5. Sunil Batra(II) v Delhi Administration (1980) 3 SCC 488.
6. Ramesh Kaushik v B L Vig Supt, Central Jail, Delhi, 1980 (3) SCR 929.
7. Rudal Shah v State of Bihar, AIR 1983 SC 1086; Sebastian M Hongray v State of J & K, AIR 1984 SC.1206 ; D K Basu v State West Bengal, JT 1996 (9) SCALE 298.
8. Section 61, Prisons Act 1894.
9. Chapter 2, Section 4- accommodation and sanitary condition; Chapter 6, Section 31-treatment of prisoners; Chapter 7, Section 35- treatment of prisoners; Chapter 8, Section 37-39 deals with the health of prisoners including the sick prisoners, Prisons Act 1894.
10. Section 39 of Prison Act 1894.
11. Article 25, paragraph 1, International Covenant on Economic, Social and Cultural Rights.
12. Article 12 , para 1, GA Resolution 2200A (XXI), 21 UN GAOR Supp (no.16), UN Doc A/6316, (1966), 993. The Covenant on Civil and Political Rights, Article 7 says that no One shall be Subjected to Inhuman or Degrading Treatment.
13. Principle 24, GA Resolution 43/173, Annex, 43 GAOR supp (No.49); UN Doc A/43/49(1988); Principle 1 Deals with the Right to be Treated with Respect and Dignity; Principle 5(2) Provides the Right to Non Discrimination Among the Prisoners.
14. Rule 23 of the Standard Minimum Rules for the Treatment of Prisoners Deals with the Special Medical Needs of Women and Nursing Infants. Adopted 30 August 1955, by the first United Nations Congress on the Prevention of Crime and the Treatment of Offenders.
15. Principle 9, Basic Principles for the Treatment of Prisoners.
16. Rule 26 of Standard Minimum Rules for the Treatment of Prisoners.
17. Balambal, V., (1998)- 'Studies in the History of the Sangam Age', Kalinga Publications, Delhi, p. 51.
18. {4:9:21, 23}. 21-for the Hindrance of Sleep, Sitting Down Meals,Aanswering Class of Nature or Movement and for Binding in a Judge's Lock-up or in a Prison House, the Fines shall be 3 Panas Increased Successively by 3 Panas for him who does it and for him who Causes it to be done; 23- for the Superintendent of the Prison House Allowing Movement to a Prisoner without Informing (the Judge or Magistrate) the Fine is 24 Panas for Using Torture Double (that), for making him Submit to Another Position or with holding Food

and Drink Ninety-six for Tormenting or Maiming him the Middle Fine for Violence, for Killing him One Thousand (panas as fine) Cited in Kangle, R.P., (1963) - 'The Kautiliya Arthasastra', Part II, University of Bombay, Bombay, pp. 323-324.

19. Datir, R.N., (1978)- 'Prison as a Social System', Popular Prakashan Pvt. Ltd., Bombay, p. 51.
20. Article 6, Code of Conduct for Law Enforcement Officials.
21. Principal 1-6, GA.Res. 37/194 annex, 37 UN GAOR Supp (No.51) at 211, UN Doc. A/37/51 (1982).
22. Velupillai, T.K., (1940) –'The Travancore State Manual', Vol. IV, (Adm), , Kerala Gazetters Department, Trivandrum, p.133.
23. Chishti, Anees. (2001) – 'Committees and Commissions in Pre-Independence India (1836-1947)', Vol. I –1836-1879, Mittal Publications, New Delhi, pp. 128-130.
24. Chapter XIII, Rules for the Superintendence and Management of the Central Prison, Trivandrum, 1919, p. 41.
25. Cochin Legislative Council Proceedings, Official Report of Legislative Session 1117, 14 Edavom 1117/27 May 1942, Wednesday, p. 1175.
26. Act XVIII of 1950, The Travancore Cochin Prisons Act.
27. The Committee Submitted Its Report on 28 January 1993, P M Aboobecker –Chairman, 9th Kerala Legislature Estimate Committee (1991-1993), p. 5.
28. National Human Rights Commission—Annual Report 1998-1999, p. 23.
29. Kerala State Human Rights Commission—Annual Report 2002, Thiruvananthapuram, p. 29.
30. The Hindu, 12 August 2004, Thursday, Vol. 127, No. 192, Thiruvananthapuram, p. 3.
31. An Interview with K.A. Kumaran, Chief Welfare Officer, 20 December 2006, Prison Headquarters, Poojapura, Trivandrum.
32. The Hindu, 8 November 2005, Thursday, Thiruvananthapuram., p. 2.
33. The Hindu, 14 January 2006, Tuesday, Thiruvananthapuram, p. 10.
34. An Interview with V.P. Mohankumar, Chairman, Kerala State Human Rights Commission on 15 March 2006, Thiruvananthapuram.
35. An Interview with Mr. Vikraman, Hospital Head Warder on 13 January 2007, Poojapura Central Prison.
36. An Interview with the Mr. K J Varghese, Jail Welfare Officer on 17 January 2007, Poojapura Central Prison.

37. The Hindu, 14 November, 2007, Wednesday, Thiruvananthapuram, p. 2.

38. The New Indian Express, 22 June 2007, Friday, Thiruvananthapuram, p. 3.

39. Written Statements Submitted by the Asian Legal Resource Centre (ALRC) a Non-governmental Organisation in General Consultative Status- 17 July 2006, 61st Session of the Commission on Human Rights, Thiruvananthapuram.

18

Rights of Prisoners in India

A Myth or Reality

Manoj K. John

Human life has always been valued and given the paramount importance under common law, while Indian traditions treat human life as inseparable from divinity.[1] All over the world a newer jurisprudence is evolving day be day, particularly with the help of judicial decisions, where prisoners are not equated with animals but as human beings.

The Universal Declaration of Human Rights and the International Covenant on Civil and Political Rights among other instruments has provided a broad platform for international community in not only providing basic definitions and postulates for human rights and fundamental freedoms , but also has created binding legal obligations among member states in the field of human rights protection.

In India we follow the adversary legal system for which a major basic premise is the presumption of innocence of an accused person, unless proved guilty.

The system requires that the prosecution is to prove what it alleges against the accused beyond the shadow of reasonable doubt. The law also provides a fair opportunity for the accused person to defend himself and prove his innocence. Hence in the normal circumstances the burden of proof is on the prosecution to prove the guilt of the accused.

For several reasons many accused has to face trial while under detention. The courts has drawn a clear distinction between an under trial prisoner and a convict. The treatments of under-trial-pre trial detainees are guided by two fundamental principles. One is the presumption of innocence and second is the obligation of the state to treat detainees with humanity and dignity, in conformity with their unconvicted status. Since the suspect or accused is presumed to be innocent until adjudged guilty by a competent court, protection of his human rights is more important in view of the hardships caused to him while in detention.

Article 10 of the International Covenant on Civil and Political rights prescribes that "all persons deprived of their liberty shall be treated with humanity and with respect for the inherent dignity of the human person"[2]. The covenant also stress that convicted and unconvicted persons should be kept in separate quarters.

In the case of a convict there is of course a judicial finding that he is guilty of an offence, but nevertheless even such conviction cannot reduce him to a non-person[3]. In our country the Right to Life has been held available to all prisoners, under trial or convict as a fundamental right[4]. The worth of the human person and dignity survives even in a prison setting.[5]

Constitutional and Legal Safe Guards

There are legal and procedural safe guards for ensuring justice and fair trial and prisoner's rights enshrined in the constitution, code of criminal procedure and various prison legislations and rules made there under.

Article 21 of the constitution guarantees the right of 'personal liberty' and thereby prohibits any inhuman, cruel or degrading treatment to any person detained, whether he is a national or foreigner. Any violation of this right attracts the provision of Article 14 of the constitution which enshrines equality before law and equal protection of laws.

The constitutional guarantee against deprival of personal liberty by Article 21 is further strengthened by Article 22 which prescribes the minimum procedural requirements that must be included in any law enacted by the legislature in accordance with which a person may be deprived of his life and personal liberty. Clauses (1) and (2) of Article 22 of the Indian constitution guaranties for rights to the persons who are arrested under an ordinary law. They are:

- The right to be informed as soon as may be in the grounds of arrest.
- The right to consult and to be represented by a lawyer of his own choice.
- The right to be produced before a Magistrate within 24 hours; and
- The freedom detention beyond the said period except by the order of Magistrate.

Article 22 (4) to (7) provide the procedure which is to be followed if a person is arrested under the law of 'Prevention Detention', which includes scrutiny by an Advisory Board for longer detentions.

The question of the amount of fundamental rights guaranteed by the constitution available to a detainee was discussed in *Sunil Batra v Delhi Administration*[6] by the Honorable Supreme Court. The court held that Fundamental Rights in Part III of the constitution does not part company with the prisoner at the gates, and judicial oversight protects the prisoner's shrunken fundamental rights, if flouted, or frozen by the prison authority. The 'reasonable restriction' for depriving personal liberty should only be according to the 'procedure established by law' and the reasonability will be tested under Article 19.

All provisions in the Code of Criminal Procedure 1973 (hereinafter referred as code) are designed to protect the interest of justice and to provide a fair trial to the accused. Section 479 of the code, prescribes that no magistrate or judge who has any interest in any manner with the case must not preside over the trial or hear an appeal tried by him.

The principle of public trial in an open court is embodied in section 327, which also provides for in camera proceedings for certain offences like rape, ensuring victim's rights.

Section 56 and 57 of the code contains similar guidelines in Article 22 (2) of the constitution. While section 56 directs a police officer arresting without warrant to produce the arrestee before a magistrate, section 57 directs arrestee not to be detained more than 24 hours without special order from a Magistrate.

Section 167 authorizes a magistrate to authorize detention in custody a person for 15 days when the investigation cannot be completed by 24 hours. An accused can be given for specified days in police custody by the Magistrate within the first 15 days, and only remand to judicial custody after the expiry of the first fifteen days.

Bailable and non-bailable offences are categorized in the code and detailed provisions regarding bails are provided in chapter 33 of the code. (A detailed discussion on Arrest and Bail are beyond the scope of this subject and hence not discussed.)

Prison Acts and Jail manuals in general ensure the minimum needs of the prisoners, including convicted prisoners undergoing sentence.

Hence collectively, the constitution, the criminal procedure, and the Prison legislations and rules tries to ensure, the rights of prisoners like rights for access to law and legal aid, right to live with human dignity, right against undue harassment, right for fair trial, bail provisions, for communication, gainful employment, against arbitrary prison punishments, etc:

Role of Judiciary

The Indian Judiciary has been playing the role of a sentinel of human rights, not to speak of the legal and constitutional rights of citizens of this country. The court has through a series of epoch making decisions, expanded the concept of 'locus standi' and promoted the concept of 'Public Interest Litigation' which has contributed a lot in ensuring human rights and cutting down of violations of detainees and under trials.

J. Bhagwati said in the historic decision of *Peoples Union of Democratic Rights v Union of India*[7]

"...where a person or a class of persons to whom legal injury is caused or legal wrong is done is by reason of poverty, disability or socially or economically disadvantaged position not able to approach the court for judicial redress, any member of the public acting bonafide ... may move to the court...and the judicial process may be set in motion by any public spirited individual or institution even by a letter addressed to the court."[8].

Thus started the growth of public interest or social action litigation, which provided a lot of human rights protections to various classes of underprivileged sections of the society.

There are many instances where court considered letters as writs and ordered release of detainees languishing in jails for 20 to 30 years[9], upholding the locus standi of law professors bringing court's notice the plight of inmates living in inhuman conditions of protective homes[10], and invoking the writ of Habeas Corpus on a public interest petition to release a person from illegal detention.[11] The creative and some times an activist Supreme Court in the eighties and nineties paved way for the growth of a new social consciousness regarding rights of underprivileged including detainees.

Judicial Decisions Establishing Prisoner's Rights

In the land mark decision of *D.K.Basu v State of West Bengal*[12], the honorable Supreme Court laid down various guide lines for arrest and detention. The Guidelines include identification labels of the arresting officer, attestation of arrest memo by witnesses, right to be informed of the arrest to a friend or relative, the right of to be made aware of his right to get his arrest known to friends, entry in police diary, any injuries to be recorded, right for medical examination every 48 hours, right to meet his lawyer, copies of documents to be send to court and information of arrest to district police control room.

The court also quoted the *Universal Declaration of Human Rights*[13] which states that "No one shall be subject to torture or to cruel, inhuman or degrading treatment or punishment".

In *S.C Advocates on Record Association V Union of India*[14], the court held that the provision of speedy justice is an obligation of state and Speedy trial is a Fundamental right an ingredient of Act. 21 of the constitution. In *Hussainara Khatoon v State of Bihar*[15], the court held that an under trial is not expected to kept in jail without any trial for a longer time. An under trial has been kept in jail for a period longer than the maximum period of expected imprisonment, release was ordered by the court. It follows that the convict should not suffer any more than what is warranted by the sentences; and not subjected to any degrading mode of execution of that sentence. If this principle is violated then the court would interfere.

In *Sohraj v Supdt*[16] the court said the court will interfere where a convict is constantly kept in fetters, day and night (reducing the prisoner from a human being into an animal) regardless of the fact of detention in the interest of security. In the same case court also said that even where the sentence is one of rigorous imprisonment having regard to the age or condition of the convict, hard labor should not be imposed, as it amounts to unnecessary harshness. In *Sanjay v Delhi Administration*[17], the court said when accepting such restrictions as are necessary in the interest of security and discipline; prisoners should not be denied opportunity of visits by family members and friends including news men. The court have guaranteed legal aid to prisoners in the case of *Hussainara Khatoom v Delhi Domestic Working women forum,* in addition to the right provided in 304 CrPC, which has now been given all over India to accused persons not represented by a lawyer, also by virtue of Legal Services Act, passed by parliament.

In *State of Rajasthan v Sukpal Singh*[18] it was held that all prisoners have got a right provided under prison laws to have copies of all the judgments convicting them so that appeals may be filed. In this case a jailer by ill will withheld the copies, it has been held to thwart the court process and thus violation of Act 21, it was held, in all such cases of delays benefit goes to the accused person.

Myth or Reality

The conscience of Indian public received a shock recently when for the first time in the history of independent India, a former Asst Commissioner of Delhi police Mr. Thyagi, was sentenced to death, for murder in the lock up. The National Human Rights Commission so motto look cognizance of a report published in a newspaper dated November 1993 captioned "Two cops suspended for custody death". It was reported that Sri Madanlal, 22 years of age had allegedly died in police custody under mysterious circumstances. On perusal of the report submitted by the Government of the capital territory of Delhi, the commission decided to have an investigation. A member of the higher judicial service was appointed to investigate the matter. The report concluded the death as a result of physical assault while in police custody. The commission made recommendations in the instant case. In this case the Government accepted the recommendations made by the commissions after inquiry.[19]

NHRC directed the Delhi Government to pay compensation of Rs. 10000 each to four victims who suffered atrocities in police custody. The commission directed a departmental enquiry against Mr.R.P..Tyagi former Asst. commissioner of police Delhi and station house officer, Anand Prabat police station, who had manipulated the records to prove his absence from the station at the time of the occurrence of the incident. The commission had utilized its investigation wing in this case.

Now after trial R.P. Tyagi is sentenced to death for murder in police custody. Never before has an Indian police man received so severe a sentence. The'Times of India' news paper ,described the conviction a landmark event and points out that the media and films also contributed to this social climate of sanctioning police excesses to root out terrorism.[20] No doubt the judgment would lead to substantial reduction of human rights violations by police personnel committing custodial violence.

The police have a significant role in the protection and enforcement of human rights of individuals. They are duty bound to maintain the rule of law and to ensure protection of rights of all sections of the society. But at many times they play negative role and some times act in excess of their powers. The major accusation, against the police is that they indulge in custodial violence and at times torture or give degrading treatment to arrested persons or individuals in lock ups.

In *Khatri v State of Bihar*[21], the Supreme Court had to deal with blinding of under trials by police by piercing their eyeballs with needles and pouring acid in them. In *Sudha Rashid v Union of India*[22], the Supreme Court awarded seven lakh rupees to the relatives of an advocate who died in police custody. There are now any number of reported decisions of Supreme Court and various high courts punishing police personnel responsible for deaths and violence in custody, and awarding compensation in many cases.

A total of 1591 deaths were recorded in various jails in the country including all states and union territories between April 2005 and March 2006 against 1357 between 2004 and 2005. One of the main reasons would certainly be poor, inhuman, overcrowding and unhygienic living condition within the jails. The National Human Rights Commission has received intimation regarding lock up deaths; of 139 deaths in police custody in 2005-2006 against 136 in 2004-2005.

Even though there are a number of constitutional and other legal and judicial safeguards with a view to protect the very basic rights of prisoner, we can never deny the fact that Indian police has a long way to go to be the real custodian of law and become a model police force which effectively protect the human rights of all, including those in their custody. The importance of realization of one's own rights by individual citizens is also necessary requirement for overall improvement in terms of respect for rights.

The National Human Rights Commission has also suggested many reform measures for ensuring more human rights to prisoners improving prison infrastructure and prison reforms. This is a very positive action in the right direction. There has to be a concerted effort from the part of the Government and the executive to take appropriate and timely measures to implement various guidelines provided for reforms and to improve the living conditions therein.

There has been substantial criticism from International Human Rights groups against successive governments in the country, for not ratifying the *International Convention against Torture*. They say that as a democratic country like India, should not shy away from the process of ratification as it owes to its citizens the minimum guarantee of protection that could be availed by the treaty obligations.

The issuance of guidelines by Supreme Court and various other courts and National Human Rights commission, in itself has not provided a total protection of human rights violations under detention. Protection of human rights of persons especially in pre- trial detention is a critical element of humanization of criminal justice system. It is true that besides protection of the accused there are also other priority interests like getting justice to the victim, but to deny the protective umbrella of human rights to a pre trial detainee is repugnant to the rule of law and the fundamental freedoms and basic right to liberty and could be counter productive in terms of crime control also.

REFERENCES & NOTES

1. D.D.Basu, (2003) . Human Rights in Constitutional Law, P. 392.
2. Article 10(1) International Covenant for Civil and Political Rights.
3. Sunil V Delhi Administration . AIR.1978 SC 1675.
4. State of AP V Challa Ramakrishna Reddy, AIR 2000 SC 2083.
5. Sohraj Vs Supdt. A . 1978 SC 1514.
6. Sunil Batra v Delhi Administration AIR 1978 SC 1675.
7. Peoples Union of Democratic Rights v Union of India AIR 1982 SC 1473.
8. ibid. p. 1477.
9. Veena Sethi v State of Bihar AIR 1983SC339.
10. Upendra Baxi v State of U.P (1983)2 SCC 308.
11. Sunil Batra v Delhi Administration AIR 1978 SC1675.
12. D.K.Basu v State of West Bengal.
13. Article 5 of Universal Declaration of Human Rights
14. SC advocate on Record Association Vs Union of India. AIR 1994 SC 268.

15. Hussainara Khatoon Vs State of Bihar. AIR 1979 SC 1360.

16. Sohraj Vs Supdt. 1978 SC 1514.

17. Sanjay v Delhi Administration (1989) supp (2) 511.

18. State of Rajasthan v Sukpal Singh AIR1984 SC207.

19. Annual Report of NHRC 1994-95. P. 34.

20. Times of India, Editorial dated Dec. 20, 2006.

21. Khatri v State of Bihar AIR 1981SC928.

22. Sudha Rashid v Union of India 1999 Cri LG 1099(Del).

19

HIV/AIDS and Human Rights

P.G.Thomaskutty & Mary George

Introduction

The issue of Human Rights of HIV/AIDS infected and affected people is of prime importance in the context of numerous cases of violation of human rights of this category of people. In this paper we use the word 'HIV/AIDS infected' to those people who are clinically diagnosed unequivocally as HIV positive. The word 'HIV/AIDS affected' is used to denote those close relatives of HIV/AIDS infected people. In the case of HIV/AIDS, unlike any other infectious disease, not only the infected but also their close relatives are subjected to harassment, sense of shame and accusing fingers. Many a case they are treated as if they are criminals.

Indian Constitution provides for equality of all citizens before law. Hence HIV/AIDS infected and affected people are eligible for equality ensured in the Constitution. The provisions that are relevant to the AIDS situation in India are found in Part III of the Indian Constitution, which deals with Fundamental Rights and in Part IV of Directive Principles of State Policy. Articles 14 to 18 guarantee equality before law and equal protection. Laws or regulations isolating AIDS patients and denying them eligible treatment at health care centers can be challenged before the Supreme Court of India or in the High Courts.

However HIV/AIDS have raised a multiplicity of legal questions, and prompted a 'juridical outburst in many quarters' (Kirby Michael 1987 & 1988). Either through legislation or litigation, many countries have recognized that their people have the right to HIV treatment as part of their human rights, confirming that economic, social and cultural rights are justiciable.

In its important verdict on case No.SU-256(1996) the Constitutional Court of Colombia observed, "It is necessary to remember that the person ill with AIDS or the person who is HIV- positive person is a human being and, as such, enjoys in accordance with article 2 of the Universal Declaration of Human Rights, all the rights proclaimed in the international human rights instruments, with out the possibility of being the object of discrimination, nor or arbitrary decision, by reason of their status. It would be illogical for a person who has illness to be treated in a manner harmful for their physical, moral or personal integrity". HIV- positive people have the right to non-discrimination, equal protection and equality before law.

On the backdrop of the above court verdict and similar other verdicts, we try to summarize some important human rights of AIDS-HIV- positive people.

Right to Work

Discrimination at work place is rampant and termination of service of those who have been diagnosed as HIV-positive is not uncommon. Though there are clear norms against this kind of treatment on HIV-positive people employers resort to this in one pretext or the other. The situation is more severe in private sector rather than in government service. The fear of being removed from job forces many to conceal their positive status, which leads to many faceted complications.

Right to Equality in Employment

People living with HIV have the right to equality in employment. The verdict of Honorable Bombay High court in its verdict No. MXV.ZY.AIR 1997 Bom.406 granted the petition by MX who sought a court order remedying the companies discriminating decision to deny him any further employment because of his HIV-positive status, including through quashing the company's discriminatory policies and reinstating him with benefits and back salaries. There are similar verdicts from other courts in India and abroad. People living with HIV have the right to work unless otherwise they are medically unfit to carry out the job assigned to them. In the case of workers who have become unfit to carryout the work assigned to him due to his HIV-positive situation he is eligible to get compensation similar in any other case of becoming medically unfit. State and public corporations can not take a ruthless and inhuman stand that they will not employ a person with HIV-positive status. Since HIV-positive persons require community support, economic support and non-discrimination, equality at work place is a necessity.

Right to Privacy

Right to privacy include privacy with respect to one's intimate life and state of health. Under the Indian Medical Council Act, the code of Medical Ethics prohibits doctors from disclosing 'the secrets of a patient that have been learnt in the exercise of your profession'. The exceptions are that such secrets 'may be disclosed only in a Court of Law under orders of the presiding judge'. Therefore the doctors who treat an HIV positive person have the duty to maintain secrecy corresponded to a right of the patient to such confidentiality.

Right to Equal Access to Education

HIV-positive children do have every right to study in any educational institution of his/her or parents' choice. Since the HIV status of a student did not pose any threat to any other student or teacher denying admission or removing from rolls on the ground of HIV-positive status is clear case of human right violation. There were cases, where admission was denied to children on unfounded apprehensions and unscientific views like fear of risk of transmission of HIV to other children as a result of insect bites, sharing of sweets and sharing of toilets. There were cases where, when a school admits children with HIV-positive, parents of rest of the children oppose the decision of school authorities and resort to agitation. (Thomaskutty & Mary George: 2007)

Right to Health Care and Medical Treatment

HIV-positive people have right to health care and necessary medical treatment, including treatment for HIV/AIDS. If the state is providing free or subsidized Medical care, the HIV-positive people also do have a right to get free/subsidized treatment funded by government outlets. Denying medical treatment for an HIV-positive person is nothing but gross discrimination. Access to medical treatment also implies availability of such services and medicine at affordable price. The International Covenant on Economic, Social and Cultural Rights (Article 12) which expressly recognizes the right to every person to enjoy the highest attainable standard of physical and mental health.

Right to Life/Right to Live with Dignity

Like any human person HIV-positive people do have the right to live with dignity. This right cannot be curtailed even when the HIV-positive person is a prisoner. The UN Standard Minimum Rules for Treatment of Prisoners (1955) state that 'All accommodation provided for the use of prisoners and in particular all sleeping accommodation shall meet all requirements if health, due regard being paid to climatic conditions and particularly to cubic content of the air, minimum floor space, lighting, heating and ventilation'. The United Nations International Guidelines on HIV/AIDS and Human Rights state that 'the isolation and segregation of the HIV-positive inmates is contrary to human rights norms' (HIV/AIDS and Human Rights: International Guidelines: Office of the UN High Commissioner for Human Rights and Joint Programme on HIV/AIDS, 1998).

Right to Freedom of Movement

HIV-positive people have the right to freedom of movement. They have the right to travel and use the mode of transportation of their own choice. They should not be forbidden from entering into any public place including place of worship. If any agency/person imposes any restriction on them by differing or denying entry to places like place of worship, educational institution, recreation centre, etc. is a clear case of human rights violation.

The Right to Marry and Found a Family

A person living with HIV has the right to marry and this right is not lost or suspended on account of the person's HIV status. A person with HIV who enters into marriage with a willing partner after disclosing his HIV status doesn't commit an offence. However, it doesn't mean that an HIV-positive person will not come under the purview of existing legal regimes governing marriage in the country.

Other Human Rights

Apart from the above listed human rights the HIV/AIDS infected people also have the right to liberty and security of person, the right to seek and enjoy asylum, the right to freedom of opinion and expression and the right to freedom of association, the right to an adequate standard of living, the right to social security, assistance and welfare, the right to share in scientific advancement and its benefits, the right to participate in public and cultural life, the right to be free from torture and cruel, inhuman and degrading treatment or punishment.

The protection of human rights is essential to safeguard human dignity in the context of HIV and to ensure an effective right-based response to HIV/AIDS. It may be noted that when human rights are protected, fewer people become infected and those people who are infected and affected can better cope with HIV/AIDS. It is of importance to protect human rights of vulnerable groups like sex workers, injecting drug users especially in marginalized sections and children.

Some of the important Guidelines issued by the office of the United Nations High Commissioner for Human Rights in association with the Joint United Nations Programme on HIV/AIDS are summarized below. The Commission on Human Rights has asked Governments to take all necessary steps to ensure the respect, protection and fulfillment of HIV-related human rights as contained in the Guidelines, and has urged Governments to ensure their laws, polices and practices comply with the Guidelines.

(See Resolutions 1997/33, 1999/49, 2001/51, 2003/47 &, 2005/84)

Guideline: 1- States should establish an effective national framework for their response to HIV which ensure a coordinated, participatory, transparent and accountable approach, integrating HIV policy and programme responsibilities across all branches of government.

Guideline: 2 - States should ensure, through political and financial support, that community consultation occurs in all phases of HIV policy design, programme implementation and evaluation and that community organizations are enabled to carry out their activities, including in the field of ethics, law and human rights, effectively.

Guideline: 3- States should review and reform public health laws to ensure that they adequately address public health issues raised by HIV, that their provisions applicable to casually admitted diseases are not inappropriately applicable to HIV and they are consistent with international human rights obligations.

Guideline: 4- States should review and reform criminal laws and correctional systems to ensure that they are consistent with international human rights obligations and are not misused in the context of HIV or targeted against vulnerable groups.

Guideline: 5- States should enact or strengthen anti-discrimination and other protective laws that protect vulnerable groups, people living with HIV and people with disabilities from discrimination in both the public and private sector, ensure privacy and confidentiality and ethics in research involving human subjects, emphasize education and conciliation, and provide for speedy and effective administrative and civil remedies.

Guideline: 6 (as revised in 2002) - States should enact legislation to provide for the regulation of HIV-related goods, services and information, so as to ensure widespread availability of quality prevention measures and services, adequate HIV prevention and care information, and safe and effective medication at an affordable price.

States should also take measures necessary to ensure for all persons, on a sustained and equal basis, the availability and accessibility of quality goods, services and information for HIV prevention ,treatment, care and support, including antiretroviral and other safe and effective medicines, diagnostics and related technologies for preventive, curative and palliative care of HIV and related opportunistic infections and conditions.

States should take such measures at both the domestic and international levels, with particular attention to vulnerable individuals and populations.

Guideline: 7 - States should implement and support legal support services that will educate people affected y HIV about their rights, provide free legal services to enforce those rights, develop expertise on HIV-related legal issues and utilize means of protection in addition to the courts, such as offices of ministries of justice, ombudspersons, health complaint units and human rights commissions.

Guideline: 8 - States in collaboration with and through the community should promote a supportive and enabling environment for women, children and other vulnerable groups y addressing underlying prejudices and inequalities through community dialogue, specially designed social and health services and support to community groups.

Guideline: 9 - States should promote the wide and ongoing distribution of creative education, training and media programmes explicitly designed to change aptitudes of discrimination and stigmatization associated with HIV to understanding and acceptance.

Guideline: 10 - States should ensure that Government and the private sector develop codes of conduct regarding HIV issues that translate human rights principals into code of professional responsibility and practice, with accompanying mechanisms to implement and enforce these codes.

Guideline: 11 - States should ensure monitoring and enforcement mechanisms to guarantee the protection of HIV-related human rights, including those of people living with HIV, their families and communities.

Guideline: 12 - States should cooperate through all relevant programmes and agencies of the United Nations system, including UNAIDS, to share knowledge and experience concerning HIV-related human rights issues and should ensure effective mechanisms to protect human rights in the context of HIV at international level.

Conclusion

In this article the authors summarize some of the important human rights of HIV/AIDS infected people. Taking stoke of the social reality we argue for the protection of human rights of not only the infected but also the affected. The guidelines issued by the office of the United Nations High Commissioner For Human Rights in association with the Joint United Nations Programme on HIV/AIDS regarding effective implementation and practices of human right law and regulations are of prime importance. Protecting the human rights of HIV/AIDS victims will go in a great way in ensuring justice to them and also enhance the dignity of human life.

REFERENCES

1. Kirby Michael Justice (1987) (High Court of Australia) Presentation at the Symposium International de reflexion sur le SIDA, Paris, 22-23 October 1987.
2. Kirby Michael (1988) The New AIDS Virus-ineffective and Unjust Laws. Journal of Acquired Immune Deficiency Syndrome 1:304-312).
3. Constitutional Court of Colombia, Decision SU-256 (1996).
4. Thomaskutty P G & Mary George'Socio-economic Implication of HIV/AIDS' *Proceedings of International AIDS Conference* Held at MG Kashi Vidyapith , Varanasi, India, 2007.
5. The UN Standard Minimum Rules for Treatment of Prisoners (1955)-Article 10) (HIV/AIDS and Human Rights: International Guidelines. Office of the UN High Commissioner for Human Rights and Joint Programme on HIV/AIDS, 1998, para. 29.
6. UNAIDS, (2006) Courting Rights, Case Studies in Litigating the Human Rights of People Living with HIV; Geneva.
7. UNAIDS (2006) International Guidelines on HIV/AIDS and Human Rights Geneva.
8. UNAIDS (2002) Report on the global HIV/AIDS epidemic Geneva.

9. UNDP (1993) Law, Ethics and HIV. Regional Project on HIV/AIDS, New Delhi.

10. ICASO (1999) HIV/AIDS and Human Rights: Stories from the Frontlines, Toronto: ICASO Available at: http://www.icaso.org/docs/stories_english.pdf

11. UNAIDS (2000)HIV and AIDS- Related Stigmatization, Discrimination and Denial: Forms, Contexts and Determinants. Research Studies from Uganda and India. Geneva: UNAIDS

12. UNAIDS(2001) Determinants of AIDS-Related Discrimination, Stigmatization and Denial in India (prepared by shalini Bharat) Geneva:UNAIDS.

20

Human Rights Violations during Internal Strife and Its Humanitarian Remedies

Sanoj Rajan

The twenty-first century has witnessed significant challenges to the traditional views on Human Rights law which regulates the conduct in peace time and International Humanitarian law which regulates the use of force in armed conflict. The death and destruction caused on various internal strife's with in the borders of the nations especially one like the insurgency/terrorist problems in Jammu and Kashmir and North East states in India and the September 11, 2001, incident in USA, which literally shook the world, reflect the increasingly complex nature of modern conflicts. Groups that rely on the benefits of globalization and technological advances to conduct operations across international borders are threatening the maintenance of international order. The novel way of conducting hostilities and the invisibility of the opponent in the so called terrorist/insurgent activities (which is usually supported and fueled by other nations) has in fact distorted the line of difference between international and internal armed conflicts. The tools for violence in this type conflicts range from conventional weapons of war to more modern weapons of mass destruction[1] and potentially asymmetric "cyber attacks."[2]

As the distinction between the International Armed conflicts, Non International Armed conflicts and Internal Strife are thinning down[3], the laws which are meant for maintaining the Human Rights of the non-combatants, *Hors de Combat* and victims are being watered down. The proliferation of internal armed conflicts points to similarly complex security challenges within nation-states. These conflicts have not always attracted the same amount of publicity as transnational conflicts and terrorism, which does not, however, make their threat to international and human security any less real. In these situations, death and human suffering largely emanate from readily available, but relatively "low-tech" means, such as antipersonnel mines, the omnipresent AK-47 rifle,[4] and even machetes and transistor radios.[5]

It is a well known fact that up keeping of the rights especially Human Rights of the people during a rebellion is well with in the ambit of the concerned nation and the International Law has nothing to do with it. The concept of rebellion in traditional international law refers to situations of short-lived insurrection against the authority of a state.[6] In part due to their brevity, situations of rebellion are considered to be completely beyond the remit of international humanitarian concern.[7] Rebels challenging the *de jure* government during a rebellion are afforded no protection under traditional international law.

When a rebellion survives suppression, it duly changes in status to a situation of insurgency[8]. The concept of insurgency in traditional international law is, however, ambiguous in the sense that its broad parameters are ill-defined. Falk describes it as a "catch-all designation" stating, "On a factual level, almost all that can be said about insurgency is that it is supposed to constitute more sustained and substantial intrastate violence than is encountered if the internal war is treated as a 'rebellion'"[9]. But in case of insurgency also International Law's protection comes into picture only if that insurgency is recognized by third party nations. Recognition of insurgency occurs out of necessity when the interests either of the *de jure* government or a third state are affected by the conflict, requiring the establishment of relations with the insurgent party. This vague criterion of necessity abbreviates much of the ambiguity surrounding the concept of insurgency in traditional international law. As the conditions for the recognition of insurgency are not clearly defined, the legal situation arising from such acts of recognition differs in each case.[10]

As this ambiguity prevails in the internal armed conflicts realm, the protection of the Human Rights in such situations is at stake. If the situation amount to rebellion only, then the law applicable will be the Human Rights law which has to be enforced by the concerned nation, on the other hand if it amount to insurgency then the insurgents get the status of combatants and the whole conduct will be governed by International Humanitarian Law. But unfortunately in today's internal strife, the states usually wage war against invisible combatants who can be classified more or less as terrorists, and hence neither the state take pains to prevent their Human Rights violations[11] nor they come under the scrutiny of International Law. Some times laws like The Armed Forces (Jammu & Kashmir) Special Power Act, 1990[12] meant exclusively for dealing emergent situation adds to this fury. These anomalies can really put non-combatants and *Hors de Combat* in jeopardy. International Law cannot intervene as it does not fall within the category of non international armed conflict.

As there should be a continuum of norms that protect human rights in all situations, from international armed conflicts at one end of the spectrum to situations of non armed internal conflicts at the other, there should be a convergence of humanitarian and human rights norms[13]. The violations of Human Rights during armed conflict are being assessed through the perspective of human rights law, as well as under international humanitarian law. This Paper explores the interface between these two normative regimes and its impact on efforts to control Human Rights violations during internal conflicts. The analysis will analyze the present provisions of the International Humanitarian Law, ie, the Geneva Conventions and its protocols, the Customary International Humanitarian law and the recent development through case law in the ICTY and ICTR(International Criminal Tribunal for Rwanda) to see whether it is sufficient to protect the civilians and non-combatants from Human Rights violations from the excesses of such Conflicts.

I. Article 3 Common to the Geneva Conventions of 1949 and Internal Armed Conflict

Before the formulation of the four Geneva Conventions of 1949, no codification of international law existed specific to internal armed conflicts. Consequently, the application of international humanitarian law to a situation of internal armed conflict depended on it being fundamentally similar to an international armed conflict. Article 3 common to the four Geneva Conventions is the first codification of international law specific to situations of internal armed conflict.

The concept of internal armed conflict resulting from the formulation of Common Article 3 differs very significantly from that assumed by state practice in traditional international law. Usually, in order for international humanitarian norms to be applied, recognition of belligerency was required by traditional international law. Arguably one of the greatest achievements of the common Article is that it lowers the threshold for the application of international humanitarian norms. It applies to all situations of non-international armed conflict, including situations of insurgency not reaching the threshold of a civil war. The concept of internal armed conflict that results is therefore much broader in scope than that assumed by traditional international law. Another significant development lies in the provisions of Common Article 3, which provide a set of humanitarian norms to be adhered to (as a minimum) in all circumstances. The text of Common Article 3 is as follows:

> In the case of armed conflict not of an international character occurring in the territory of one of the High Contracting Parties, each Party to the conflict shall be bound to apply, as a minimum, the following provisions:
>
> 1. Persons taking no active part in the hostilities, including members of armed forces who have laid

down their arms and those placed hors de combat by sickness, wounds, detention, or any other cause, shall in all circumstances be treated humanely, without any adverse distinction founded on race, colour, religion or faith, sex, birth or wealth, or any other similar criteria.

To this end, the following acts are and shall remain prohibited at any time and in any place whatsoever with respect to the above-mentioned persons:

(a) Violence to life and person, in particular murder of all kinds, mutilation, cruel treatment and torture;

(b) Taking of hostages;

(c) Outrages upon personal dignity, in particular humiliating and degrading treatment;

(d) The passing of sentences and the carrying out of executions without previous judgment pronounced by a regularly constituted court, affording all the judicial guarantees which are recognized as indispensable by civilized peoples.

2. The wounded and sick shall be collected and cared for.

An impartial humanitarian body, such as the International Committee of the Red Cross, may offer its services to the Parties to the conflict.

The Parties to the conflict should further endeavour to bring into force, by means of special agreements, all or part of the other provisions of the present Convention.

The application of the preceding provisions shall not affect the legal status of the Parties to the conflict.[14]

A further noteworthy departure from traditional international law is that the implementation of Common Article 3 does not, in principle, require reciprocity since it is binding irrespective of agreements (of lack thereof) between parties to an armed conflict. As customary international law, the common

Article forms part of the strongest corpus of international law. The section that follows focuses on how this helps to prioritize its implementation in situations of non-international armed conflict.

The strength of Common Article 3 as a provision relating to situations of non-international armed conflict is highlighted by its status as customary international law. The International Court of Justice (ICJ) in the *Nicaragua* case states:

Article 3 which is common to all four Geneva Conventions of 12 August 1949 defines certain rules to be applied in the armed conflict of a non-international character. There is no doubt that [. . .] these rules also constitute a minimum yardstick [. . .] and they are rules which, in the Court's opinion, reflect what the Court in 1949 called "elementary considerations of humanity."[15]

The ICJ's position on the customary status of Common Article 3 is supported by the ICTY's jurisprudence. The Appeals Chamber of the ICTY in the *Tadic* case referred to the common Article as a provision embodying "certain minimum mandatory rules."[16] These rules "reflect 'elementary considerations of humanity' applicable under customary international law to any armed conflict, whether it is of an internal or international character."[17] The Appeals Chamber goes on to state "customary international law imposes criminal responsibility for serious violations of Common Article 3."[18] This view of the common Article as customary international law is upheld in the subsequent case law of the ICTY.[19] It is also supported in the jurisprudence of the ICTY's sister institution, the International Criminal Tribunal for Rwanda (ICTR). According to the *Akayesu* case before the ICTR, "It is today clear that the norms of Common Article 3 have acquired the status of customary law in that most States, by their domestic penal codes, have criminalized acts which if committed during internal armed conflict, would constitute violations of Common Article 3."[20]

Although a consensus exists concerning the customary status of the Common Article 3, the grounds for its application have been fraught with controversy. The Article states that it applies "in the case of armed conflict not of an international character." The Geneva Conventions, however, do not define or explain what an "armed conflict not of an international character" consists of. The absence of a definition has arguably undermined the implementation of the international humanitarian law, allowing states latitude to deny the existence of armed conflict.[21] The ambiguity in the scope of Common Article 3 effectively allows states the opportunity to evade the responsibility to adhere to its provisions. States are often reluctant to recognize the applicability of the common Article due to the perception that it increases the authority of the insurgents.

As there is no formula for the recognition of armed conflict in the Geneva Conventions, the implementation of Common Article 3 is largely dependent on the will of parties engaged in hostilities to acknowledge the applicability of international humanitarian law. This is perhaps the most problematic aspect of the law governing situations of internal armed conflict. Without a formula for the recognition of armed conflict, it is possible for states wishing to avoid the application of international humanitarian law to simply deny its relevance. A definition of non-international armed conflict was included in Additional Protocol II to the Geneva Conventions of 1949 to help avoid this problem. The following section examines how the definition contained in Additional Protocol II affected its scope after first investigating how Additional Protocol I narrowed the concept of internal armed conflict to exclude wars of national liberation.

II. The Concept of Internal Armed Conflict in the Additional Protocols of 1977

After Common Article 3, the next major development in international humanitarian law was the formulation of two Additional Protocols to the Geneva Conventions of 1949.[22] Here we have two sections to analyze, the section studies Additional Protocol I, demonstrating how the concept of non-international armed conflict is narrowed to exclude wars of national liberation. The second part scrutinizes Additional Protocol II, paying specific attention to provisions governing its application. The distinctions introduced into the notion of internal armed conflict by the Additional Protocols are held not to be advantageous to the cohesiveness of the concept.

A. Additional Protocol I

The significance of Additional Protocol I to the present discussion concerns its characterization of internal wars of national liberation as situations of international armed conflict. The title of the instrument states it relates to "the Protection of Victims of International Armed Conflicts."[23] Article 1(4) expands on this to include armed conflicts which peoples are fighting against colonial domination and alien occupation and against racist regimes in the exercise of their right of self-determination, as enshrined in the Charter of the United Nations and the Declaration on Principles of International Law concerning Friendly Relations and Co-operation among States in accordance with the Charter of the United Nations.[24]

Before the formulation of this instrument, wars of resistance against colonial powers were viewed through the lens of international humanitarian law as situations of internal armed conflict. Common Article 3 was thus considered to be the main applicable standard. Article 1(4) expands the laws governing the conduct of hostilities in wars of national liberation. According to Professor Leslie C. Green, "So long as an internal conflict is directed towards self-government, the Protocol provides for its recognition as an international conflict governed by the Conventions and the Protocol, as well as the ordinary law regarding international armed conflicts."[25] The drafters of the instrument, however, interpreted Article 1(4) more restrictively: the ICRC Commentary states the three cases recorded therein (colonial domination, alien occupation, and racist regimes), constitute "an exhaustive list" of internal armed conflicts deemed now to be international.[26] On the other hand, it does not include cases in which, without one of these elements, people takes up arms against authorities which it contests, as such a situation is not considered to be international.[27] It is thus clear the protocol excludes the majority of internal armed conflicts, not fitting into any of the important categories of such conflicts.

B. Additional Protocol II

The concept of non-international armed conflict contained in Additional Protocol II, however, sets a much higher threshold of application than Common Article 3. While Common Article 3 applies to all situations of non-international armed conflict, Article 1(1) of Additional Protocol II states that it applies only to armed conflicts which take place in the territory of a High Contracting Party between its armed forces and dissident armed forces or other organized armed groups which, under responsible command, exercise such control over a part of its territory as to enable them to carry out sustained and concerted military operations and to implement this Protocol.[28]

While Article 1(1) provides a positive definition of non-international armed conflict, Article 1(2) of the Protocol provides a negative definition. This provision states that the protocol "shall not apply to situations of internal disturbances and tensions, such as riots, isolated and sporadic acts of violence and other acts of a similar nature, as not being armed conflicts."[29]

The clause in Article 1(2) providing for the exclusion of internal disturbances and tensions was retained from the original draft of the Protocol, which assumed the same threshold of application as Common Article 3. According to the ICRC Commentary on the Protocol, the purpose of this provision "was to define the lower threshold of the concept of armed conflict, assuming that the field of application of common Article 3 and the Protocol would be identical. The paragraph was not questioned and was retained and adopted without lengthy debates."[30]

Given the list of objective criteria in Article 1(1), it would appear unnecessary to include a further provision excluding situations of internal disturbance. The inclusion of Article 1(2) is significant, however, as it demarcates the lower threshold of non-international armed conflict and thus the application of Common Article 3. Commenting on the distinction between situations of non-international armed conflict and internal disturbances, Professor Dietrich Schindler lists the following four conditions determining the existence of armed conflict:

> In the first place, the hostilities have to be conducted by force of arms and exhibit such intensity that, as a rule, the government is compelled to employ its armed forces against

> insurgents instead of mere police forces. Secondly, as to the insurgents, the hostilities are meant to be of a collective character, that is, they have to be carried out not only by single groups. In addition, the insurgents have to exhibit a minimum amount of organisation. Their armed forces should be under responsible command and be capable of meeting humanitarian requirements. Accordingly, the conflict must show certain similarities to a war without fulfilling all conditions necessary for the recognition of belligerency.[31]

It should be emphasized, however, that the distinction between situations of internal disturbance and internal armed conflict is not always apparent. The conditions outlined by Schindler, above, approximate those contained in Article 1(1) of Additional Protocol II. Situations of low-intensity armed conflict outside the remit of the Protocol, necessitating the application of Common Article 3, are more difficult to differentiate.[32]

Each of the Additional Protocols created a distinction in international humanitarian law that previously had not existed. Article 1(4) of Additional Protocol I, providing for the internationalization of wars of national liberation, has effectively narrowed the concept of internal armed conflict, and, in doing so, lessened interest in the development of applicable laws.[33] The creation of a new threshold of application by Article 1(1) of Additional Protocol II is, however, a much more regressive development—rather than bolstering the implementation of international humanitarian law, the heightened threshold serves to strengthen the discretionary power of states to deny the existence of armed conflict. As pointed out by Medard R. Rwelamira, "Individual states are . . . left with a *carte blanche* to decide when the Protocol or common Article 3 should be invoked."[34]

III. The Concept of Internal Armed Conflict Propounded in the Tadic Jurisdiction Decision

On 2 October 1995, the appeals chamber of the ICTY issued its decision on the Defence Motion for Interlocutory Appeal on Jurisdiction (the *Tadic* Jurisdiction Decision).[35] This decision concerning the first case before the tribunal considerably influenced the development of international humanitarian law. The decision affected many aspects of international humanitarian law—the discussion here is restricted to the definition of armed conflict provided in that decision:

> An armed conflict exists whenever there is a resort to armed force between States or protracted armed violence between governmental authorities and organized armed groups or between such groups within a State. International humanitarian law applies from the initiation of such armed conflicts and extends beyond the cessation of hostilities until a general conclusion of peace is reached; or, in the case of internal conflicts, a peaceful settlement is achieved. Until that moment, international humanitarian law continues to apply in the whole territory of the warring States or, in the case of internal conflicts, the whole territory under the control of a party, whether or not actual combat takes place there.[36]

The appeals chamber in the *Tadic* case related the above concept to the situation in the Prijedor region of Bosnia-Herzegovina. In doing so, the chamber clarified grounds for asserting the existence of "a legally cognizable armed conflict,"[37] triggering the application of international humanitarian law:

> Applying the foregoing concept of armed conflicts to this case, we hold that the alleged crimes were committed in the context of an armed conflict... . There has been protracted, large-scale violence between the armed forces of different States and between governmental forces and organized insurgent groups. Even if substantial clashes were not occurring in the Prijedor region at the time and place the crimes allegedly were committed-a factual issue on which the Appeals Chamber does not pronounce-international humanitarian law applies. It is sufficient that the alleged crimes were closely related to the hostilities occurring in other parts of the territories controlled by the parties to the conflict.[38]

The existence of armed conflict is interpreted in broad terms by the appeals chamber, which states, "the temporal and geographical scope of both internal and international armed conflicts extends beyond the exact time and place of hostilities."[39] This position, which strengthens the reach of international humanitarian law, is also voiced by the trial chamber in the *Delalic* case: "whether or not the conflict is deemed to be international or internal, there does not have to be actual combat activities in a particular location for the norms of international humanitarian law to be applicable."[40] Furthermore, the use of the term "protracted" in the tribunal's definition of non-international armed conflict ("protracted armed violence between governmental authorities and organized armed groups or between such groups"), implies that hostilities need not be continuous.[41] As interruptions in fighting do not suspend the obligations of the parties under international humanitarian law, the use of this term allows for a broad, practical interpretation of internal armed conflict.

The *Tadic* Trial Chamber applied the concept of armed conflict introduced by the appeals chamber.[42] In doing so, it posited the following interpretation of the definition provided by the appeals chamber:

> The test applied by the Appeals Chamber to the existence of an armed conflict for the purposes of the rules contained in Common Article 3 focuses on two aspects of a conflict; the intensity of the conflict and the organization of the parties to the conflict. In an armed conflict of an internal or mixed character, these closely related criteria are used solely for the purpose, as a minimum, of distinguishing an armed conflict from banditry, unorganized and short-lived insurrections, or terrorist activities, which are not subject to international humanitarian law.[43]

The two aspects of internal armed conflict stated by the *Tadic* Trial Chamber—the intensity of the conflict and the organization of parties to the conflict—provide grounds for the recognition of *de facto* armed conflict (and thus also for the application of Common Article 3). The trial chamber in the *Delalic* case supports this interpretation of non-international armed conflict, stating that "in order to distinguish from cases of civil unrest or terrorist activities, the emphasis is on the protracted extent of the armed violence and the extent of organisation of the parties involved."[44] The ICTR also employs this approach: In determining the existence of armed conflict in Rwanda, the tribunal held that it is "necessary to evaluate both the intensity and organization of the parties to the conflict."[45]

Besides being utilized to determine the applicability of international humanitarian law in the former Yugoslavia and Rwanda, the formula propounded in the *Tadic* Jurisdiction Decision has also been applied to a number of other situations. These include the Occupied Palestinian Territories of the Middle East and Somalia. The UN Special Rapporteur on the situation of human rights in the Palestinian territories, John Dugard, has used the *Tadic* formula repeatedly in evaluating the status of the situation in the Palestinian territories under Israeli occupation. In a report issued on 4 October 2001, he stated the situation could be characterized, "on an irregular and sporadic basis," as an armed conflict due to the "frequent exchanges of gunfire between the Israel Defense Forces and Palestinian gunmen."[46] Mona Rishmawi, an independent expert of the Commission on Human Rights, applied the *Tadic* formula to the situation in Somalia to determine the existence of armed conflict and thus the application of international humanitarian law. She held that,

> as long as the faction leaders, the militias and other irregular armed forces continue their conflict in Somalia and until a peaceful settlement is reached, international humanitarian law related to internal armed conflict applies in the whole territory of Somalia irrespective of whether the specific area is engulfed in active fighting.[47]

Providing a basis for determining the existence of armed conflict, the *Tadic* formula now arguably forms part of the conceptual framework for the application of international humanitarian law to situations of internal armed conflict. The section that follows examines how it has been adapted in the Rome Statute of the International Criminal Court, highlighting the broad scope of non-international armed conflict as a positive development of the law.

C. The Adaptation of the Tadic Formula in Article 8(2)(f) of the Rome Statute

The ICTY's characterization of non-international armed conflict as "protracted armed violence between governmental authorities and organized armed groups or between such groups" has had a significant impact on its contemporary conceptualization in international humanitarian law. Perhaps the strongest evidence of this influence is the adaptation of the formula in the Rome Statute of the International Criminal Court. Although the issue of jurisdiction over non-international armed conflicts was one of the most controversial to be dealt with at the Rome Conference,[48] its inclusion in the statute of the court eventually was agreed upon despite opposition from countries including India, China, Turkey, Sudan, and the Russian Federation.[49]

A question that subsequently arose at the Rome Conference concerned the scope of the Court's jurisdiction over non-international armed conflicts. The wording of Article 1(2) of Additional Protocol II received general approval when proposed as part of a definition of internal armed conflict and is now included in Article 8(2)(f) of the Rome Statute. This clause provides for jurisdiction over war crimes committed in "armed conflicts not of an international character" and thus notes the exclusion of "situations of internal disturbances and tensions, such as riots, isolated and sporadic acts of violence or other acts of a similar nature."[50] The second sentence of Article 8(2)(f) (stating that the Statute applies "to armed conflicts that take place in the territory of a State when there is protracted armed conflict between governmental authorities and organized armed groups or between such groups"),[51] originated in a proposal submitted by the Sierra Leone delegation.[52] This proposal adapted the *Tadic* formula to provide a positive definition of non-international armed conflict.

Sierra Leone's proposal received support as an alternative to the one restricting the Court's jurisdiction according to the text of Article 1(1) of Additional Protocol II. As elucidated in the previous section, this article defines situations of non-international armed conflict as taking place

> in the territory of a High Contracting Party between its armed forces and dissident armed forces or other organized armed groups which, under responsible command, exercise such control over a part of its territory as to enable them to carry out sustained and concerted military operations and to implement this Protocol.[53]

If accepted as a positive definition of non-international armed conflict, this provision would have imposed an excessive restriction on the Court's jurisdiction, effectively excluding situations of internal armed conflict such as those in Liberia and Somalia.[54] The adaptation of the *Tadic* formula in Article 8(2)(f) of the Rome Statute has had the effect of lowering the threshold of intensity required for the recognition of internal armed conflict. This has been welcomed by a number of commentators.

For Professor Theodor Meron, the recognition of *de facto* armed conflict as possibly existing between organized armed groups is "both welcome and realistic."[55]

In contrast to the restrictive standard set by Article 1(1) of Additional Protocol II, the inclusive breadth of Article (8)(2)(f) is highlighted by Andreas Zimmerman, pointing to its coverage of the following three situations: Armed conflicts between governmental authorities and dissident authorities; armed conflicts between governmental authorities and organised armed groups; and armed conflicts between several organised armed groups.[56]

The use of the term "governmental authorities" has further broadened the parameters of the provision. According to Zimmerman, the term "has to be understood as including not only regular armed forces of a State but all different kinds of armed personnel provided they participate in protracted armed violence, including, where applicable, units of national guards, the police forces, border police or other armed authorities of a similar nature."[57] The less restrictive nature of the definition contained in Article 8(2)(f) is further demonstrated by the absence of any requirement for the existence of responsible command, sustained and concerted military operations or effective control over part of the territory of a State. Zimmerman remarks this was due to the "experiences of the last twenty years after the adoption of the Second Additional Protocol."[58] In contrast to Article 1(1) of Additional Protocol II, it is also worth noting that the concept of internal armed conflict in Article 8(2)(f) does not require organised armed groups to have the ability to implement international humanitarian law.

In order to reassure states with concerns over the broadness of the provision and its low threshold of application, Article 8(3) states that none of the provisions in the Statute relating to non-international armed conflicts "shall affect the responsibility of a Government to maintain or re-establish law and order in the State or to defend the unity and territorial integrity of the State, by all legitimate means."[59] This clause is taken from Article 3(1) of Additional Protocol II and serves to emphasise that the Statute's provisions on internal armed conflict may not be interpreted as intruding on state sovereignty.[60]

The concept of internal armed conflict provided by *Tadic* and its adaptation in Article 8(2)(f) of the Rome Statute arguably represent progressive developments in international humanitarian law. Providing a basis for the application of Common Article 3, the formula distinguishes broadly the terms for determining the existence of armed conflict, showing it to be distinct from situations of internal disturbance. As previously illustrated, prior to the *Tadic* Jurisdiction Decision the only standard provided by international humanitarian law demarcating situations of internal armed conflict was that contained in Article 1(1) of Additional Protocol II. The high threshold of application set by the Protocol had proved problematic, measuring the existence of armed conflict according to a standard similar, in certain respects, to that required in traditional international law for the recognition of belligerency.

The lowering of the threshold requirements posited by Article 1(1) of Additional Protocol II has resulted in the broadening of the concept of internal armed conflict to include situations of insurgency that until now were not recognised as requiring the application of international humanitarian law. Common Article 3 is now a recognized applicable standard in situations of guerrilla warfare where hostilities take place between organized armed groups without the involvement of government authorities. Prior to the *Tadic* Jurisdiction Decision, the characterization of such situations as manifestations of *de facto* armed conflict would have been inappropriate due to non-involvement of *de jure* state authorities. This development of international humanitarian law to include situations where state structures have disintegrated, takes into account the experiences of countries such as Somalia and Liberia.[61]

Implicit in the *Tadic* formula is the fact that situations of insurgency are now included within the concept of internal armed conflict, necessitating the application of international humanitarian law. The *Tadic* Jurisdiction Decision summarizes succinctly four reasons for the historical extension of international humanitarian law to cover situations of insurgency:

> First, civil wars have become more frequent, not only because technological progress has made it easier for groups of individuals to have access to weaponry but also on account of increasing tension, whether ideological, inter-ethnic or economic; as a consequence the international community can no longer turn a blind eye to the legal regime of such wars. Secondly, internal armed conflicts have become more and more cruel and protracted, involving the whole population of the State where they occur: the all-out resort to armed violence has taken on such a magnitude that the difference with international wars has increasingly dwindled . . . . Thirdly, the large-scale nature of civil strife, coupled with the increasing interdependence of States in the world community, has made it more and more difficult for third States to remain aloof: the economic, political and ideological interests of third States have brought about direct or indirect involvement of third States in this category of conflict, thereby requiring that international law take greater account of their legal regime in order to prevent, as much as possible, adverse spill-over effects. Fourthly, the impetuous development and propagation in the international community of human rights doctrines,

particularly after the adoption of the Universal Declaration of Human Rights in 1948, has brought about significant changes in international law, notably in the approach to problems besetting the world community. A State-sovereignty-oriented approach has been gradually supplanted by a human-being-oriented approach.[62]

The move from a state-sovereignty approach to a human-being-oriented approach is to be welcomed as it allows for and supports a greater degree of humanitarian protection for the victims of non-international armed conflicts. The adaptation of the *Tadic* formula in the Rome Statute represents a positive development which strengthens this protection, helping to ensure accountability for crimes committed in situations of internal armed conflict.

Conclusion

Prior to the formulation of the Geneva Conventions of 1949, situations of internal armed conflict were generally viewed as falling outside the remit of international law. Situations analogous to international armed conflict were exceptions only when recognition of belligerency had taken place. In traditional international law, the existence of insurgency was not viewed as necessitating the application of international humanitarian law. It was through the recognition of belligerency, either by the *de jure* government or by a third state, that parties to an internal armed conflict were categorically obligated to comply with the laws of war. Soon after the Spanish Civil War, the doctrine of belligerency was viewed to be redundant because of the absence of acts recognizing the existence of armed conflict in the practice of states.[63] The strict criteria governing the recognition of belligerency, together with its high threshold of application, were undoubtedly considerations for the drafters of Common Article 3.

The formulation of Common Article 3, despite its failings, has come to be recognized as the first major achievement in the codification of a universally acceptable standard specific to situations of internal armed conflict. Now recognized as customary international law, the common Article embodies a set of minimum standards of humane treatment to be adhered to in all circumstances. The cardinal problem with the application of Common Article 3, however, is not with its humanitarian provisions, but with the actual recognition of the existence of armed conflict. As there is no set of criteria indicating conditions manifesting an armed conflict "not of an international character" in the Geneva Conventions, the implementation of the common Article is based on the willingness of parties to recognize its applicability. When a state refuses to recognize the existence of armed conflict, it also avoids the application of the common Article. As discussed earlier, the lack of a formula for determining the existence of armed conflict has in many ways facilitated states wishing to avoid the application of international humanitarian law.

In the process of drafting the Additional Protocols of 1977, it is likely that delegates were mindful of how the absence of a formula weakened the efficacy of Common Article 3. The drafters of Additional Protocol II attempted to strengthen the instrument by including a set of criteria demarcating its field of application. This resulted, however, in the establishment of an excessively high threshold for its implementation and also effectively created another category of internal armed conflict in international humanitarian law. Additional Protocol I, relating to situations of international armed conflict, narrowed the concept of internal armed conflict by internationalizing internal wars of national liberation. As a consequence, situations of internal armed conflict against racist regimes or colonial occupation were now viewed as wars governed by the Geneva Conventions in their entirety and not by Additional Protocol II. Both Protocols had the effect of creating new, and in certain respects, problematic distinctions in the concept of internal armed conflict. The distinction created by Additional Protocol II delineated situations of a particular threshold, excluding completely from its remit internal armed conflicts of low intensity. Additional Protocol I distinguished particular kinds of *prima facie* internal armed conflict as international on the grounds of their cause or intended outcome. These distinctions were included due to the pragmatism of drafters, responding to the political pressure exerted during negotiations. Now accepted features of international humanitarian law, they narrow the notion of internal armed conflict, further exacerbating problems that surround the formulation of a cohesive concept. For this reason, the formula propounded in the *Tadic* Jurisdiction Decision and adapted in Article 8(2)(f) of the Rome Statute of the International Criminal Court is an especially welcome development.

The concept of internal armed conflict as "protracted armed conflict between organized armed groups and government authorities or between such groups" is welcome for a number of reasons. It expands the concept of internal armed conflict beyond that contained in Additional Protocol II and, in doing so, provides a basis for the application of Common Article 3. The formula is broad enough to include situations of low intensity armed conflict and yet exclude situations of internal disturbance. By realistically defining the concept of internal armed conflict in broad terms, Article 8(2)(f) of the Rome Statute expands the protection offered by international humanitarian law in such situations. The practice of guerrilla warfare may now be included in the concept of armed conflict as a result of the provision's lower threshold of application. The definition provided in Article 8(2)(f) lacks the excessive restrictions imposed by Article 1(1) of Additional Protocol II such as the existence of territorial control, responsible command over troops, and the use of sustained and concerted military operations by insurgents. Furthermore, the definition in Article 8(2)(f) specifically provides for the existence of armed conflict between warring factions without the involvement of a *de jure* governmental authority. Before the *Tadic* Jurisdiction Decision, such situations, irrespective of their scale, were generally not recognised in international humanitarian law as constituting armed conflicts. The broad, inclusive language of the definition is of significant help in ensuring a greater degree of protection to the victims of such situations.

The more recent developments outlined in this article show an expansion of the concept of internal armed conflict in international humanitarian law. This is to be welcomed as it enables a greater degree of humanitarian protection. The progress that has been achieved in the area of international humanitarian law governing situations of internal armed conflict has been slow, attained by progressively pulling against interests of state sovereignty. Although the concept of internal armed conflict codified in Article 8(2)(f) of the Rome Statute is a significant attainment, further development is required for its evolution into a more substantive measure for determining the existence of armed conflict. It is important to recognize, however, that there should not be a quantitative threshold set for either intensity of hostilities or the organization of insurgents, as flexibility in the application of the formula could well be stifled by such an action. The concept being phrased in an abstract manner will allow future case law to develop without being constricted by the kind of restrictive stipulations set out in Additional Protocol II. This is vital. In order for the formula to strengthen the application of international humanitarian law, it must possess an optimum degree of flexibility. The concept is a positive contribution to the body of law governing internal armed conflict and no doubt will be further utilized in the future to ensure a greater degree of humanitarian protection in situations once deemed to be the exclusive concern of state sovereignty.

REFERENCES

1. Weapons of Mass Destruction are Identified as "a Chemical, Biological, Radiological, or Nuclear Weapon, or High-yield Explosives" in the NATIONAL STRATEGY FOR COMBATING TERRORISM 9 (Feb. 2003), *at* <http://www.whitehouse.gov/news/releases/2003/02/counter_terrorism/counter_terrorism_strategy.pdf>.
2. NATIONAL STRATEGY FOR HOMELAND SECURITY 9 (July 2002), *at* <http://www.whitehouse.gov/homeland/book/sect2-1.pdf> (Indicating that "Terrorist Groups are Already Exploiting New Information Technology and the Internet to Plan Attacks, Raise Funds, Spread Propaganda, Collect Information, and Communicate Securely"). "Asymmetric Warfare" has been Defined As Fighting for Different Ends, or in Different Ways, or with Different Means from those of One's Opponent. Mark Clodfelter, *Airpower Versus Asymmetric Enemies: A Framework for Evaluating Effectiveness,* 16 AIR & SPACE POWER J. 37, 37 (2002).
3. The Good Examples for Such Conflicts are which Frequently Taking Place in Kashmir. This So Called Insurgency is Undoubtedly Supported and Aided by Foreign Hands. This can Even Aggravated to an Extend where the Other Nation will Conduct Hostilities in Disguise of Insurgents and that May End Up in Full Fledged Conflict, Just Like what Happened in Kargil Conflict.

4. Mass-produced Weapons Such As the AK-47 and Similar Small Arms Stand Out As Late-twentieth-century Symbols of Warfare by the "people." As John Keegan Notes, the Industrialization of Modern Society Militarized the Populations of Both Rich and Poor States. JOHN Keegan, A History Of Warfare 57 (Vintage Books 1994) (1993).

5. Not all Killing Results from Modern Weapons. The Genocide of Eight Hundred Thousand Rwandans was carried out Largely by Local Populations, who were "Spurred on by Their Radio Station RTLM, Spewing Racist Propaganda, Exciting Hutus to Kill All Tutsis as well as Elements of UNAMIR." Romeo A. Dallaire, *The End of Innocence: Rwanda 1994, in* Hard Choices: Moral Dilemmas In Humanitarian INTERVENTION 71, 78 (Jonathan Moore ed., 1998).

6. *See* Richard A. Falk, *Janus Tormented: The International Law of Internal War, in* James N. ROSENAU, INTERNATIONAL ASPECTS OF CIVIL STRIFE 197-99 (1964). Heather Wilson Defines Rebellion As "A Sporadic Challenge to the Legitimate Government." Heather A. Wilson, International Law And The Use of Force by National Liberation Movements 23 (1988).

7. R.P. Dhokalia, *Civil Wars and International Law,* 11 INDIAN J. INT'L L. 219, 224 (1971).

8. According to Erik Castren, "Recognition of Insurgency Means Acknowledgement of the Existence of An Armed Revolt of Grave Character and the Incapacity, At Least Temporarily, of the Lawful Government to Maintain Public Order and Exercise Authority Over All Parts of the National Territory." Erik Castren, Civil War 212 (1966). For Further Reading on the Concept of Insurgency in Traditional International Law, William V. O'Brien, *The Jus in Bello in Revolutionary War and Counter-Insurgency, 18 VA. J. INT'L L. 193 (1978);* George Grafton Wilson, *Insurgency and International Maritime Law, 1 AM. J. INT'L L. 46 (1907).*

9. Falk, *supra* note 6 , at 199.

10. Castren, *supra* note 8, at 212.

11. The Human Rights Violation in J&K, North East Provinces in India and in the Present Afghanistan and Iraq are Good Examples for this.

12. Act No. 21 of 1990, this Act Gives the Armed Forces Members Indiscriminate Powers and Pay Scanty Regards to Human Rights, for Example Special Powers of the Armed Forces Under Section 4 of the Act Reads as follows:

    Any Commissioned Officer, Warrant Officer, Non-commissioned Officer or Any Other Person of Equivalent Rank in the Armed Forces may, in a Disturbed area:

(a) If he is of Opinion that it is Necessary so to do for the Maintenance of Public Order, After Giving Such Due Warning as he may Consider Necessary, Fire Upon or Otherwise Use Force, Even to the Causing of Death, Against Any Person who is Acting in Contravention of Any Law or Order for the Time Being in Force in the Disturbed Area Prohibiting the Assembly of Five or more Persons or the Carrying of Weapons or of Things Capable of Being Used As Weapons or of Fire-arms, Ammunition or Explosive Substances.

13. See generally Meyrowitz, Le Droit de la guerre et les droits de l'homme, 88 REV. DROIT PUBLIC & SCIENCE POLITIQUE EN FRANCE & A L'ETRANGER 1059 (1972); Draper, Humanitarian Law and Human Rights, 1979 ACTA JURIDICA 193; Draper, The Relationship Between the Human Rights Regime and the Law of Armed Conflicts, 1 ISR. Y.B. HUM. RIGHTS 191 (1971); Partsch, La Protection Internationale des droits de l'homme et les Conventions de Geneve de la Croix-Rouge, 26 REV. INT'LE DROIT COMPARE 73 (1974); Aldrich, New Life for the Laws of War, *75 AJIL 764 (1981);* Robertson, Human Rights as the Basis of International Humanitarian Law, in PROCEEDINGS OF THE INTERNATIONAL CONFERENCE ON HUMANITARIAN LAW 55 (San Remo 1970); A. CALOGEROPOULOSTRATIS, DROIT HUMANITAIRE ET DROITS DE L'HOMME: LA PROTECTION DE LA PERSONNE EN PERIODE DE CONFLIT ARME (1980); M. BOTHE, K. PARTSCH, & W. SOLF, NEW RULES FOR VICTIMS OF ARMED CONFLICTS (1982). For a List of the Principal Humanitarian Conventions and a Discussion of the Scope of Humanitarian Law, see Partsch, Humanitarian Law and Armed Conflict [Instalment], 3 ENCYCLOPEDIA OF PUBLIC INTERNATIONAL LAW 215 (R. Bernhardt ed. 1982).

14. Richard Guelff & Adam Roberts, Documents on The Laws of War 302 (3d Ed. 2000).

15. Case Concerning Military and Paramilitary Activities in and Against Nicaragua (Nicar. v. U.S.), 1986 I.C.J. 4 para. 114 (Judgment of June 27) (Merits).

16. Prosecutor v. Dusko Tadic (a/k/a Dule), No. IT-94-1-AR72, para. 102 (Oct. 2, 1995) (Decision on the Defence Motion for Interlocutory Appeal on Jurisdiction).

17. *Id.*

18. *Id.* para. 134.

19. *See* Prosecutor v. Mladen Naletilic, and Vinko Martinovic, No. IT-98-34-T, para. 228, (Mar. 31, 2003) (Trial Chamber Judgment); Prosecutor v. Miroslav Kvocka, Milojica Kos, Mlado Radic, Zoran Zigic, &

Dragoljub Prcac, No. IT-98-30/1-T, para 124 (Nov. 2, 2001) (Trial Chamber Judgment); Prosecutor v. Dragoljub Kunarac, Radomir Kovac, & Zoran Vukovic, No. IT-96-23-T & IT-96-23/1-T, para. 406 (Feb. 22, 2001) (Trial Chamber Judgment); Prosecutor v. Zejnil Delalic, Zdravko Mucic, Hazim Delic, & Esad Landzo, No. IT-96-21-A, paras. 136-139 (Feb. 20, 2001) (Appeals Chamber Judgment); Prosecutor v. Dusko Tadic, No. IT-94-1-AR72, para. 609 (May 7, 1997) (Trial Chamber Judgment).

20. Prosecutor v. Akayesu, No. ICTR-96-4, para. 608 (Sept. 2, 1998) (Judgment).

21. Examples of Armed Conflicts in which the Application of International Humanitarian Law has been Denied include Situations in the West Bank, Kuwait, and East Timor. The Parties Denying Applicability in these Situations are, Respectively, Israel, Iraq, and Indonesia. *See* Theodor Meron, *The Humanization of Humanitarian Law, 94 AM. J. INT'L L. 239, 261 n.119 (2000).*

22. Unlike the Geneva Conventions of 1949, the Additional Protocols of 1977 have yet to be Ratified by all 191 Member states of the United Nations. To date, 162 States Ratified Additional Protocol I while 157 have Ratified Additional Protocol II. The Non-ratification of Additional Protocol I and II by states such as India, Pakistan, Indonesia, and the United States does not Impact Significantly on how the Internal Armed Conflict is Conceptualized Contemporaneously in International Humanitarian Law. David J. Scheffer, the Former U.S. Ambassador at Large for War Crimes Issues, in an Address to I Corps Soldiers and Commanders on 4 May 2000 Stated, "We Continue to Recognize that many of the Substantive Provisions of both Protocol I and Protocol II, which Covers Internal Armed Conflicts, Reflect the Development of Customary International Norms." In the Same Speech he Stated, "Thirteen Years Ago, President Reagan Asked the Senate for Its Advice and Consent to Additional Protocol II to the 1949 Geneva Convention, which Governs Internal Armed Conflicts. President Clinton Renewed that Request in January 1999." David J. Scheffer, Address to I Corps Soldiers (May 4, 2000) (Transcript on File with Author).

23. Protocol Additional to the Geneva Conventions of 12 August 1949, and Relating to the Protection of Victims of International Armed Conflicts, Dec. 12, 1977, art. 1, 1125 U.N.T.S. 3 [hereinafter Additional Protocol I]

24. *Id.* art. 1(4).

25. Leslie C. Green, *Strengthening Legal Protection in Internal Conflicts: Low-intensity Conflict and the Law, 3 ILSA J. INT'L & COMP. L. 493, 503 (1997).*

26. ICRC, Commentary on The Additional Protocols of 8 June 1977 to The Geneva Conventions of 12 August 1949 1325 (1987) At 1354.

27. *Id.* at 1355-56.

28. Additional Protocol II to the Geneva Conventions of 12 August 1949, and Relating to the Protection of Victims of Non-International Armed Conflicts, *Adopted* 8 June 1977, *Entered into Force* 7 Dec. 1978, U.N. Doc. A/32/144 Annex II, 1125 U.N.T.S. 609 [hereinafter Additional Protocol II], art. 1(1).

29. Id.

30. ICRC, *supra* note 26, at 1354.

31. Dietrich Schindler, The Different Types of Armed Conflicts According To The Geneva Conventions And Protocols 163 (1979); 163 Recueil Des Cours 117, 147.

32. *See* James E. Bond, The Rules of Riot: Internal Conflict And The Law of War 52 (1974).

33. David A. Elder, The Historical Background of Common Article 3 of the Geneva Conventions of 1949, 11 CASE W. RES. J. INT'L L. 37, 39 (1979), at 69.

34. Medard R. Rwelamira, The Significance and Contribution of the Protocols Additional to the Geneva Conventions of August 1949, at 236.

35. Prosecutor v. Dusko Tadic (a/k/a Dule), No. IT-94-1-AR72, para. 70 (Oct. 2, 1995) (Decision on the Defence Motion for Interlocutory Appeal on Jurisdiction).

36. *Id.* para. 70.

37. *Id.* para. 66.

38. *Id.* para. 70.

39. *Id.* para. 67.

40. Prosecutor v. Delalic, Mucic, Delic, & Landzo, No. IT-96-21-T, para. 185 (Nov. 16, 1998) (Trial Chamber Judgment); *see also* Prosecutor v. Blaskic, No. IT-95-14-T, Trial Chamber Judgment, P 100-101 (Mar. 3, 2000). The *Blaskic* Case Before the ICTY Refers to the Definition Provided by the *Tadic* Appeals Chamber as a Criterion Applicable "To All Conflicts Whether International or Internal. It is Not Necessary to Establish the Existence of An Armed Conflict within Each Municipality Concerned. It Suffices to Establish the Existence of the Conflict Within the Whole Region of which the Municipalities are a Part." *Blaskic,* No. IT-95-14-T, para. 64.

41. *See* Andreas Zimmermann, *War Crimes Committed in an Armed Conflict Not of An International Character, in* Otto Triffterer, Commentary On Statute Of The International Criminal Court 285 (1999).

42. *See* Prosecutor v. Dusko Tadic, No. IT-94-1-AR72, para. 628 (May 7, 1997). The ICTY has Consistently Employed this Test in Determining the Existence of Armed Conflict. *See* Prosecutor v. Kunarac, Kovac & Vukovic, No. IT-96-23, para. 56 (June 12, 2002) (Appeals Chamber Judgement); Prosecutor v. Jelisic, No. IT-95-10-T, paras. 29, 30 (Dec. 14, 1999) (Trial Chamber Judgment); Prosecutor v. Furundzija, No. IT-95-17/1, para. 59 (Dec. 10, 1998) (Trial Chamber Judgment).

43. *Tadic,* No. IT-94-1-AR72, para. 562

44. *Delalic,* No. IT-96-21-T, para. 184.

45. Prosecutor v. Akayesu, No. ICTR-96-4, para. 620 (Sept. 2, 1998) (Judgment).

46. *Report of the Special Rapporteur of the Commission on Human Rights on the Situation of Human Rights in the Palestinian Territories Occupied by Israel since 1967* para. 13, U.N. Doc. A/56/440 (2001).

47. *See Report on the Situation of Human Rights in Somalia, Prepared by the Independent Expert of the Commission on Human Rights, Mona Rishmawi, Pursuant to Commission Resolution 1996/57 of 19 April 1996* para. 54 U.N. Doc. E/CN.4/1997/88 (1997).

48. Darryl Robinson & Herman von Hebel, *War Crimes in Internal Conflicts: Article 8 of the ICC Statute,* 1999 Y.B. INT'L HUMANITARIAN L. 193, 198 (1999).

49. *Id.* at 198 n.37.

50. Rome Statute of the *International* Criminal Court, U.N. Doc. A/ CONF.183/9, July 18, 1998, as Amended Through Jan. 16, 2002, *Entered into Force* July 1, 2002 [hereinafter Rome Statute] art. 8(2)(f).

51. *Id.* The Wording of this Definition of Non-international Armed Conflict Differs Slightly from that Provided by the *Tadic* Jurisdiction Decision. Instead of "Protracted Armed Violence," The Term "Protracted Armed Conflict" is used in the Rome Statute. This, However, is not to be Interpreted as Either Changing the Scope of Internal Armed Conflict or Creating a Threshold of Applicability Distinct from that of the *Tadic* Definition. *See* Meron, *supra* note 63, at 260; THEODOR MERON, WAR CRIMES LAW COMES OF AGE 309 (1998); Clause Kress, *War Crimes Committed in Non-International Armed Conflict and the Emerging System of International Criminal Justice,* 2001 ISRAEL Y.B. ON HUM. RTS. 103, 117-18; ICRC Working Paper, *supra* note 74.

52. U.N. Doc. A/CONF.183/C.1/L.62 (on File with Author).

53. Additional Protocol II, *supra* note 28, art. 1(1).

54. *See* ICRC, *Armed Conflicts Linked to the Disintegration of State Structures: Preparatory Document Drafted by the International Committee of the Red Cross for the First Periodical Meeting on International Humanitarian Law,*

Geneva (Jan. 19-23, 1998), *Available at* http://www.icrc.org/web/eng/siteeng0.nsf/iwpList74/02CED570ABFDD384C1256B66005C91C6 [hereinafter ICRC, Armed Conflicts Linked to the Disintegration of State Structures].

55. Theodor Meron, *Classification of the Conflict in the Former Yugoslavia: Nicaragua's Fallout, 92 AM. J. INT'L L. 236, 237 (1998).*

56. *See* Andreas Zimmermann, *War Crimes Committed in an Armed Conflict Not of An International Character, in* Otto Triffterer, Commentary on Statute of The International Criminal Court 285 (1999), at 286.

57. *Id.*

58. *Id.*

59. Rome Statute, *supra* note 50, art. 8(3).

60. Additional Protocol II, *supra* note28, art. 3(1).

61. ICRC, *supra* note 54.

62. Prosecutor v. Dusko Tadic (a/k/a Dule), No. IT-94-1-AR72, para. 97 (Oct. 2, 1995) (Decision on the Defence Motion for Interlocutory Appeal on Jurisdiction).

63. Lieutenant Colonel Yair M. Lootsteen, *The Concept of Belligerency in International Law, 166 MIL. L. REV. 109 (2000)*; at 111.

21

Demanding Ergonomically Designed Working Environment

A Basic Right to Health

Visalakshi Rajeswari

Introduction

Ever heard of Aesulapius, a pioneer in Medicine, about whom the Greeks are still proud of? This leader had two daughters: Hygiea and Panacea. The former was worshiped as the Goddess of Health and the latter, the Goddess of Medicine – one pertains to man and the other to the environment. Thus the dichotomy between curative medicine and preventive medicine had grown roots very early. Hippocrates, 'the father of medicine', in his concept of health and disease had stressed the relation between man and his environment, focusing on the innate capacity of the body of responding to disturbances in the equilibrium that constitutes health; a statement, which is more or less on par with the Greek belief. The Romans were more practical - minded and had a keen sense of sanitation. Public health was thus born in Rome. Then came the sanitary awakening in England. Now modern medicine is a dual mix of both preventive and curative medicine. Evidently, health, disease and medicine have started receiving a 'person – centric' attention, by which is implied that man is also responsible for his health – an agent to prevent diseases he may fall prey to.

Modern preventive medicine is defined as the art and science of health promotion, disease prevention, disability limitation and rehabilitation (Clark, D. W. *et al* - 1981). With this, emerged the concept of social medicine- the study of man as a social being in his total environment. Similarly, the social engineering phase of public health brought in its wake, the concept of 'risk factors'. Despite such decentralisation of health aspects, man's role in personal health maintenance still remains to be defined.

Health and disease lie along a continuum (Park, K. - 2002). Through his Spectral concept of health, he emphasizes that the health of an individual is not static; it is a dynamic phenomenon and a process of continuous change, subject to variations – caused by very many factors. Health, is multi factorial, is thus a known fact. It is influenced by factors, which lie both within the individual and external ones. Health connotes 'absence of disease' according to the biomedical concept of health, but ecologists view health as a dynamic equilibrium between man and his environment. Psychosocial domain addresses health issues to be influenced by social, psychological, cultural, economic and political factors of the people concerned. The holistic model currently used is a perfect blend and synthesis of all these concepts. Now, health implies a sound mind in a sound body in a sound environment. One's health and the diseases to which one may fall victim to (if exposed) may depend on the combi- factors of genetic and environmental origin. The interaction between the two factors can be health promoting or harming- the essence of human ecology.

As stated earlier, Hippocrates, was the first to relate disease to environment, followed, centuries later, by a German, Pettenkofer, (Park, K. 2002), who revived the concept. Though there is an endless list of indicators, the most promising ones determining one's health status are environment and personal lifestyle. Environment is classified as internal and external. The former relates to each and every component part, tissues, organs, systems and their harmonious functioning within the system. The external or macro environment consists of those things to which man is exposed. It encompasses all that is external to the individual human host- physical, biological and psychological and psychosocial components (Last, J.M. – 1983). The microenvironment (domestic environment) or personal environment includes the individual's way of living, lifestyle and the much evaded and neglected occupational environment.

The environmental components, albeit being internal or external, are so inextricably linked with one another that it is realistic and fruitful to view the human environment in toot, while considering the influence of the same on the health status of the individuals. Favourable conditions enable individual's full use of their physical and mental capabilities and vice versa. For the sake of convenience interactions in environments are categorised (Banister, E. W. *et al.* –1988, and Park, J. E. *et al.* - 1989), under three types:

- *Physical:* which includes all physical factors like air, water, land, housing, climate, geography, heat, light, noise, debris, radiation and the like,
- *Biological:* where the causative factors of disease and ill health to man are the living things which surround him like microbes, rodents etc.,
- *Psychosocial:* which stem from the psychosocial makeup of individuals and the structure and functions of the social groups and includes 'people'? Their behaviour, customs, attitudes, beliefs and traditions, can be aggravated by factors like poverty, migration, housing occupation/work and stressful situations.

The key to man's health lies largely on his environment. Protection and promotion of environmental health, thus receives special address today. Not only modulation of the environment, but, making them more plastic, is imperative for safeguarding one's health. From another standpoint, adoption and practice of a healthy lifestyle by individuals is also solicited. Health is thus an offspring and a precursor of desirable lifestyle.

Health, but, is multi-dimensional, relating to one's physical, mental (knowing or cognition) and emotional (feeling) disposition.

In this modern era with an ever-increasing number opting to work for a livelihood, the vocational aspect of life, further adds a new dimension, especially when work is not fully adapted to human goals, capacities and limitations. Therefore, non-medical dimensions- social, cultural and environmental, - also leave tell-tale influences on the health of an individual. Analysis on such varied tangents project health to embody a state of physical, mental and social well-being. What is well-being? It is a mix of subjective (quality of life) and objective (standard of living and levels of living) components.

Quality of life is a composite measure of physical, mental and social wellbeing as perceived by each individual or groups and pinpoint to the, happiness, satisfaction and gratification experienced through such life concerns like human values cherished (especially health), work and human and non-human resources one has (Nagpal, R. *et al.* - 1985). The demand in recent years is for a better quality of life. Quality of life is best assessed from a composite index incorporating a number of health indicators, focusing further attention to the indicator called 'health'.

Though, health is an integrated theme in all cultures, it still continues to be a neglected entity; mostly taken for granted. Recently, however, health is considered a fundamental human right and a global- social goal. It is an essential ingredient to the satisfaction of basic human needs and to an improved quality of life. While being an end in itself, it has become a major instrument of the overall socio- economic development of an individual.

Right to health is not a proclaimed component in many of the Constitutions of the world. Only the Declaration of Human Rights, at the international level stated in its Article 25 thus: 'Everyone has the right to a standard of living adequate for the health and wellbeing of himself and his family'. Among the important indicators of health, one major element is environmental indicators. Man is living and working today in a highly complicated environment, which is getting complex with the passing of time, when he is becoming more and more ingenious and technologically advanced. Use of electrical, electronics and telecommunication systems etc. have enhanced the possibility for human exposure to electromagnetic charges. If this trend continues, the quality of life, people cherish may also be endangered. This is the story of the well educated, most sophisticated, working community. The other side of the population lives and works (farms, factories, industries, mines, quarries, hospitals etc), in most deplorable conditions.

Environment constitutes the physical, biological and ambient conditions in which diseases occur and in which people also live and work. Pollution of air, water, land, radiation, solid wastes, noise, exposure to toxic substances, extreme heat/cold, electromagnetic charges, all but, belong to this category. A major element questioned and is well disputed under the concept of right to health is right to a healthy environment-may it be the domestic front or the work situation. Salutations to all the pioneers who had invented many a labour-saving gadgets which have lent a big hand in reducing stress and relieving the women from household drudgery, and making the home front a less polluting and minimum accident prone area. But, what about the working environment and individual's occupational safety and health?

A stable and a harmonious equilibrium between man and his environment is a must to reduce man's vulnerability to disease and to permit him to lead a productive and satisfying life. This aspect has made us think of health in a new two-pronged perspective: Health care and self care. Self-care is a person's responsibility for his own health, which will be discussed later on in this chapter. Health care on the contrary is an expression of concern for fellow human beings – among blood relations, friends, co- workers and above all Employer-employee relationships - which is the core concept of this article, in varied working environments, that is, occupational health care and safety. For enabling one to understand the facts underlying these factors, knowledge on the importance of working conditions and their influence on workers receives attention. A safe and healthy working environment is the basic right of every worker. However, the global situation falls far short of this right.

The International Labour Organisation (ILO. - 1949), aims at encouraging a culture of safety at the workplace with an emphasis on prevention. To quote The Hindu (2006), two million are estimated to die annually owing to work related injury and illness, 250 million suffer occupational accidents and another 160 million falls ill on account of exposure to hazards in the workplace. There has been a corresponding increase in the type of risks owing to a transformation in the relations of production. Additional hazards to life from machines and tools, biological and socio-psychological hazards and musculo-skeletal disorders are also emerging as serious challenges. Though this may seem a global scenario, India is a great contributor to this statistic.

Health and safety of the employees are important aspects in an organisation's smooth and effective functioning. Healthy and safe environment ensures an accident-free industrial set up. Management through concern for OH&S (Occupational Health and Safety) matters demands adoption of a structured approach for the identification of hazards, their evaluation and control of risks (WHO –1986).

Our country has a very dismal health and safety record. Though much legislation exists to protect workers rights and health, they are not implemented properly and only influential workers enjoy the benefits. Of the total workforce only less than ten per cent are organised. Naturally the workforce (without jobs) is abundant, low skilled, easily available and the mounting rate of unemployment leaves them susceptible to exploitation. For Indians, getting work is more important than the hazard involved in it, though jobs have become more of a problem than a pleasure for many (Kirkman, B. - 2005).

NCERT's comments on Directives relating to economic policies begin thus: "Man partly is and wholly hopes to be a God. If proper environment is made available, he can develop the godly qualities. Rights provide that environment." It further describes rights as those claims of an individual that are necessary for the development of his own self (http://www.ncert.nic.in/textbooks/xi/indi-cont/chap4). Now what are these rights? How can they be related to one's occupation? There are mainly three rights that help safeguard a worker. They are:

Right to Equality: This guarantees Equality of opportunity in all matters of public employment.

Right against Exploitation: According to this no individual can be forced to do work without wages (Art: 23). Women and children should not be exploited. Children below 14 years shall not be employed in work in any factory, mine or in any dangerous works (Art: 24).

Right to Freedom: As freedom of the individual is the essence of democracy, all Indians have the liberty to form associations and unions. (www. textbooks online.tn.nic.in).

At the International level, the Universal Declaration of Human Rights established a breakthrough in 1948, by stating in Article: 25 thus: "Everyone has the right to a standard of living adequate for the health and wellbeing of himself and his family". The preamble of the WHO contribution also affirms that. "It is one of the fundamental rights of every human being to enjoy the highest attainable standard of health". Inherent in the right to health, is the right to health or medical care. Some countries also use the term, right to health protection, which is assumed by a comprehensive system of social insurance/ social security (WHO, 1976).

In an increasing number of societies, health is no longer accepted as a charity or the privilege of the few, but demanded as a right for all, as health is one of the indicators of Quality of Life (QL). As Quality of Work Life (QWL) is a subset of quality of life, QWL also gains attention.

Work environment can seriously affect the performance of workers. It is an important ergonomic consideration (Rohmert, W. - 1985), because Ergonomics is concerned with the relationships between the individual and the work environment- the determinants of quality of living, which is the ultimate aim of total development. Quality of working life is increasingly used to describe certain environmental and humanistic values neglected by the industrial society, (Biswas, S. K. - 1993). Referred to, also as a perspective concept, it attempts to design the work environment (De Cenzo, D. *et al.* - 1993). In many ways, QWL represents a blending of real concerns for human values in today's society with awareness that all individuals devote a greater part of their mature lives to work. It recognizes, moreover, that work is the chief determinant of an individual's freedom, growth and self-respect, as well as his or her standard of living. QWL was found to reflect the favourableness or unfavourableness of a job environment for people (Davis, K. *et al.* – 1989). The thrust on this can be gauged by the standards putforth (Venkata Ratnam, C. S. (1993), concerning freedom of association, prohibition of forced labour, equality of opportunity and treatment, employment and human resources, labour administration and relations, wages, hours of work, weekly rest and paid leave, occupational safety and health, social security and the like as necessary ingredients in our Constitution.

India is a developing country with innumerable public, private and government undertakings employing millions of workers-breadwinners of families. These workers are employed to work in varied working conditions and situations. Society is as dependent on the quality of this day to day living decisions and interchanges as are the individuals and families themselves. This composite activity is reflected not only on their quality of life, but also in that of other communities and in the broader society as well. The relationships between the family system and the workers are, in some cases, compartmentalised with rather impermeable boundaries around the work system. In this context, the view that (Deacon, R. E. *et al.* – 1988) organisations that made extensive demands on the family system have often provided benefits and services to families to increase their understanding of and commitment to the organisation sounds true. We have ample evidence in the Software (MNC) companies functioning in India on this score. Considering all these factors, specialists try to measure how adequately work design and management practices meet the demands of human beings in their respective work environments.

The basic concept underlying the QWL is therefore, what has come to be known as "humanisation of work", (Biswas, S. K. - 1993); the four basic principles which summarise this concept of work identified being:

1. *Principle of security:* Which stresses on the safety of working conditions and working without fear of economic want.
2. *Equity:* Which requires that there is a just way of evaluating the conditions of employees and refers to paying for knowledge and skill to carry out the task and not for the task alone.
3. *Democracy:* Which implies that greater authority and responsibility be vested in the workforce; and
4. *Individualism:* That warrants availability of freedom and autonomy in deciding their own pace of activity and design of operations.

QWL, therefore, attempts to design work environments so as to maximise concern for human welfare, by administering various dimensions like improvement in work conditions, fair compensation and job security (Nag, A. - 1993). To make QWL favourable to workers , thoughts and actions have to be channelised in terms of working environment, occupational health,occupational stress and ergonomic considerations as four important factors (Robbins, S.P. - 1994).

Working Environment

Work environment is the place where an individual performs job-related tasks (Francis, G. J. *et al* - 1988). Two important factors that have potential to affect the performance efficiency of jobs, identified are provision of appropriate working conditions and physical environment of work (Monappa, A. *et al.* - 1996).

Analysis of the working environment, is found to include cleanliness, light, heat, ventilation, physical energy required, length of working day, regularity of working hours, physical hazards, exposure to possible industrial diseases and also those social, group and managerial conditions that directly or indirectly influence the worker's happiness, satisfaction or dissatisfaction at work (Bhangoo, K. S. – 1995); indeed a very long list. Maintenance of optimum temperature and humidity and public amenities were qualifying aspects too (Prasad, L. *et al.* - 1990). Factors like avoidance of dust, smoke and fumes, overcrowding and noise also receive special mention. New and easy to operate machines and safety measures are found to determine the efficiency, satisfaction and productivity of the workers. This connotes to fencing of machines, restrictions on work on or near machines in motion, striking gear and devices for cutting of power, self-acting machines, prohibition of employment of women and children in hazardous situations, testing and examination of appliances, supply of safety gear to workers, precautionary measures against fumes, gases, fire and dust. Supervisory behaviour is also an important constituent of working conditions.

Restrictions were laid relating to hours of work, overtime work, holidays and leave and provision of welfare facilities like canteen, crèches, rest and lunch rooms recreational facilities, sanitary and medical amenities (first-aid, ambulance, nursing room, medical staff etc.,), transport, and basic needs like safe drinking water which employers have to satisfy. These were recommended almost 40 years ago (National Commission on Labour India. - 1969). Other components, which may have an impact on workers, figure as the design of jobs and the subsequent relationships with other tasks (Heneman, H. - *et al.* - 1993). Experimenting with job redesign as a way of making the job more compatible with the ability and motivation of employees has encouraged the development of 'quality circles' that solicit ideas on how to improve productivity, an other attempt at ensuring worker satisfaction. This would facilitate identifying problem shooters and help thrash out the same without endangering their health status in the occupational milieu.

The sum of the prevailing external conditions and influences which have a bearing on the health status of the working population thus, refer to occupational environment. Basically, there are three types of interactions in a working environment (Park, K. - 1997).

Man and Physical Environment

Physical environment is means the cumulative effects of physical agents (ambient atmospheric conditions, radiation, noise, vibrations and ionizing radiation), chemical agents (toxic dusts and gases, fumes, smoke, particulate matter etc.,) and biological agents like viral, parasitic and bacterial origin (Gupta, R.D. - 2000). The factors act in different ways on health and efficiency of the workers singly or in different combinations. The amount of working and breathing space made available too can affect one's productivity, especially during hot humid days and when the task requires high precision.

Man and machine: An industry or factory implies the use of machine driven by power with emphasis on mass production. There may be another wing that does not utilise mechanised effort, but relies entirely on the human resource potential, with his crude tools and unsophisticated, non- electric, gadgets, which may leave the user in any kind of a predicament at any time. The unguarded machines, protruding parts and moving components, poor installation, lack of safety measures and tools, equipment and machinery that is not compatible to the worker, are all trouble-shooters that can indirectly affect their health status.

Man and man: There are numerous psychological factors, which operate at the place of work. These are the human relationships amongst workers themselves on the one hand and those on authority over them on the other. Psychological factors include the type and rhythm of work, work stability, service conditions, job satisfaction, security, communication, system of payment, welfare conditions, degree of responsibility, trade union activities, incentives and a host of other factors, all entering the field of human relationships. According to ecological approach, occupational health represents a dynamic equilibrium or adjustment between the worker and his occupational environment.

Occupational Health

Occupational health is essentially preventive medicine because both have the same aim (Park, J.E. *et al.* - 1995). The levels of application of preventive measures are the same- health promotion, specific protection, early diagnosis and treatment, disability, health screening, education and the like. Occupational health therefore, is the application of preventive measures aimed at providing a safe occupational environment. With due consideration to these factors, job related health concerns can be viewed to belong to any of these three types, namely, occupational diseases, occupational stress and occupational injuries (Greene, W. H. *et al.* - 1984), which should be strategically controlled and contained.

- Occupational diseases are closely linked to the prolonged exposure to inclement weather conditions, hazardous agents and conditions, inhalation of toxic gases, radiation, etc, unique to occupational settings.
- Occupational stress is linked to job dissatisfaction and mental and physical illness (Konar, C. - 1996). Stressors could be physical (noise, temperature, radiation, overwork, infection, inadequate nutrition etc) social or psychological (Chawla, S. – 1998).
- Occupational injuries are primarily a product of unsafe working conditions and equipment, compounded by the lack of a safety ethic among workers and exacerbated by fatigue and carelessness. Both these factors can contribute and supplement to 'risk factors' in a large measure (Greene, W.H. *et al.* - 1984).

Occupational Stress

The basic fact about stress is that, like feelings, stress is experienced. The determinants as stressors are, conditions of work like worker's earning/wages, perks, gratuity, overtime payment, working hours, leaves and holidays, social security (ESI and insurance) and labour welfare, and working conditions encompassing nature of the job, physical situations, supervision, communication, trade unionism etc. (Singh, J. K. – 1998). The joint ILO/WHO Committee on occupational health had way back in 1950 proposed that "Occupational health should aim at:

- the promotion and maintenance of the highest degree of physical, mental and social wellbeing of workers in all occupations;
- the prevention among workers of departures from health caused by their working conditions;

- the protection of workers in their employment from risks resulting from factors adverse to health;
- placing and maintenance of the worker in an occupational environment adapted to his physiological and psychological equipment (Park, K. - 2002).

To summarise, it connotes the 'adaptation of work to man and of each man to his job' (Grandjean, E. 1985). This contains in a nutshell the ethos of Ergonomics.

Ergonomics

Ergonomics is concerned with the design, manufacture and arrangement of products and environments so as to ensure safety, health and comfort of the human beings who use them. It is about ensuring a good fit between people, the things they do, the objects they use and the environments, in which they work and live. It is an engineering science where the ergonomist 's objective is to improve the efficiency of operation by taking into account a typical person's size, strength, speed, visual acuity and physiological stresses such as fatigue, speed of decision making and demands on memory and perception (Mc Atamney, L. *et al.* – 1992). Applications range from the design of the work area to the disposition of switches, gauges and control panels of machinery. It is a discipline involving the three basic human sciences of Anatomy, Physiology and Psychology. They are applied in ergonomic studies towards achieving two main objectives, namely, the most productive use of human capabilities and the maintenance of human health and wellbeing. As all kinds of activities insist on the use of the different parts of the human body and as all the internal organs and systems are involved in such endeavours, a comprehensive approach wherein, both the external and internal responses are considered is imperative; and this is what Ergonomics, as a discipline does. It studies man's external attributes, that is, how he does work and his internal reactions, relating to the way he responds to his own self-inflicted strain combined with the external stressors.

Poorly designed equipments/implements or products often require workers to compensate and exert themselves unnecessarily (Glendon, A. I. *et al.* – 2006). All too often, such an exertion leads to both jobs – related errors and an increased level of risk. Moreover, the stressors transmit the stress onto the workers directly reducing their ability to do their job safely and effectively (Kathirvel, K *et al.* - 2005). Designing work conditions and the job itself in such ways as to minimise physical labour, effort and stress, simultaneously, ensuring health, safety and satisfaction of the workers is the aim of ergonomics, also called Human factors engineering (Salvendy,G. – 1987 and Sanders, M. S. et al – 1993). It is used to designate equally a body of knowledge, a process and a profession. It is a body of knowledge, acting as a repository of data pertaining to human characteristics, capabilities and limitations in relation to machines, jobs and environments. As a process, it refers to the conception of designing machines, machine systems, work methods and environments to take into account the safety, comfort and productiveness of the users/ operators (Encyclopaedia Britannica, 1980).

Fire Prevention and Protection: in-built fire resistance capabilities, prohibiting potential ignition sources, providing ample fire-fighting devices and warning systems, education on personal responsibilities in emergencies.

Layout and Housekeeping: designing layout, accommodating ample window area, floor area, wide traffic aisles, enough air movement, neatly finished walls and ceiling, non-slip/skid floors, clean and hygienic locations, safe disposal of solid, effluent and gaseous wastes, provision of safe drinking water and clean working gear.

Lighting and Climate Conditioning: good quality illumination at recommended levels, based on task, proper placement of sources, sufficient and uniform distribution, provision for entry of natural light, control of environmental temperature, efficient heat exchange, natural and artificial ventilation, controlled air flow and air movement (Rao, M. P. – 1998).

Noise and Vibration: exercising control at source and transmission, protective gear (ear plugs), reducing exposure duration, limiting speed of moving parts, damping of joints of moving parts, use of resilient bumper at the point of impact, isolation of vibrating machinery, resilient flooring and padding.

Ergonomics: successful application of tools and techniques, comfortable lighting, noise level, climatic condition, minimum physical work-load, improved/correct work postures, ergonomically designed displays/controls/tools/furniture and working heights, safe lifting and handling, alternating static and dynamic effort, application of work simplification techniques and principles, work studies, research and development wings, regular participatory ergonomics sessions, and forming quality circles. Lack of awareness among doctors and physicians regarding occupational diseases, is another dimension to be looked into (Shepherd, E. – 2001).

Ergonomics, thus is concerned with the whole man – his physical dimensions, mental processes, emotions, relationship with other workers and ability to deal with information of all workers (Cowling, A. *et al.* – 1990) and working condition, has emerged as a multi-attribute function (Pal, M. N. *et al.* – 2001). Ultimately the aim of all ergonomic efforts is to harmonize the influence resulting from the configuration of worker, work, and work environment, equipment and work organisation with one's physical and mental capabilities and his/ her psychological needs. These factors buttress the need for the working community to demand ergonomically designed environments as a basic right to health.

The management of all the employer population has to perfunctorily satisfy these demands, failing which, the employee population's health status would be endangered. A study conducted among workers in a refinery and petrochemicals industry, revealed that more than the relational and job factors, working and financial factors presented a dismal picture, highlighting that the mental frame of the workers relating to what they need and what is satisfied also dictates their health status (Baglari, J. et al. – 1999). The following data summarizes a few common ailments, which they may fall prey to if exposed to conditions not conducive for the jobs relegated to them.

Extreme Heat, Cold and Humidity: Excessive sweating, headache, nausea, heat stroke, chill blains, cramps, vasoconstriction of the peripheral blood vessels, paralysis.

Noise: Temporary/permanent hearing loss, headache, irritation, annoyance, nervousness, and mental disorders.

Insufficient Lighting: Eye strain, headache, lack of concentration, fatigue, monotony with work, accidents, injuries, falls, low productivity, reduced motivation and taking frequent breaks, etc.

Vibration: Fatigue, loss of sense of touch, muscular weakness, loss of mental dexterity, pain and stiffness in joints, degenerative changes in bones and joints and lastly, Raynaud's syndrome.

Radiation: Allergies, cancer, infertility and impotence - even though a controversy exists (Parthasarathy, K. S. - 2008).

Biological: Various infectious and communicable diseases, physical disabilities, mental disorders, paralysis, effects on various bodily systems and death.

Chemical: Respiratory disorders, allergies, asphyxia, suffocation, cancer, paralysis, memory loss, and death.

Particulate Matter, Dust and Fumes: respiratory problems, lung diseases, allergies, cancer, asthma, metal and food poisoning.

Work Related: Added to those mentioned above, musculo-skeletal disorders, degenerative changes in bones and joints, fractures, ligament/tissue ruptures, injuries in different parts of the body etc., leading to pain, sprain, wounds, dislocation of bones (especially in the spinal region, shoulders, hip etc), burns, affected tendons, even hospitalisation and death can occur. For those engaged in sedentary activities, that too for long hours, cramps, muscle catch, obesity, osteoarthritis and stiff joints set in.

Stress: Either physiological or psychological, can cause, hypertension, diabetes, obesity, stomach disorders, fear complex, nervousness, atrophy, allergies, respiratory and skin problems, stroke and cardiac problems.

Lifestyle: Heart diseases, blood pressure, intestinal disorders, ulcers, diabetes, obesity, stress- both, physiological and psychological, infections, musculo-skeletal problems and the like.

Posture: Musculo-skeletal disorders, fractures, ligament/tissue/tendon disabilities, and degeneration in the discs, spinal problems, and permanent disabilities.

Technology Induced: Continuous use of mobile phones can cause tendinitis, carpal bone problems and affect the eardrum and hearing. Prolonged use of computers also can contribute to physical discomfort, stress and damage to the user's body. Constant tapping away at the keyboard can cause serious damage to the fingers, hands, elbows and shoulders (The Hindu. - 2008). Maintenance of a more or less sedentary/awkward posture, in furniture not suited to their anthropometry and duration of work render them unsafe for health. Isolation in individual cubicles, lack of verbal communication, supervision through cyber networking, changes in diurnal rhythm, long working hours, lack of leisure and meeting deadlines, the perils of modern day work situations, further add to psychological discontentment.

Tools, Machinery and Furniture: use of tools, machinery and furniture incompatible to individuals, those not conducive for a specific task, those not accommodative to one's anthropometry cause injuries, wounds and accidents not thought of. Use of furniture which does not support user's back (especially lower), thigh, arms and knees comfortably and make them adopt distorted postures are another group of vector causing musculo-skeletal disorders and permanent repair of the spinal column.

Aging: factors inherent to age like presbycusis, presbyopia, general debility, bone and joint problems, osteoporosis, anaemia etc., can complement other disabilities.

Women Related: Employed mostly in unorganised sector as unskilled labour, get low wages, which are not on par with men. Problems faced are dual work syndrome, menstrual disorders, gynaec problems, abortions, sexual harassment (www.amrc.org.hk/alu/Alu39/013901.html) and a host of problems linked to work environment plus the discomforts endured by their co-workers belonging to the opposite sex in the same working milieu.

Children: all problems affecting adults attack them in a much more pronounced manner. Loss of tenderness, youthfulness and self-esteem are additional ones.

As far as women and children are concerned, a higher proportion is engaged only in unskilled, field activities, with low pay and deplorable working conditions. They are not covered under any social security schemes or are assured job security. Research studies conducted with women workers as samples in cashew industries, farm activities, mine/quarry labour and tea plantations have proved that they are not in a position to claim any recognition in these matters (Sathyadas, A. *et al.*- 1995; War. I. *et al.* – 1997; Sreemani, S. *et al.* – 1998 and Vijayarani, P. *et al.* – 2002.). As many of the household activities like mopping, sweeping and washing, are strenuous and fatiguing for Indian women, especially those who maintain a poor nutritional status, engaging in manual labour further deteriorates their health (Visalakshi Rajeswari, S. *et al.* –1997). For these unfortunate groups (who enjoy a poor reproductive health too) none of the clauses stated in the Fundamental Rights, or in the Directive Principles are found to be obligatory. In many instances, children are found employed in their tender age, well below 14 years, and some were bonded labourers too.

According to the Directives relating to economic policies of the Directive Principles of State Policy, clause.4 assures equal pay for equal work, while clause.5 ensures to protect health and strength of workers (both men and women) and affirm that the tender age of children are not abused and citizens are not forced by economic necessity to enter avocations unsuited to their age and strength. Similarly, clause (9) delineates the suitable provisions made for just and humane conditions of work, for maternity relief, secure work, a living wage and conditions of work ensuring a decent standard of life. These have been framed with all good intentions. Lamentably, these are not enforceable by any court, though now and again people keep questioning about its enforcement as a law (Mahesh, A. - 2001). To correct anomalies, the employers and workers should come to a compromise to settle working environment related issues to the benefit of both the groups. But who will bell the cat? Situations where it cannot be obtained by Gandhian measures, their rights have to be demanded. This can materialise only when our workers can gain literacy, training on occupational health and safety and knowledge of Fundamental Rights (Appendix -1).

Workers' compensation is yet another neglected sector, notwithstanding the two main laws, namely, Workman's Compensation Act and the Employees State Insurance, as, the procedure involved for redress is quite cumbersome to ordinary laymen (Pandita, S. - 2001).

The other aspect that has created many ripples in recent years is the concept of self-care. Health is on one hand a highly personal responsibility. From the person's side, health has to be earned and maintained by the self (Levin, L. S. et al. – 1983). So, man has to learn lessons on self care and practice it too. Self-care is defined as those health generating activities that are undertaken by the person's themselves like promoting their own health, preventing their own diseases, limiting their own illness and restoring their own health. They dictate observance of simple rules of behaviour relating to diet, sleep, work, attention to personal hygiene and sanitation, inculcation of healthful habits (use of safe drinking water, avoidance of outside food, renouncing addiction to smoking, drugs, tobacco, alcohol etc) and hygienic, nutritious lifestyle.

From the standpoint of the employers and management, five factors for consideration in managing health and safety in the premises are, complying with health and safety rules, avoiding the costs of illness, accidents/incidents at work, improving their reputation through health and safety practices, correlating these practices to insurance costs and planning ahead to get these measures met (www.businesslink.gov.uk/bdotg/action). For exemplary performance, Vishwakarma Rashtriya Puraskar and National Safety Awards are also being awarded in India (http://labour.nic.in/annrep).

It is evident that occupational health is a joint objective of both the employment-givers and employment-seekers alike. Individuals have to accept greater responsibility for sustained health. Their active interest and participation in solving their own health problems are a clear manifestation of social awareness and self-reliance. Creating public understanding of these health and safety issues and human rights in the working environment parlance can help immensely in reducing incidents and also promote self motivation to move the correct pawn to lay hands on the Rights, justified to them.

Observing the World Day for Safety and Health at Work (28 April of each year) doesn't alone help reach any targets, (www.ilo.org/safework), but realistic and a spiritual adoption of the preventive and safety culture will bear fruits. In the long run this will promise a very strong, healthy, worker populace across the globe. This may also dictate developing a fresh genre of doctors and physicians well versed in occupational medicine, enforcing ratification of the ILO conventions by all countries, and interlacing them into the web and fabric of occupational standards set as obligatory for individual sectors.

Thus, Ergonomics, the science that deals with man and his work environment, is now a well-recognised discipline and constitutes an integral part of any advanced occupational health service. What was not known was the concept by this name, Ergonomics. It lays emphasis upon the people, the conditions in which they live and work, their hopes and fears, attitudes towards their job, their fellow workers and employers. The major hurdles looming in the current scenario pertain to changing job patterns and working relationships, greater out-sourcing, (bare) minimum interrelationships, homework, overwork, inhumane deadlines, out of sight boss (a total stranger), increasing number of employees working away from their establishment, sleepless, restless slogging jobs, toiling against diurnal rhythm, stress and surmounting tension, and constant use of computers, that too in awkward postures. It is high time we start reacting to such harsh job related verbal jargons like, zero hour deadlines, sweatshops, work-free weekends, flexi-work, the corporate India culture...When, then, will we adopt the 'work-life balance' logic and have the intelligence to realise that a relaxed and happy workforce could and would be more productive. Let the working community internalise and induct this logic for the betterment of the self-at least now.

It is but ethical on the part of the employer to make all possible efforts to eliminate such hurdles and provide a labour friendly environment. Situations where it is denied or is not satisfied the employees' strength and duty vests in demanding ergonomically designed work environments as a basic right to health.

"The mere fact of knowing what hurts you

Has an inherent curative value"

–Hans Selye

REFERENCES

1. Bhangoo, K. S., (1995) – *'Dynamics of Industrial Relations'*, Deep and Deep Publications, New Delhi, pp.48-71.
2. Clark, D. W and MacMahon, B. (1981) – *'Preventive and Community Medicine'*, Little Brown and Company, Boston, p. 22.
3. mFrancis, G. J and Milbourn, G. J. R. (1988) – *'Human Behaviour in the Work Environment, a Managament Perspective'*, McGraw-hill, USA, pp. 24, 25.
4. Heneman, H. G. et al. (1993) – *'Persona/Human Resource Management'*, Universal Book Stall, New Delhi, p. 13.
5. Last, J. M., (1983) – *'A Dictionary of Epidemiology'*, Oxford University Press, p. 9.
6. Monappa,A and Mirza, S. S. (1996) – *'Personnel Management'*, Tata McGraw Hill, New Delhi, pp. 373, 374.
7. Nag, A., (1993) – *'The Management Refresher'*, Vikas Publishing house, New Delhi, p. 19.
8. Nagpal, R and Sell, H. (1985) – *'Subjective Wellbeing'*. Reg. Health Papers, No. 7, SEARO, WHO, New Delhi.
9. Park, K., (1995, 1997 and 2002) – *'Preventive and Social Medicine'*, Banarasidas Bhanot, Jabalpur, pp. 5, 6-18, 23, 431-443.
10. Prasad,L and Bannerjee, A. M. (1990) – *'Management of Human Resources'*, Sterling Publishers, pp. 158-164.
11. Robbins, S. P. (1994) – *'Organisational Behaviour'*, Prentice Hall, New Delhi, p. 720.

22

Environment Education for Sustainable Future

S. Prema & A. Venmathi

Introduction

In recent years there has been a growing concern in India regarding the steady deterioration in the country's environment. Unplanned development, rapid industrialization and unprecedented growth in population are recognized as being the main cause of environmental degradation. Over the last few decades, human activities have led to resource degradation, loss of biodiversity, land degradation, global climate changes and release of chemical, radioactive and other toxic wastes. While these activities have enabled a significant portion of the world to improve the condition of life, they are now showing their adverse effects on the quality of air, water and land, moving the ecological balance of the planet to a new equilibrium. Whether the new equilibrium is conducive to human activities or whether it will prove adverse to the coming generations is a very complex question. But present indications are that there is urgency by taking corrective measures at the global as well as regional levels to prevent environmental degradation. In such a scenario the importance and need for switching over to sustainable development holds the vision of a more equitable world.

Need For Sustainable Development

Sustainable development aims at improving the living standards and the quality of people's lives, both now and for the future generations. All countries strive to ensure that citizens both in urban and rural areas have clean air to breathe, safe drinking water, and adequate supplies of clean renewable energy. Agriculture and industry are the important sectors in which natural resources – land, soil, forests, rivers, oceans and mineral deposits upon which they rely – have to be used efficiently and effectively. Environmental problems are linked to economic issues like poverty. They are also liked to social issues like population growth. Population growth puts pressure on natural resources as well as on the capacity to provide amenities like housing, health care, education, safe drinking water and sanitation.

The concept of Sustainable development had its origins in the world Conservation Strategy (WCS) Report, published in 1980. It says, "Conservation is the management of human use of the biosphere so that it may yield the greatest sustainable benefits to present generations, while maintaining its potential to meet the needs and aspirations of future generations." Sustainable development was formally defined for the first time in the Brundtland Report, published in 1987. It said, "Sustainable development is development that meets the needs of the present without compromising the ability of future generations to meet their own needs."

If Sustainable development is to give the priority that it deserves, the following measures should be adopted to sensitize or educate the decision-makers.

- Environmental education cannot be confined to any one group in our society. It is responsibility for everyone – government, industry, the media, educational institutions, community groups – as well as individuals.
- Effective environmental education must encourage the pursuit of environmental goals in a way that acknowledges other powerful and legitimate social and economic goals – it should not be taught in a vacuum, or simply equip people to pursue an agenda on the margins of society.

- Set up training programmes for school and university graduates to help them achieve sustainable livelihoods.
- Encourage all sectors of the society, including industry, universities, governments, non-governmental organizations and community organizations to train people in environmental management.

The sustainable development of the Indian future should be:

- The stratospheric ozone layer will be preserved intact and the changes in climate caused by people will be small enough to allow for natural adjustment.
- Transboundary water and air pollution will be on such a small scale that every country will independently be able to determine the state of its own environment.
- Levels of air pollution and noise will not impair people's health or well – being, and the threats to our cultural heritage will have been eliminated.
- Lakes and seas will support viable, balanced populations of naturally occurring species, and their value for fishing, recreation or water supplies will not be impaired by pollution.
- The productivity of agricultural and forest soils will be sustainable on a long-term basis. Pollution will not be permitted to disturb natural biological soil processes or restrict the use of groundwater.
- Renewable resources will be used within the limits of ecosystem productivity, non-renewable resources sparingly and responsibly.
- The potential of biotechnology will be harnessed for the benefit of environmental protection and its many applications in other areas will be scrutinized and controlled so that harm to the environment is avoided.
- The flow of goods will be characterized by producer liability "from cradle to grave", and economic growth will be used for consumption that spares natural resources and the environment.

Conclusion

The sustainable development is one in which the natural environment, economic development and social life are seen as mutually dependent – and the interaction between them contributes to the sustainability and enhancement of the quality of people's lives of the natural environment. It should develop the knowledge skills, perspectives and values which will empower people at all ages to assume responsibility for creating and enjoying a sustainable future for both developed and developing countries.

REFERENCES

1. Chris Park (1997): The Environment, Principles and Application London and New York.
2. Shalini Raj (2000): Teaching Environment Education Published by IVY New Delhi.
3. Krishnamacharyulu.V(2006): Environmental Education, Neelkamal Publications New Delhi.
4. Purushotham Reddy & Narasimha Reddy (2001): Environmental Education, Neelkamal Publications Pvt. Ltd. Hyderabad.

23

Genetic Privacy and Human Rights

An Analytical Study

Dinkar V.R

Introduction

The discovery of Deoxyribonucleic Acid (DNA) revolutionized not only the scientific discipline, but also the legal setting. More and more scientific inventions are being made establishing extensive scope for application of DNA and achievements in forensic examination and their related studies. The Human Genome Project is one such advanced potential application of DNA, by which its mystery is resolved for human benefit. In fact, DNA contains vital information relating to an individual, which he/she doesn't know. No doubt, it is clear that inherent rights of human beings lie ingrained in genome. Therefore, each and every use of genomic information has enormous potential for controversy.[1] Nowadays the DNA information is being widely used for scientific research, law enforcement purposes and medical and diagnostic purposes. Such use unleashes a list of problems linked to human rights, ethical and legal issues based on confidentiality and privacy of genomic information.

The ultimate aim of Human Genome Project is to establish complete human genetic code and thereby enlarging scope of research on unresolved problems in medicine and to develop new techniques for genetic analysis.[2] The project was started in 1990 and completed recently. Moreover, in some countries discussions are going on regarding the implementation of universal DNA database i.e. inclusion of the whole population in the DNA database system. These and other issues would directly intrude into the human rights like right to privacy.

The paper explores two things viz.: (1) whether the dissemination of information on one's DNA would result in violation of human rights; (2) International and India's safeguard mechanism on genetic privacy.

DNA and its Analysis

DNA the acronym of Deoxyribonucleic acid is a genetic material, which directs the entire bodily functions of living beings. George Annas said DNA as "an individual's probabilistic future diary."[3] The mystery about DNA was exposed to the world by the discovery of the structure of DNA in 1953 by James Watson and Francis Crick. DNA profiling then began its voyage into the armoury of genetic research, forensic science, medicine etc. DNA is a long filament, which is compressed inside the chromosome. Human cell contains 23 pairs of chromosome. In this set 44 are autosomes and two are sex chromosomes. There are two 'X' chromosomes in females and one 'X' and one 'Y' chromosome in females. The chemical nature of DNA is that it is a polymer consisting of monomeric units called nucleotides. The nucleotide consists of three monomeric units called nitrogen base, pentose sugar and phosphate group. The nitrogen base may be either purine or pyrimidine. The purines are adenine and guanine and pyrimidines are cytosine and thymine. DNA is a double stranded molecule, the backbone of which consists of a regular alteration of sugar and phosphate groups. The two strands are both coiled around a common fibre axis. Both strands are connected by a weaker hydrogen bond. DNA is situated in the nucleus, mitochondria and plastids of a cell. Almost 99% of DNA in a human being is similar. It is the remaining one percent that distinguishes persons (the polymorphism) and allows scope to profile.

There are different methods to develop a DNA profile. The most frequently used and the old method was the Restriction Fragment Length Polymorphism (RFLP) analysis, which was replaced by another sophisticated technique known as Polymorphic Chain Reaction[4] (PCR) amplification technique.

The most advanced method of DNA analysis is mitochondrial DNA profiling. It can be performed successfully though there is no enough nuclear DNA as well as on severely degraded cells. The number of copies of mtDNA is higher than nDNA; hence, in forensic cases it can be more successfully typed than nDNA, even in samples with low DNA load.[5] The main problem in mtDNA fingerprinting is that it cannot be used for paternity testing because mtDNA is inherited only from mother.[6] The other important feature of mtDNA is that it does not undergo recombination;[7] so it is useful as a reference sample of maternal relatives.[8] MtDNA is also more likely to survive in a dead cell than nDNA.[9] Moreover, the mutation rate in an mtDNA is very higher than nDNA; hence, the mtDNA supplies more individuality to a person than nDNA[10].

How much Information About an Individual can be Discovered from one's DNA?

The advocates who are arguing in favour of DNA database justify it by saying that the DNA used for analysis is only junk DNA, which carries no genetic information. However, it is not clear how far this statement is correct because recently scientists at Centre for Cellular and Molecular Biology (CCMB), Hyderabad, discovered that junk DNA in human Y-chromosome control the function of a gene that is not limited to sex located in another chromosome. "The study shows unequivocal evidence, for the first time, that 40 mega base repeat block of the Y-chromosome, which was earlier perceived as junk DNA, is transcribed into RNA and controls the expression of a protein by a mechanism described as trans-splicing"[11] Therefore, it is high time to check the ethical aspects of DNA analysis on the basis of privacy rights. Here one prominent question posed against the scientific community is that how much of privacy would be affected by DNA analysis, presuming that the DNA analysis carries genetic information. It is also possible that in future more functions of junk portions of DNA may be discovered and at that time, it is expected that the scientists would conduct more analysis on the junk portions of DNA already collected.

The private genetic information derived from DNA must be protected because it is more sensitive than any other information about a person. For e.g., information that a person's portion of DNA that makes it possible that the individual may suffer Alzheimer's disease later in life is private information and it would be lethal to his career development, if such type of information comes to the knowledge of general public. The more serious one is the collecting genetic secrets from the family history of the person affected by some heredity-supplied disease. In this case not only the affected person but also his other family members are affected by the genetic research.

Owing to these advancements, it is likely that he/she may be discriminated in future for any employment. Potential employers may use screening to select the most fit persons in order to increase productivity or insurance companies may begin to require personal genetic data for consideration when fixing premiums and granting coverage,[12] if his or her DNA analysis results are not provided confidentially. Adoption agencies and adopting parents may use the results of genetic tests to determine the quality of a child. Thus extensive institutionalised screening practices may create a genetic underclass and cause high discrimination from friends, family members, and society as a whole.

Similarly the creation of universal DNA databases i.e. including all persons in DNA database system would generate fear in the mind of persons that at any time they may be wrongly inculpated due to any error in conducting DNA analysis.

The other prominent area where fright may arise is genetic research.

Human Rights Facets of Personal Genetic Information

The fight against genetic privacy violations is an issue of contemporary human rights jurisprudence. It is doubtful, how many persons are aware of their genetic privacy and human right violations. Respect for human dignity and belief in justice are rooted deep in the intellectual mores of the world. The human rights became fundamental law of the world only after it was codified by United Nations. The International human right laws were evolved from various international instruments, which include: (1) Universal Declaration of Human Rights (UDHR),[13] (2) International Covenant on Civil and Political Rights (ICCPR)[14] and its Optional Protocol,[15] and (3) International Covenant on Economic, Social and Political Rights (ICESCR).[16] International Scholars named these Covenants as International Bill of Human Rights (IBHR).

Article 12 of UDHR prohibits arbitrary interference with an individual's privacy, family or home. Article states as follows: "No one shall be subjected to arbitrary interference with his privacy, family home or correspondence, or to attacks to his honour and reputation. Everyone has the right to the protection of the law against such interference or attacks." Same wording is also there in Article 17 of ICCPR. Article 7 of ICCPR mandates that, "no one shall be subjected without his free consent to medical or scientific experimentation." Moreover, various other United Nations declarations have documented possible hazards that may affect the human rights by novel scientific advancements.[17]

Universal Declaration on the Human Genome and Human Rights

The aforementioned articles only generally protect the privacy of the person; however, this is not enough to guard a person's genetic privacy. Since more and more scientific inventions on DNA and its related disciplines compelled human rights scholars to draft a special Bill for protecting genetic privacy. In view of that in its 27th Session, held on 15th October 1993, the General Conference of UNESCO invited the Director-General to prepare an international instrument for protection of the human genome. The Legal Commission specially authorized for that drafted the Bill, Universal Declaration on the Human Genome and Human Rights and it came out on 25th July 1997. The 29th Session of the General Conference adopted unanimously the declaration on 11th November 1997. The subsequent year, the United Nations General Assembly authorized the Declaration. Recognizing the prospects of the research on human genome for health, the General Conference of UNESCO emphasize that "such research should fully respect human dignity, freedom and human rights, as well as the prohibition of all forms of discrimination based on genetic characteristics."

The UNESCO declaration gave sacredness to human genome by emphasizing it as the "heritage of humanity."[18] The declaration distinguished human dignity from genetic characteristics of an individual and mandates not to reduce individuals to their genetic characteristics.[19] Article 5 to 9 of the Universal Declaration on the Human Genome and Human Rights guarantees certain rights to the persons disturbed with genomic research, treatment or diagnosis. The rights enumerated in these articles are:

1. Research, treatment or diagnosis affecting an individual's genome shall be undertaken only after rigorous and prior assessment of the potential risks and benefits pertaining thereto and in accordance with any other requirement of national law.[20]
2. The prior free and informed consent of the person concerned shall be obtained before his/her genome is used for the said purposes. If the person concerned is not in a position to give proper consent, it shall be obtained in the manner prescribed by law.[21]
3. In the case of research, protocols shall, in addition, be submitted for prior review in accordance with relevant national and international research standards or guidelines.[22] If according to the law a person does not have the capacity to consent, research affecting his or her genome may only be carried out for his or her direct health benefit. If the research is intended to contribute to the health benefit of other persons in the same age category or with the same genetic condition, subject to the conditions prescribed by law, and provided such research is compatible with the protection of the individual's human rights.[23]

4. No one shall be subjected to discrimination based on genetic characteristics that is intended to infringe or has the effect of infringing human rights, fundamental freedoms and human dignity.[24]

5. Genetic data associated with an identifiable person and stored or processed for the purposes of research or any other purpose must be held confidential in the conditions set by law.[25]

6. Every individual shall have the right, according to international and national law, to just reparation for any damage sustained as a direct and determining result of an intervention affecting his or her genome.[26]

7. In order to protect human rights and fundamental freedoms, limitations to the principles of consent and confidentiality may only be prescribed by law, for compelling reasons within the bounds of public international law and the international law of human rights.[27]

Article 10 gives emphasis to human rights than to research or research applications of human genome. Article 16 gives direction to the States for the establishment of independent, multidisciplinary and pluralist ethics committees to assess the ethical, legal and social issues raised by research on the human genome and its applications. The General Conference of UNESCO endorsed its implementation in 1999. It provides for an evaluation of both the results obtained through the guidelines and of the impact of the Declaration worldwide. The Guidelines were intended for:

1. UNESCO (Headquarters and field offices);
2. The International Bioethics Committee (IBC);
3. The Intergovernmental Bioethics Committee (IGBC);
4. Bodies and specialized institutions of the United Nations system;
5. Competent governmental and nongovernmental organizations at the international, regional and national levels;

6. Public and private decision-makers, especially in science policy;
7. Lawmakers;
8. Ethics committees and similar bodies;
9. Scientists and research workers;
10. Individuals, families and populations with genetic mutations that may lead to illnesses or disabilities.

The Declaration warrants a new outlook regarding genetic human rights violations. It guarantees genetic equality by prohibiting discrimination based on genetic traits. However, the provisions in the Declaration are not much effective to control processing, using and storing human genetic data.[28] Science is becoming more and more advanced and in this epoch there is no difficulty in collecting human bodily samples. A used teacup or cigarette is enough to get sufficient DNA for analysis. The genetic data is far and wide. Therefore it is necessary to have common ethical guidelines. The UNESCO Director-General Matsuura in his speech to the General Conference stressed the urgency in enacting an ethical guideline for controlling human genetic data. The task was handed over to its agency International Bioethics Committee (IBC), which submitted two reports viz. (1) Confidentiality and Genetic Data (June 2000) and Human Genetic Data: Preliminary Study by the IBC on its Collection, Treatment, Storage and Use (May 2002). In October 2003, UNESCO's General Conference adopted the International Declaration on Human Genetic Data, which sets out the ethical principles that governs the collection, processing, storage and use of these data, extracted from biological samples (blood, tissue, saliva, sperm, etc.).[29]

The Declaration recognized that human genetic data have a special status on account of its sensitive nature. The aims and scope of the Declaration are provided in Article 1. They are as follows:

(a) To ensure the respect of human dignity and protection of human rights and fundamental freedoms in the collection, processing, use and storage of human genetic data, human proteomic data and of the biological samples from which they are derived, referred to hereinafter as "biological samples", in keeping with the requirements of equality, justice and solidarity, while giving due consideration to freedom of thought and expression, including freedom of research; to set out the principles which should guide States in the formulation of their legislation and their policies on these issues; and to form the basis for guidelines of good practices in these areas for the institutions and individuals concerned.

(b) Any collection, processing, use and storage of human genetic data, human proteomic data and biological samples shall be consistent with the international law of human rights.

(c) The provisions of this Declaration apply to the collection, processing, use and storage of human genetic data, human proteomic data and biological samples, except in the investigation, detection and prosecution of criminal offences and in parentage testing that are subject to domestic law that is consistent with the international law of human rights.

Article 5 states that human genetic data may be collected, processed, used and stored only for diagnosis and health care, medical and scientific research, forensic medicine, civil, criminal and legal proceedings or for any other purpose consistent with the Universal Declaration on the Human Genome and Human Rights. Article 7 exclusively mandates that human genetic data should not be used for discriminating people so as to infringe human rights. Part B to E of the Declaration deals with the provisions regarding the collection, processing, use and storing of genetic data. According to article 8, prior free informed and express consent must be obtained for the collection of human genetic data. If the person is incapable to give consent, it must be obtained from his interested person. It is also possible to collect data without consent if there are compelling reasons by domestic law consistent with the international law of human rights. The collection of human genetic data, *in vivo* or post mortem for forensic, civil, criminal or other legal proceedings must be conducted in accordance with the domestic law consistent with the international law of human rights.[30] Articles 13 to 15 deal with processing. Article 14 mandates that state should protect the privacy and confidentiality of the genetic data and it should not be made accessible to third parties especially to employers, insurance companies, educational institutions and family except with consent of the person concerned or in accordance with domestic law consistent with the international law of human rights. Human genetic data should not be kept in a form which allows the data subject to be identified for any longer than is necessary for achieving the purposes for which they are collected or subsequently processed.[31] The persons or entities responsible for processing and interpreting genetic data should ensure their accuracy, reliability, quality and security and it should be done with rigour, caution, honesty and integrity in view of their ethical, legal and social implications.[32]

According to Article 16, the genetic data collected for one purpose should not be used for different purpose, contrary to the consent for which it was obtained unless the prior, free, informed and express consent of the person concerned is obtained or allowed by the domestic law for an important public interest reason which is consistent with the international law of human rights.

Article 22 mandates that human genetic data and bodily samples collected from a suspect in the course of criminal investigation, forensic purpose and civil proceedings should be destroyed unless otherwise provided for by domestic law consistent with the international law of human rights.

The genetic data is collected from human beings with authority of law and it may be used for diverse purposes. If it is used for private purpose without the consent of the owner, it may result in serious violations of the enjoyment of other prominent rights. No doubt the Declaration would serve as a framework and an encouragement for those States, which did not yet establish a legislative framework on genetic privacy.

Judicial Approach to Genetic Privacy

The trend in United States shows that the court would strike down the action of either public or private institutions violating person's genetic privacy. There are only few reported decisions, which give information with reference to the way in which court may determine privacy issue related to genetic information. One of the foremost decisions in this area is *Doe* v. *High-Tech Institute, Inc.*[33] In this case the cause of action for the plaintiff, a student in Cambridge's medical assistant training programme arose due to an unauthorized testing of blood sample and subsequent publication of the results of that test. The facts of the case reveal that the High-Tech Institute obtained consent from the plaintiff to test his blood for rubella, but without his consent the school performed a further test for detecting human immunodeficiency virus (HIV) and the test result was disclosed by the school to the Department of Health. Court observed that a person has a claim under the common law definition of invasion of privacy by intrusion upon seclusion as set forth under the *Restatement (Second) of Torts 652B* (1981).[34] Rejecting the argument of the defendant that a person's privacy interest ends once the blood was removed from the body and plaintiff had no reasonable expectation of privacy in his blood sample once it was drawn, court held, an additional or unauthorized test could be sufficient to state a claim for relief for intrusion upon seclusion.[35] Citing *Skinner v. Railway Labour Executives' Ass'n,*[36] court held personal information concerning a person's health might be obtained through one's blood, urine, and other bodily products, such products could not be extracted from a person or initially tested without either consent or proper authorization.[37]

In *Norman-Bloodsaw* v. *Lawrence Berkeley Laboratory,*[38] court reiterated the same stand and held that a person has a constitutional right of privacy in his or her genetic information and other sensitive personal information that restricts unauthorized testing of bodily fluids. In this case court thoroughly distinguished general medical examination from sensitive genetic examinations and held that giving one's consent "to a general medical examination does not abolish one's privacy right not to be tested for intimate, personal matters involving one's health - nor does consenting to giving blood or urine samples, or filling out a questionnaire."[39] The court agreed that genetic tests for sickle cell trait might reveal sensitive information about family history and implications for reproductive decision-making.[40]

The U.S. Senate enacted the *Genetic Nondiscrimination Act*, 2003. The Act prohibits discrimination and promotion in employment and health insurers on the basis of genetic information and family history.[41] Moreover in U.S. they have a Federal legislation, the Genetic Privacy Act that controls the collection, analysis, disclosure of genétic information and research on genetics.

In India, the Constitution does not guarantee the right to privacy as a fundamental right; however, the Supreme Court read it into Article 21 of the Constitution. In *Govind* v. *State of M.P.*,[42] court observed that both right to personal liberty and right to move freely and speech establishes the right to privacy. In *R. Rajagopal* v. *State of Tamil Nadu*,[43] Supreme Court clarified the extent of the right by saying that the right was available to the citizen to safeguard his privacy, his family marriage, procreation, motherhood, child bearing and education and no one could publish anything regarding the matters abovementioned. Court postulated that the right to privacy included the right to be let alone.

India is a signatory to the International Covenant on Civil and Political Rights, 1966. Therefore, it is the duty of the Indian judiciary to implant human rights enshrined by the International Covenants into the valuable rights provided in the Constitution. Thus in *Peoples Union for Civil Liberties* v. *Union of India*[44], court interpreted Article 21 in conformity with Article 17 of the International Covenant on Civil and Political Rights, 1966 and Article 12 of the Declaration of Human Rights, 1948.

In India, though right to privacy is a constitutional right, there is no legislation on privacy. At the same time there is legislation on right to information. The right to information is also a constitutional right, which is embodied under Article 19 (1) (a) i.e., freedom of speech and expression. The object of right to information is to make governmental functions more transparent. The Freedom of Information Act, 2002 was passed with the said object.[45] The Act was intended to penetrate the mask of governmental confidentiality and to open agency action to the light of public scrutiny. Its object is to encourage the accountability of public officials through citizen monitoring and exchanges of information between agencies and citizens as well as between different agencies. Disclosure, not secrecy, is the dominant objective of the Act. In *Essar Oil Ltd.* v. *H.U. Samiti,*[46] court held that the citizens had a right to know the decision of the government, which affect the health, life and livelihood. Thus due to the existence of a full-fledged Statute governing freedom of information, there is a possibility of conflict between right to information and right to privacy. Since the strategy of government is to allow access to the official records, the interest in protecting certain sensitive matters should be balanced against the freedom to attain information freely. The Right to Information Act, 2005 gives power to the authorities to withhold certain information. Section 8(1) (a) to (j) of the Act provides certain matters in which the authorities are not obliged to give information. In these exceptions, exception (e) and (j) specifically deals with information affecting the individual privacy.[47]

The authorisation given by the Act to the authorities regarding nondisclosure of information is only discretionary and not mandatory, hence the outcome is that the government may disclose any information even though it is barred from disclosure.

How far the Provisions in Right to Information Act Affect Genetic Privacy of a Person

The records maintained by a body owned, controlled or substantially financed non-Government organization; substantially financed□directly or indirectly by the appropriate Government are matters to disclosure under the Act. Once DNA typing had been conducted, the DNA profile becomes the official record of the governmental agency and it will be converted as data material detained in any electronic form, which is accessible to the general public. From the language of section 8 it is clear that the authority may withhold the information in the DNA profile, if it would make unwarranted invasion of the privacy of an individual or if it would come under the fiduciary relationship between the affected person and the authority. Notwithstanding, the authority may disclose the information if it satisfies that the larger public interest justifies the disclosure of such information.

The Act is silent regarding the situations in which the invasion would amount to an unwarranted one. Here it is important to know whether the disclosure of information contained in ones DNA would amount to an unwarranted invasion. No doubt, the information can be used if it satisfies the larger public interest. Thus in order to justify disclosure of information provided in exceptions, a strong public interest should outweigh the private interests. However, it is doubtful whether the safeguards guaranteed by the Act are adequate to protect the sensitive information contained in one's DNA. In the Act there are no terms like 'medical information' or 'genetic information' and regarding its disclosure.

The judicial approach in India also seems to be in favour of disclosing medical information, if it would facilitate in advancing public morality or public interest. In almost all cases in which the conflict arose between the right to privacy and right to lead a healthy life, court showed compassion towards right to lead a healthy life. In *Mr. 'X' v. Hospital 'Z,'*[48] the Supreme Court observed:

> Where there is a clash of two Fundamental Rights, as in the instant case, namely, the appellant's right to privacy as part of right to life and Ms. 'Y' right to lead a healthy life which is her Fundamental Right under Article 21, the right which would advance the public morality or public interest, would alone be enforced through' the process of Court, for the reason that moral considerations cannot be kept at bay and the Judges are not expected to sit as mute structures of clay, in the Hall, known as Court Room, but have to be sensitive, in the sense that they must keep their fingers firmly upon the pulse of the accepted morality of the day.

Approach of the Indian Judiciary Regarding DNA Testing and Right to Privacy

Through various decisions, judiciary has made a consensus regarding DNA testing and right to privacy. The court on DNA analysis gave divergent views. In criminal adjudication DNA evidence can be used against the accused if it would facilitate the prosecution in establishing guilt against the accused. But in civil cases court cannot conduct a roving inquiry with the help of DNA evidence and the parties in a suit cannot compel the opposite side to give his/her bodily samples for DNA analysis. However, courts took a clear stand by saying that cases in which the respondent refuses to submit himself to medical examination, the court would be entitled to draw an adverse inference against him.

Mr. 'X' v. Mr. 'Z'[49]: in this case the respondent filed a petition directing All India Institute of Medical Science to prepare a slide containing blood samples of the petitioner and the respondent for a DNA test to ascertain whether respondent was the father of the removed foetus of the petitioner. The application was opposed by the petitioner saying that it would infringe her right to privacy guaranteed by Article 21 of the Constitution. The brief facts of the case were that the wife had filed a divorce petition alleging cruelty and adultery against her husband. The husband also raised a similar contention that wife had adulterous affairs with a person. The husband contended that he came to know that the pregnancy of his wife was a tubular pregnancy and he was not the father of the child. Unfortunately the pregnancy was terminated and husband applied to prove the paternity of the foetus. In this case the prominent question came up for consideration was whether the petitioner could resist the request of the respondent from taking slides and conducting DNA tests for establishing the paternity of the foetus. The petitioner contended that since the foetus is a part of her body and without her consent DNA test couldn't be conducted and for that she couldn't be compelled. After referring various decisions court came to the conclusion that in the present case foetus was not part of the body of the petitioner, since it was discharged from her body. Court was of the view that the bond between the foetus and the mother would come to an end when it was discharged and it couldn't be treated as a part of the mother, but as a unique organism.[50] Therefore, court came to the conclusion that there was no need of any consent or compulsion of the petitioner for conducting any test on foetus. Regarding right to privacy court observed that it was not an absolute right and once the subject of privacy became a matter of public record, the privacy right no longer subsists.[51] Court held that "when the right to privacy has become a part of public document, in that event a person concerned indeed cannot insist that any such test would infringe his/her right of privacy."[52]

It is submitted that the reasoning of the decision is disquieting. It is well settled that if a person who is not capable to give consent for genetic testing, his biological relative must give it. In the case of removed foetus, though it is considered as a unique organism, consent should be obtained from its mother because it is genetic part of the mother. Each and every genetic test conducted on it would affect the genetic privacy of its mother and father. Moreover, a mere public document does not itself create any right for the public to have access to the document unless law permits it. In genetic data's genetic secrets of a person are there and it is dischargeable only if there is strong public interest outweighing the interest of the person affected. Court ought to have distinguished mere public documents from highly sensitive public records like genetic data. Foetus is a unique combination of genetic traits of the parents and therefore, any tests or research on it should be conducted only after obtaining informed and express consent of the parents.

It is high time to distinguish mere medical information from genetic information. Medical information does not penetrate deep into the privacy of an individual; at the same time, genetic information exposes the biological personality of a person. Moreover, other distinguishing feature of genetic test is that it discloses not only the information of the person concerned but also information about his biological relatives. An important thing to be reckoned is that genetic information provides only the probability that there is possibility in future for a hereditary transmitted disease. However, this prophecy cannot be equated with medical information because the concerned person may not be affected with the disease predicted.

Bioethical Policies in India for Safeguarding Genetic Privacy

In 1999, a national bioethics committee was constituted to harmonise the guidelines made by the Universal Declaration on the Human Genome and Human Rights. The committee had drafted various policies regarding human genome. The object of the policies are to enhance genetic research for the benefit of the human being, at the same time to control it by implementing national ethical policies for the human genome, genetic research and services. According to the policy of consent, before conducting genetic research or services consent of the participant shall be obtained and it must be documented. The consent is valid only for primary purpose for which the samples are collected unless specific consent has been obtained for secondary purposes. The consent shall be obtained from close biological relatives in the case of persons who are incapable to give consent due to physical or mental problems. In view of the policy of genetic privacy and discrimination the individual subjected to genetic testing shall not be discriminated on the basis of genetic characteristics or information.

In sum, this part presents a complicated interdisciplinary issue in a very simple manner. The international development on the topic prompts the writer to give certain suggestions for the law reform in India. At the outset, it is high time to insert a clause against genetic discrimination under Article 15 and 16 of the Indian Constitution in order to prevent genetic discrimination.

Since Article 15 of the constitution is applicable only in the case of public employment; it is necessary to enact a special law in tune with U.S. Genetic Nondiscrimination Act, 2003, to prevent genetic discrimination on genetic grounds in employment both in public sector and private sector.

The Parliament may consider the need for enacting a Genetic Privacy Act.

DNA Fingerprinting Database for Identifying Criminals and Privacy Issues

This part discusses the scope of developing a DNA database system similar to the fingerprint database system for the law enforcement authorities. It also discuses the constitutionality and privacy of the citizens while implementing such database system.

DNA Database System in United States

Initially the database system was formed as an effective tool for crime solving. It was in United States, the world's first DNA information system introduced. The FBI under the United States Department of Justice (DOJ) created this in 1989. FBI started this project as a combined DNA index system (CODIS). This system was created in accordance with the provisions in the *DNA Identification Act*, 1994. The CODIS is a software-based system, which contains three indices: Forensic Index; Convicted Offender Index; and Population File Index. Forensic Index consists of DNA profiles from crime scenes.[53] The Convicted Offender Index consists of DNA profiles of convicted persons for felony sex offences and other violent crimes and Population Index is for statistical purpose. A network in a hierarchical order, local, state and national level, connects all these indices. In fact, the bio-data and DNA profile of a person will enter into the system through the crime laboratory. In 1998, the FBI created another system known as the National DNA index System (NDIS). This is an electronic system in which the Federal, State and local law enforcement agencies can contribute DNA samples and thereby activate the DNA database system in finding culprits.[54] In U.S., Virginia was the first State, which implemented a criminal DNA database.[55] Following this all fifty States formed their own DNA database system.[56]

Canadian DNA Database System

In Canada, the DNA databank system was established by the enactment of the *DNA Identification Act*. The databank consists of two indices viz. (1) crime scene index and (2) convicted offenders index. The crime scene index is composed of with DNA profiles collected at the time of investigation and convicted offenders index consists of data's collected from the offenders convicted for the designated offences under section 487.04 of the *Criminal Code*. Every DNA sampling should be conducted with the warrant of the court. The authorized person may take bodily substances by plucking hairs, taking of buccal swabs and taking small quantities of blood without consent of the suspect and he may also use reasonable force for that.[57]

DNA Database System in England

In 1995, the world's first DNA database of persons convicted of an offence punishable by imprisonment was established in UK.[58] By March 1998, the database contained the DNA profiles of more than 2,55000 suspects and convicted persons and 30,000 profiles developed from materials found at crime scenes.[59] It was in 1995, the British government for the first time formed a criminal DNA database system. In 1998 three other European countries, Austria, Germany and Netherlands introduced their DNA databases.[60]

DNA Database System in Australia

In Australia, at Federal level a national DNA database system known as the National Criminal Investigation DNA Database (NCIDD) has been established. The Australian DNA database system was formed according to the provisions in the *Crimes Amendment (Forensic Procedures) Act* 1998. It is operated by the Federal government agency known as Crim Trac.[61] The database contains DNA profiles from each of the participating States and Territories. Profiles will be shared between jurisdictions. The DNA profiles in New South Wales databases will be available on the national database system. Indexes in New South Wales include a missing persons index; offenders index; suspects index; unknown deceased persons index; volunteers (limited purposes) index; and a volunteers (unlimited purposes) index. Australian database system is under the strict control of *Crimes (Forensic Procedures) Act* 2000.[62]

The unresolved issue in connection with this topic is regarding the determination of the list of persons who may be included in the DNA database system. The type of person to be included in the DNA database differs from jurisdiction to jurisdiction, which includes sex offenders, persons convicted of felony offences, all persons convicted, persons arrested for felony offences, all persons arrested, and total population. In UK by March 2003 it was announced that the UK police would have the right to retain indefinitely the DNA profiles from all people from whom DNA is collected, whether the person was charged with a crime or not.[63] Robert William and Rony Dunkan in their scientific commentary published in *Nature* have opined that it was better to take DNA profile of all individuals at birth.[64] According to them this tendency would not only act as a deterrent from crime for all members of the community, but would make the task of catching criminals easier for police.[65]

Privacy Issues Arising from Forensic DNA Data Banks

The use of DNA database to identify suspects in effect creates some personal liberty issues in the mind of persons arguing for human rights.[66] They argued that DNA profile contains data of person's genetic characteristics and if it were disclosed to some others, his privacy would be infringed.

In almost all countries in which DNA databases were introduced, the issue of privacy arose as a major concern. The issue gained strength by the policy of some Countries like Britain, United States and Canada to collect DNA samples from all persons who are arrested including ordinary citizens who are not involved in any crime. The persons arguing for privacy established it on two aspects: (1) sampling privacy and (2) informational privacy. As far as the issue is concerned with the second one is significant. However, in U.S. challengers of universal DNA databases argues that it would violate the Fourth Amendment protection against unwarranted and unreasonable searches.[67] On the other hand, the people who appreciate universal DNA database say that it would build up the conviction rates, prevention of crime and cutback erroneous convictions.

The informational privacy argument is based on the fact that every person has his own information to be kept undisturbed by others. The argument favouring informational privacy would lie only if it outweighs the societal interest of protection against crime. It is well accepted by courts that the person who is arrested by police for any crime committed by him would lose his privacy right to some extent. But the information stored in DNA and the chance that it may come to someone's knowledge must be thoroughly evaluated, because the degree of information stored in ones DNA is quite higher than the information stored in ones fingerprint or footprint. Here also one should differentiate the information stored in ones DNA with information stored in ones DNA profile. It is clear from the observation made by some scientists that there is no room for privacy violation in the case of stored DNA profile because the forensic scientists use only 'non-coded' or junk DNA for identification purpose. In a non-coded region of DNA, genes are not available; therefore, storing of DNA database would not raise any issue against genetic privacy.[68] However, the general trend is that usually almost all DNA databanks store the original samples; therefore, authorities should take extreme care in disposing of forensic samples after conducting DNA analysis. The justification for keeping body samples is to avoid further body sampling from the same person for retesting.

Legalising DNA Databases Through Legislation

In United States, the DNA database system had been legalised by the State through suitable legislations. All fifty states and the District of Columbia have enacted laws requiring convicted criminals to present their DNA to the authorities so that it may be stored in databases. A statute was also enacted at the federal level for legalizing DNA databank. The key legislations in U.S. are *DNA Identification Act* of 1994, *DNA Analysis Backlog Elimination Act* of 2000, (DNA Act of 2000) and *Justice for All Act* of 2004/*Debbie Smith Act* of 2004. The *DNA Analysis Backlog Elimination Act*, 2000 was enacted to overcome some pitfalls in *DNA Identification Act*, 1994. The provision in the 1994 Act does not permit the authorities to collect DNA samples from federal offenders. On the other hand, the object of Justice for All Act is something negative. It primarily aims to protect the innocent than to convict the guilty and it also give prominence to improve fairness.[69] In England, *Criminal Justice and Public Order Act*, 1994 allows the authorities for sampling and storing of DNA from any individual who had been convicted, cautioned, or suspected of committing a recordable offence.[70] The *Criminal Investigations (Blood Samples) Act*, 1995 enables the Australian law enforcement authorities to collect and include the DNA samples in their database.

PRECEDENTIAL OVERVIEW REGARDING THE LEGITIMACY OF DNA DATABASE

Position in United States

In United States the DNA database faced the Constitutional challenges on diverging aspects. The most important is the Fourth Amendment challenge regarding the search and seizure for body samples and DNA database system. However, courts have upheld the legislations permitting law enforcement authorities to collect DNA samples for database.[71] The courts opined that the actual physical incursion was minimal and once a person was convicted for an offence, his privacy rights would be reduced.[72]

In United States the leading decision in connection with the issue is *Landry* v. *Attorney General*.[73] In this case the plaintiff challenged the Massachusetts DNA database statute as unconstitutional because it allows involuntary collection of blood samples from all persons convicted of thirty-three different types of offences. The Massachusetts Supreme Court held that though the statute allows the authorities search and seizure, it was not unreasonable. Court held that the prisoner's reasonable expectation of privacy would reduce in the interest of the State to form a reliable identification of the accused. Court gave more weight to State interest and upheld the statute.

Thus in U.S. all courts decided the issue in the line of *Landry* decision and upheld the database statutes enacted by the States.[74]

DNA Database and the Fourth Amendment

The Fourth Amendment[75] attack against DNA database was rejected by almost all courts on the basis of two approaches evolved by the Supreme Court: (1) *Balancing approach* and (2) *Special needs approach*.

Balancing Approach

Jones v. *Murray*[76] was one of the first cases in which court evaluated the constitutionality of a statute permitting the establishment of an offender DNA database. In this case the undertrial prisoners challenged extraction of blood samples by the State for creating DNA database for identifying criminals.[77] The prisoners argued that the statute permitting authorities to extract blood samples without any individualized suspicion that they had committed a crime would amount to an unreasonable search and hence violation of the Fourth Amendment.[78] The court though noted that there was a lessened expectation of privacy on a suspect, specifically held that the government's interest in detection and prevention of crime would outweigh the prisoner's lessened expectation of privacy.[79]

Thus court has evolved a balancing approach and balanced the interest of the Sate in detecting crimes with the individual's lessened expectation of privacy and reached an amicable solution to the issue. However, courts took a very different approach in the case of the privacy rights of the ordinary individuals and held they have a greater expectation of privacy and any intrusion into their privacy in the name of government interest would become unreasonable and it doesn't get the protection of the balancing approach. For e.g., in *Schmerber* v. *California*,[80] the mere prediction of the law enforcement authorities that the collection of forensic samples might become valuable evidence was held by the Supreme Court as unreasonable under the Fourth Amendment.

Nearly all courts in United States considered the database system positively; some courts decided the issue in a negative sense. For e.g., in *United States* v. *Kincade*[81] the Ninth Circuit Court reversing the district courts ruling, found that the compulsory collection of body materials under DNA Act would violate the right to privacy of an individual and held the Act unconstitutional.[82] In this case the appellant was released after completing imprisonment for ninety-seven months and at the time of release the Probation Office directed him to submit to a blood extraction for DNA analysis, which was refused by the appellant. The district court found that the refusal would amount to a violation of the terms of his supervised release.[83]

Special Needs Approach Doctrine

In United States, it is generally accepted by courts that search of a person's body can be conducted only if there is a warrant issued by the proper authority after considering the probable cause. However there are certain situations in which search could be conducted without observing this mandatory probable cause rule. Thus in *New Jersey* v. *T.L.O.*,[84] Supreme Court introduced a new doctrine known as the 'special needs.' According to the doctrine, if the State satisfies a special need than mere law enforcement, the intrusion into the body of an individual could be justified. If special need is satisfied by the State, there is no need of any warrant or probable cause for the intrusion. Thus in *State* v. *Olivas*,[85] applying the special needs doctrine, court upheld the statute authorizing the authorities to collect blood samples for creating DNA database. The State argued that the DNA database system, which contains the data of the released prisoners, would retract them from committing further offences. Accepting the argument, court held that the interest of the State in deterring released criminals with the help of DNA database system could be considered as "beyond normal law enforcement" and therefore, it would come under the doctrine of special need.[86] Regarding maximum extent of the expectation of privacy of a convicted person, Utter, J., observed:

> The final, and in my view, determinative consideration in conducting a minimally intrusive search balancing test is the privacy interests upon which the search in question intrudes. In these cases, [DNA databank legislation] the privacy interest is that of a convicted sex or violent offender in his or her identity. Under any form of analysis, this interest is minimal. It has been recognized that convicted persons, particularly those who are ultimately incarcerated, have a significantly diminished privacy interest. Furthermore, such individuals have a particularly limited privacy interest in the mere fact of their *identity*. The analogy to fingerprinting is extremely persuasive, in that both DNA typing and fingerprinting impinge on similar privacy interests. While the Fourth Amendment does impose certain constraints upon the fingerprinting of free persons, the constitutionality of fingerprinting convicted persons, even accused persons, is unquestioned. Since DNA typing is functionally equivalent to fingerprinting, nonconsensual blood extraction for DNA typing therefore intrudes upon a necessarily diminished privacy interest.[87]

Position in Canada

In Canada, the constitutional challenge against the creation of DNA database is different from United States. The Canadian search and seizure protection is highly sensitive in the case of collection of DNA samples. Even minor irregularities in conducting search and seizure would be fatal and violate section 7 and 8 of the Charter of Rights. The Canadian DNA database is strictly limited to criminal investigation purposes and employers, insurance companies or other non-criminal investigation agencies could not use it. The *DNA Identification Act*, 2000 was enacted in the line of the privacy protection provided in the Charter of Rights. The Act strictly limits the access to the information provided in the DNA database. The ultimate purpose and limits of Canada's *DNA Identification Act* is clear from section 4 of the Act:

(a) the protection of society and the administration of justice are well served by the early detection, arrest and conviction of offenders, which can be facilitated by the use of DNA profiles;

(b) the DNA profiles, as well as samples of bodily substances from which the profiles are derived, may be used only for law enforcement purposes in accordance with this Act, and not for any unauthorised purpose; and

(c) to protect the privacy of individuals with respect to personal information about themselves, safeguards must be placed on (i) the use and communication of, and access to, DNA profiles and other information contained in the national DNA data bank, and (ii) the use of, and access to, bodily substances that are transmitted to the Commissioner for the purposes of this Act.

The Act explicitly limits the type of offences for which DNA sample can be collected. It is provided that DNA samples can be collected only for serious offences and in special cases in which it is necessary in the interest of society. As per the provisions of the DNA Act, the expectation of privacy is different in different situations. For example, the expectation of privacy of an ordinary person is different from the expectation of privacy of a suspect in a crime or a convicted person. The DNA Act insists that the body samples can be collected for DNA database only after convicting a person. In *R.* v. *Stillman*[88] Cory, J., obviously laid down the extent of privacy of a convict:

> '...an accused person will have a lower expectation of privacy following his or her arrest and subsequent custody. That expectation of privacy will be even lower when serving

a sentence after conviction. Therefore, it may well be that certain kinds of searches and seizures may validly be performed on a person in custody which could not validly be performed on persons who have not yet been arrested or convicted'.

However, Canadian courts were of the view that even though the convicted persons have only a very lower expectation of privacy, it is not completely extinguished and bodily integrity remains vital.[89] Thus in the Canadian background it is clear that courts would not allow taking of samples and including it in the DNA database unless there is proper justification.

Conclusion

To conclude, it is one of the distinguishing features of genetic privacy as a human right that it is not only the right of a particular person whose genealogical secrets are in jeopardy but also the right of the persons who are biologically related to him. Disclosure of a man's genetic secret has the same effect of disclosing his kith and kin's. Therefore, there is correlative duty on the person or institution conducting genetic research to warn biological relatives that there is a genetic risk, which may arise through genetic research or analysis. The more serious problem regarding genetic testing and human rights is that whether it is good to say that genealogical rights can be curtailed by proper consensus. Genetic discrimination is something that should be given special attention than any other discrimination like sex, religion or race. Above all, it is crucial that whatever scientific and technological advancements are made; they should not override the traditional values, ethics and morality of a nation. Genetic information though highly sensitive is based on mere probabilities. Therefore, utmost care should be taken in concealing the information, the disregard of which may result in irreparable loss to the affected persons. Genes are the natural status and identity of a human being, which are not amenable to any manipulation.

In future it is expected that the crime investigating authorities would depend on DNA database for solving crimes than any other techniques. Its potential is not only limited as an absolute identifier but also as a good crime fighter without using third degree methods. The decisions in United States and Canada show that DNA databases survived the constitutional and other legal challenges; however, it should be reckoned that these are only minimum. The courts allowed it because it affects only a lesser quantum of privacy level. The convicted persons or offenders have only a minimum expectation of privacy, but it would be unwarranted to include free persons who are not suspected or convicted for any crime. Therefore, any attempt to create a universal DNA database, including all members of the society would create tension and would fail to satisfy the constitutionality because they have a higher expectation of privacy.

REFERENCES

1. See Charles H. Sanders, "Genetic Secrets: Protecting Privacy and Confidentiality in the Genetic Era," 11 *Harv. J.L. & Tech.* 865 (1998) (book review); Robyn B. Nicoll, Comment, "Long-Term Care Insurance and Genetic Discrimination - Get It While You're Young and Ignorant: An Examination of Current Discriminatory Problems in Long-Term Care Insurance Through the Use of Genetic Information", 13 *Alb. L.J. Sci. & Tech.* 751 (2003); Natalie Anne Stepanuk, Comment, "Genetic Information and Third Party Access to Information: New Jersey's Pioneering Legislation as a Model for Federal Privacy Protection of Genetic Information", 47 *Cath. U. L. Rev.* 1105 (1998); Recent Case, "Comparative Law - Genetic Privacy - Icelandic Supreme Court Holds that Inclusion of an Individual's Genetic Information in a National Database Infringes on the Privacy Interests of His Child, Gu<eth>mundsdottir v. Iceland, No. 151/2003 (Nov. 27, 2003) (Ice.)", 118 *Harv. L. Rev.* 810 (2004).

2. Francis S. Collins et al., "New Goals for the U.S. Human Genome Project: 1998-2003," 282 *Science* 682, 685 (Oct. 23, 1998). For more details about Human Genome Project, see Generally Alasdair T. Iles, Comment, "The Human Genome Project: A Challenge to the Human Rights Framework," 9 *Harv. Hum. Rts. J.* 27 (1996) (Advocating the Use of Human Rights Analysis to Confront Potential Social Consequences of the Human Genome Project); Jennifer Elle Tauer, "International Protection of Genetic-Information: The Progression of the Human Genome Project and the Current Framework of Human Rights Doctrines", 29 *Denv. J. Int'l L. & Pol'y* 209 (2001); Symposium, "The Human Genome Project, DNA Science and the Law: The American Legal System's Response to Breakthroughs in Genetic Science Washington, Dc, Friday, October 19, 2001:□Panel One: Intellectual

Property and Genetic Science: The Legal Dilemmas," *51 Am. U.L. Rev. 371*(2002); Alexander M. Capron, "Which Ills to Bear?: Reevaluating the "Threat" of Modern Genetics," in Tom L. Beauchamp & LeRoy Walters (eds.) *Contemporary Issues in Bioethics* 629 (4th ed. 1994).

3. George J. Annas, "Rules for Gene Banks: Protecting Privacy in the Genetics Age", in Timothy F. Murphy & Marc A. Lappe (eds.) *Justice and the Human Genome Project* 75, 82 (1994).

4. This Method Permits One to Conduct DNA Analysis from Smaller Stains.

5. See Reinhard Szibor et al., "Efficiency of Forensic Mitochondrial DNA Analysis Case Examples Demonstrating the Identification of Traces", 113 *Forensic Sci. Int.* 71 (2000).

6. Different from nDNA, mtDNA is Inherited Maternally. Therefore, Except in Case of Mutations, the mtDNA Sequence will be Identical for All Maternal Relatives. Similarly the Transmission of mtDNA is Consistent Across many Generations. See A. Carracedo et al., "DNA Commission of the International Society for Forensic Genetics: Guidelines for Mitochondrial DNA Typing", 110 *Forensic Sci. Int.* 79, 80 (2000). However, some Scientific Papers Pointed out that there Might be some Transfer of Paternal mtDNA into the Fertilized Egg with Recombination Leading to Hybrid mtDNA Molecules. See P Awadalla et al., "Linkage Disequilibrium and Recombination in Hominid Mitochondrial DNA", 286 *Science* 2524 (1999).

7. See Hutchison et al., "Maternal Inheritance of Mammalian Mitochondrial DNA", 251 *Nature* 536-538 (1974).

8. See Bruce Budowle et al., *Forensics and Mitochondrial DNA: Applications, Debates, and Foundations* (hereinafter Budowle, DNA applications), Annual Review, Genomics - Human Genetics 119, 122 (2003).

9. *People* v. *Holzer,* 660 N.W. 2d 405, 408 (Mich. App. 2003). Due to the Strong Protein Membrane, mtDNA can Survive Degradation than nDNA. See *Proceedings of the American Academy of Forensic Sciences* 81 (February 2006), Vol. XII.

10. See Tully, *Mitochondrial DNA Profile*.

11. See Bureau Report, "Junk DNA in Y-chromosome Control Functions" Wednesday, November 29, 2006, Available at www.zeenews.com

12. Ruth Hubbard & Elijah Wald, *Exploding the Gene Myth* 131 (1993); Joanne Seltzer, "The Cassandra Complex: An Employer's Dilemma in the Genetic Workplace," 27 *Hofstra L. Rev.* 411 (1998); Melinda Kaufmann, "Genetic Discrimination in the Workplace: An Overview of Existing Protections," 30 *Loy. U. Chi. L.J.* 393 (1999); Katherine Brokaw, Comment, "Genetic Screening in the Workplace and Employers'

Liability," 23 *Colum. J.L. & Soc. Probs.* 317 (1990); Bryce A. Lenox, Comment, "Genetic Discrimination in Insurance and Employment: Spoiled Fruits of the Human Genome Project," 23 *U. Dayton L. Rev.* 189 (1997); Laura F. Rothstein, "Genetic Discrimination: Why Bragdon Does Not Ensure Protection," 3 *J. Health Care L. & Poly.* 330 (2000); Roger Clegg, "Bragdon v. Abbott, Asymptomatic Genetic Conditions, and Antidiscrimination Law: A Conservative Perspective," 3 *J. Health Care L. & Pol'y* 409 (2000).

13. Universal Declaration of Human Rights, G.A. Res. 217(A), U.N. Doc. 810 (1948). The United Nations Human Rights Commission Drafted it and the U.N. General Assembly Adopted the UDHR Unanimously in 1948. When it was Enacted the Commission did not Intended it to Carry Inding Legal Force but later due to the International Consensus it is now Binding on all U.N. Members and Arguably on All Nations as Customary International Law.

14. International Covenant on Civil and Political Rights, Dec. 19, 1966, 999 U.N.T.S. 171, Reprinted in 6 I.L.M. 368. The U.N. Commission Drafted the ICCPR.

15. Optional Protocol to the International Covenant on Civil and Political Rights, Dec. 16, 1966, U.N.G.A. Res. 2200 (XXI), Reprinted in 6 I.L.M. 383 (1967). The Optional Protocol Allows Individual Victims of Human Rights Violations to File Complaints with the Human Rights Committee Against State Parties.

16. International Covenant on Economic, Social and Cultural Rights, Dec. 16, 1966, 993 U.N.T.S. 3, Reprinted in 6 I.L.M. 360.

17. For e.g., see the Tehran Declaration of 1968, Issued by the International Conference cn Human Rights.

18. Article 1 of Universal Declaration on the Human Genome and Human Rights.

19. Article 2.

20. Article 5(a).

21. Article 5(b).

22. Article 5(d).

23. Article 5(e).

24. Article 6.

25. Article 7.

26. Article 8.

27. Article 9.

28. Human Genetic Data Means "Information About Heritable Characteristics of Individuals Obtained by Analysis of Nucleic Acids or by Other Scientific Analysis." See the International Declaration on Human Genetic Data (UNESCO, October 2003).

29. Adopted Unanimously and by Acclamation on 16 October 2003 by the 32nd Session of the General Conference of UNESCO.

30. Article 12.

31. Article 14 (e).

32. Article 15.

33. 972 P.2d 1060 (Colo. App.1998).

34. The law is "One who Intentionally Intrudes, Physically or Otherwise, Upon the Solitude or Seclusion of Another or his Private Affairs or Concerns, is Subject to Liability to the Other for Invasion of his Privacy, if the Intrusion would be Highly Offensive to a Reasonable Person." Id. at 1068.

35. *Id*.

36. 103 L. Ed. 2d 639 (1989).

37. *Id*. at 1069.

38. 135 F.3d 1260 (9th Cir. 1998).

39. *Id*. at 1270.

40. *Id*.

41. See Genetic Privacy, Electronic Privacy Information Center, Available at www.epic.org , last modified July 23, 2004.

42. AIR 1975 S.C. 1378.

43. AIR 1995 S.C. 264.

44. (1997) 1 S.C.C. 301.

45. The Act was Amended in 2005.

46. AIR 2004 S.C. 1834.

47. Sections (e) and (j) are as follows: (e) Information Available to a Person in his Fiduciary Relationship, Unless the Competent Authority is Satisfied that the Larger Public Interest warrants the Disclosure of such Information; (j) Information which Relates to Personal Information the Disclosure of which has no Relationship to any Public Activity or Interest, or which would cause Unwarranted Invasion of the Privacy of the Individual Unless the Central Public Information Officer or the State Public Information Officer or the Appellate Authority, as the Case may be, is Satisfied that the Larger Public Interest Justifies the Disclosure of such Information.

48. 1998 (8) S.C.C. 296.
49. AIR 2002 Del. 217.
50. *Id.* at 221.
51. *Id.* at 222.
52. *Id.* at 223.
53. See Paul E. Tracy and Vincent Morgan, "Big Brother and his Science Kit: DNA Databases For 21st Century Crime Control", 90 *J. Crim. L. & Criminol.* 635, 642 (2000).
54. *Id.*
55. Allison Puri, "An International DNA Database: Balancing Hope, Privacy, and Scientific Error", 24 *B. C. Int'l. & Comp. L. Rev.* 341 (2001).
56. See John P. Cronan, "The Next Frontier of Law Enforcement: A Proposal for Complete DNA Databanks", 28 *Am. J. Crim. L.* 119, 131-32 (2000).
57. Section 487.06 and 25 of the *Criminal Code.*
58. Adrian Linacre, "The UK National DNA Database", 361 *The Lancet* 1841 (2003).
59. Mike Redmayne, "The DNA Database: Civil Liberty and Evidentiary Issues", [1998] *Crim. L. R.* 437.
60. See P.M. Schncider, DNA Databases for Offender Identification in Europe-the need for Technical, Legal and Political Harmonization, in Proceedings of the 2nd European Symposium on Human Identification, (Promega Corporation, Madison, WI, USA, 1998), pp.40-44, as quoted in Peter D. Martin, Hermann Schmitter, Peter M. Schneider, "A Brief History of the Formation of DNA Databases in Forensic Science within Europe", 119 *Forensic Sci. Int.* 225-231, 228 (2001).
61. See Rekha Lakra and Fannie Dimitriadis, "Forensic DNA Data Banks: Considerations For The Health Sector", 22 *Health L. Canada* 57 (2002).
62. See Legal Information Access Centre (LIAC) - Hot Topics, http:// www.austlii.edu.au /databases.html
63. Adrian Linacre, "The UK National DNA Database", 361 *The Lancet* 1841(2003).
64. Robert Williamson and Rony Duncan, Commentary, "DNA Testing for All", 418 *Nature* 585, 586 (2002).
65. *Id.*
66. See Peter Alldridge, Sanneke Berkhout, Van Poelgest and Katherine Williams, "DNA Profiling and the Use of Expert Scientific Witnesses in Criminal Proceedings", in Christopher Harding, Phil Fennel, Nico Jorg and Bert Swart (eds.) *Criminal Justice in Europe* (Oxford: Clarendon Press, 1995), pp.281-282; see Also Ralph Kirby, Correspondence, "The Many Dangers of Relying on a DNA Database", 419 *Nature* 247-8 (2002).

67. D.H. Kaye & Micheal E. Smith, "DNA identification Databases: Legality, Legitimacy, and the Case for Population-Wide Coverage", 2003 *Wis. L. Rev.* 413.
68. The Authorities use Only Autoradiograph to Compare the Identity of the Accused with Other Person. The Autoradiograph does not Contain any other Information Regarding that Particular Person.
69. See Kimberly A. Polanco, "The Fourth Amendment Challenge to DNA Sampling of Arrestees Pursuant to the Justice for All Act of 2004: A Proposed Modification to the Traditional Fourth Amendment Test of Reasonableness", 27 *U. Ark. Little Rock L. Rev.* 483 (2005).
70. Lynn Fereday, "Comments at the Meeting of the National Commission on the Future of DNA Evidence" (July 26, 1999), *at* http://www.ojp.usdoj.gov/nij/dnamtgtrans6/trans-i.htm
71. See, *Landry* v. *Attorney General*, 709 NE 2d 1085, 1090 (Mass 1999) (State DNA Database was Upheld Against the Fourth Amendment Challenge); *Danzey* v. *State*, 703 So 2d 1019, 1020 (Ala. Crim. App. 1997) (Court Rejected the Defendants Argument that Guilty Plea was Involuntary because he was Ignorant that State would Submit his DNA to Database); *Kruger* v. *Erickson*, 875 F. Supp. 583 (D. Minn. 1995) (Court Rejected the Challenge Based on Fourth Amendment, Ex Post Facto, and Due Process Against State Offender DNA Database).
72. See *Boling* v. *Romer*, 101 F.3d 1336, 1340 (10th Cir. 1996); *Cooper* v. *Gammon*, 943 SW. 2d 699, 704-705 (Mo. Ct. App. 1997); *Doles* v. *State*, 994 P.2d 315, 318-19 (Wyo. 1999); *Johnson* v. *Commonwealth*, 529 SE. 2d 769, 779 (Va. 2000) and *State* v. *Maas*, 64 P.3d 382, 389 (Kan. 2003).
73. 709 NE. 2d 1085 (Mass. 1999).
74. See *Jones* v. *Murray*, 962 F.2d 302, 307 (4th Cir. 1992).
75. The Fourth Amendment says that "the Right of the People to be Secure in their Persons, Houses, Papers, and Effects, Against Unreasonable Searches and Seizures, shall not be Violated, and no Warrants shall Issue, but upon Probable Cause, Supported by Oath or Affirmation, and Particularly Describing the Place to be Searched, and the Persons or things to be Seized."
76. 962 F.2d.307.
77. *Id.* at 304-305.
78. *Id.* at 306.
79. *Id.* at 308.
80. 384 U.S. 757, 769-70 (1996).
81. 345 F.3d 1095 (9th Cir. 2003).

82. *Id.* at 1102.
83. *Id.* at 1098. See also *United States* v. *Miles,* 228 F. Supp. 2d 1130 (ED. Cal. 2002) (Held that the Statute Permitting the Authorities to Compel DNA Samples for DNA Database was Unconstitutional).
84. 469 U.S. 325 (1985).
85. 856 P.2d 1076 (Wash. 1993).
86. *Id.* at 1086.
87. *Id.* at 1093.
88. 113 C.C.C. (3d) 321, 348.
89. See *R.* v. *Minhinnick,* [2001] S. J. No. 18 (Sask. Prov. Ct).

24

Rights of Students and Development of Multiple Intelligence

Sreejith. B

The state of the World's Children 1999 report on the efforts of the international community to ensure that all its children enjoy their human right to a high – quality education, efforts that are resulting in an education revolution. Towards that aim, the work of governments, non-governmental organisations (NGOs), educators, communities, parents and children are informed by a definition of education that includes, but goes for beyond, schooling. With in this definition education is an essential human right, a force for social change – and the single most vital element in combating poverty, empowering women, safe guarding children from exploitative and hazardous labour and sexual exploitation, promoting human rights and democracy protecting the environment and controlling growth. Education is a path towards international peace and security.

The denial of the right to education hurts people's capacity to work productively, to sustain and protect themselves and their families. On a society wide scale the denial of education harms the cause of democracy and social progress.

The quality of education is also of paramount concern. How knowledge skills and values are transmitted is an important as what is learned. Children must also be able to participate fully in the educational process. It is their right to be treated with dignity and allowed to develop from their school experience a level of self esteem, self discipline and sheer enjoyment of learning that will stand them in good stead throughout their lives. Offering child-centered learning experience in the class room that elicits the best in each individual, start from the environment of community and learning the local language. The overall development student can be achieved only through education based on latest trend in pedagogy.

The theory of multiple intelligence conceived by Howard Gardner has a number of pedagogical implications. The National curriculum frame work (2005) recommends the incorporation of this theory in the teaching learning process. Hence it is the right of the student to get opportunity for developing their multiple intellectual potentialities. If the teacher is not giving emphasis for the development all nine intelligences of multiple intelligence theory it will be the negation of the right of the children because modern world demands the integrated overall development of the individual.

This paper highlights how the multiple intelligence theory can be used in the language class room. In the language classroom, the learner should get opportunity to engage in language works which emphasizes the multiple intelligence of the learner so that through the language class both the language competence and the multiple intelligence of the learner develop.

Background

Multiple Intelligence (MI) refers to a learner – based philosophy that characterizes human intelligence as having multiple dimensions that must be acknowledged and developed in education. Traditional IQ or intelligence tests are based on a test called the Stanford – Binet, founded on the idea that intelligence is a single, unchanged, inborn capacity. However, traditional IQ tests, while still given to most school children, are increasingly being challenged by the MI movement. MI is based on the work of Howard Gardner of the Harvard Graduate School of Education. Gardner notes that traditional IQ tests measures only logic and language, yet the brain has other equally important types of intelligence. Gardner argues that all humans have this intelligence, but people differ in the strength and combinations of intelligence. He believes that all of them can be enhanced through training and practice. MI thus belongs to a group of instructional perspectives that focus on differences between learners and the need to recognize learner difference in teaching. Learners are viewed as possessing individual learning styles, preferences, or intelligence. Pedagogy is most successful when these learner differences are acknowledged, analyzed for particular groups of learners, and accommodated in teaching. In both general education and language teaching, a focus on individual differences has been a recurring theme in the last 30 or 50 years, as seen in such movements or approaches as individualized instruction, Autonomous Learning, Learner Training, and Learner Strategies. The Multiple Intelligence model shares a number of commonalities with these earlier proposals.

Gardner proposed a view of natural human talents that is labeled the 'Multiple Intelligence Model'. This model is one of a variety of learning style models that has been proposed in general education and has subsequently been applied to language education. Gardner claims that his view of intelligence (s) is culture – free and avoids the conceptual narrowness usually associated with traditional models of intelligence (eg: the Intelligent Quotient -IQ- testing model). Gardner points nine native 'intelligence', which are described as follows:

- *Linguistic:* the ability to use languages in special and creative ways, which is something lawyers, writers, editors and interpreters are strong in.
- *Logical/mathematical:* the ability to think notionally, often found with doctors, engineers, programmers and scientists.
- *Spatial:* the ability to form mental models of the world, something architects, decorators, sculptors and painters are good at.
- *Musical:* a good ear for music, as is strong in singers and composers.
- *Bodily/kinesthetic:* having a well coordinated body, something found in athletes and craftspersons.

- *Interpersonal:* the ability to be able to work well with people, which is strong in salespeople, politicians and teachers.
- *Intrapersonal:* the ability to understand oneself and apply one's talent successfully, which leas to happy and well – adjusted people in all areas of life.
- *Naturalist:* the ability to understand and organize the patterns of nature.
- *Existential Intelligence:* the ability to perceive one's own existence as a part of the universe. It also involves the ability to think of the meaningfulness and meaninglessness of existence in terms of physical and mental domain.

The idea of Multiple Intelligence has attracted the interest of many educators as well as the general public. School that use MI theory encourage learning that goes beyond traditional books, pens, and pencils. Teaches and parents who recognize their learners'/children's particular gifts and talents can provide learning activities that build on those inherent gifts. As a result of strengthening such differences, individuals are free to be intelligent in their own ways. The National Curriculum document recommends the incorporation of this theory in the teaching-learning process. Teachers who have to design and implement learning processes should have an insight into how this theory can be put into practice. The activities suggested in the Source book have been developed taking into consideration the classroom implication of MI theory.

Verbal-Linguistic Intelligence

All activities where the learners have to construct various discourses are capable of activating this side of intelligence.

Logical-Mathematical Intelligence

- Predicating events, based on the narratives they listen to and read
- Establishing cause and consequence relationship
- Selecting expressions appropriate to a given context
- Sequencing various events for developing narratives

Visual-Spatial Intelligence

- Drawing pictures based on a story or a given piece of information
- Interpreting a picture
- Preparing posters, greeting cards etc.
- Designing wall magazines
- Deciding the layout of a chart

Bodily-Kinesthetic Intelligence

- Role-plays
- Manifesting body language
- Miming

Musical-Rhythmic Intelligence

- Singing songs and rhymes
- Adding lines to a poem keeping its rhythm
- Identifying the rhythm of a poem

Interpersonal Intelligence

- Participation in discussion
- Agreeing or disagreeing with other's opinions
- Asking questions to elicit information
- Sharing ideas with others
- Comparing mutually

Intra-personal Intelligence

- Diary writing
- Realising one's own potentials as well as limitations
- Initiating linguistic activities
- Creative language expressions

Naturalistic Intelligence

- Developing familiarity with nature
- Translating science details of nature into linguistic expressions of pictures
- Talking about nature

The concept of language learning under went a series of changes in the last a few decades. Constructionists like Bruner (1986), Vygotsky (1962) etc proposed the idea that linguistic development happens in a constructive way. Chomsky (1994) argued that the child has an innate cognitive ability to acquire any language. This concept along with the multiple intelligence theory of Gardner (1993) implies that learning a language is not mere development of the basic skills. Hence it is the duty of the teacher to arrange activities with special focus to multiple intelligence in the class room and there by ensure the protection of rights of students in association with their overall development.

REFERENCES

1. Bruner (1986): Actual Minds Possible Worlds, Cambridge: Harward University Press.
2. Chomsky (1994): Language and Thought, London: Mayer Bell.
3. Gardner (1993): Multiple Intelligence, The Theory in Practice, New York: Basic Books.
4. Vygotsky (1962): Thought and Language Cambridge: MIT Press.

25

Transaction of Human Rights Education in the Classroom

A Review of Appropriate Instructional Methodologies

Ajitha Nayar

Introduction

Human Rights are the rights a person has simply because he or she is a human being. Human rights are held by all people equally, universally and for ever.

Human Rights Education is concerned with making students aware of the rights they have being born as Humans on this earth. "Human Rights Education is a human right, a precondition for sustainable development, the civil society and democracy "(UNESCO-1993).Education was recognized by the UNESCO as an important means for development of the Human Personality and to the strengthening of respects for Human rights and fundamental freedoms. Through Human Rights Education Students recognize the importance of using these rights which have been classified as Right to freedom, Legal Rights, Equalitarian Right and Economic rights for their successful living. The Universal Declaration of Human Rights (UDHR) states that all members of the Human Family are created free and equal in dignity.

The student population is the voices of tomorrow and the spear headers of the future. They should be properly and adequately geared and armored to face the trials and tribulations of the future. They should be made self confident and articulate in voicing their concerns. They should be equipped to be aware of their power to control their lives rather than blame it on destiny, society, Government or the country to which they were born into. This preparation can be most effectively done in the classrooms.

The classrooms are the most important place where destiny of tomorrow is being shaped as the Report of Kothari Commission (1966) puts it. So it is in the classrooms that attempts to realize the goals of Human rights education be made .The classrooms become effective places only if teachers make use of the time at their disposal to achieve this end.

The present day teaching learning process has become quite complex in the light of technological advances, changing attitudes to learning, and changes in the attitudes of teachers and last but not least the emerging influences of Globalization. What is required of teachers and what is it that students are expected to do have emerged as relevant questions in the light of vast information sources, technological explosion in the learning environment and changing perceptions of both teachers and students to the process of learning.

Instructional methodologies are means and ways by which learning is affected. It looks at the whole process of instruction from the student's point of view. It pertains to the techniques student employ for active learning when the student is involved with the process of learning, concentrating on what he is doing, focusing on the present task.

Each topic is framed with underlying objectives and the part and parcel of learning is working towards the goal of realizing these objectives. It is important here to ask what the relevance of instructional methodologies is. A teacher who is confused as to which method to be used has to bear in mind the nature of the topic, the purpose of including the topic, the underlying intention that lies behind including the topic for the particular age group (the hidden curriculum) and the objectives to be realized while learning the topic/lesson. When the hidden curriculum implies instilling values in Human Rights the Teacher has to resort to social models of Learning

Details of the Study

Objectives of the study: The major objective of the study was to identify the instructional methodologies for realizing the goals of Human Rights Education

Need and significance of the study: The present age of Liberalization, Globalization, Privatization and Technologization has made Human rights and the awareness of it very essential. It is amazing that Globalization has increased the gap between the technologically literate and the illiterate manifold. In spite of 50 Glorious years of independence the gaps continues to widen between the haves and the have-nots. A majority of people are still ignorant of their constitutional safeguards and the rights at their disposal. They cry not because they believe it is their destiny. They are not aware that their voice has the power and the spirit to drive the machinery. They ask not because they are aware not. Many of these cross sections represent the most Poor and the educationally backward. To loft them from their present state of doom and despair it is necessary that these teeming millions become aware of their rights as Humans in this earth.

No one strategy or Instructional Methodology is appropriate for all content and for all students. Role Play, Simulation, Case Studies, Discussion, Inquiry, Brainstorming, Investigative approach, Independent research, Co-operative learning, Field trips and Guest Speakers are appropriate for Human rights Education (K S Pillai- 2001).

In this study a review of Instructional Methodologies in association to the topics that can be taught in the area of Human Rights Education is attempted.

Methodology: A review of Various Instructional Methodologies was conducted. The investigator conducted a field trial of various methodologies in the classroom. The Instructional methodologies described here were those which were found effective in four viz.,

1. Whole class participation
2. Whole class involvement
3. Feedback from the students
4. Understanding of the topics taught

Tools and Techniques: An observation schedule was used to make recordings for whole class participation and whole class involvement. A questionnaire was prepared for collecting feedback from students. An achievement test was constructed based on the topic taught.

Findings of the Study

The instructional methodologies selected have high scores in whole class participation and whole class involvement. There was better awareness of Human Rights issues. Excellent opportunities were possible for data gathering, problem identification, problem solving, and conflict resolution and value clarification. The Instructional Methodologies selected comprised of:

1. Group investigation model
2. Role Play; and
3. Jurisprudential model

These Co-operative learning procedures facilitate learning across all curricular areas and ages improving self esteem, social skill and solidarity and academic goals ranging from acquisition of information and skill through the modes of inquiry of the academic disciplines.

1. Group Investigation Model

Here a problem was selected and the class was divided into groups. The student investigated the problem in groups. Since a topic could not be devoted exclusively to Human Rights Education what was done was to address the Human Rights aspects in the lesson using the instructional methodology. For example, while teaching a topic on Environment or Natural resources the following was incorporated into the presentation viz., Protection of the Environment and the Rights to livelihood of Villagers living close to Forests, Protection of the Environment and banning of Plastics (Devising alternative employment to those who are employed in the Plastic industry).Students collect data/ information related to the topic and investigated the issues related to the problem. They also identified other problems closely associated with this problem and suggested remedial measures .They brought about solutions to the problem viz., how both the Environment and the community could live close together without harming each other.

2. Role Play

Role Play was another instructional methodology that was selected and employed in the classroom when Human related issues are taught. The Teacher suggested a topic related to the content that could be enacted in the classroom. The topic was of current relevance or an enactment of a current event. Teacher introduced the situation which forms the theme on which the play was enacted. For example tell the student to suppose that he or she is a child laborer forced to work in a factory. Then ask him or her that how would he or she get the approval of his or her parents to Education and escape from the tyranny of child labor. A Model parliament is also an excellent means for developing concept of Democracy, getting awareness of ideals of Democracy, acquaintance with Assembly/Parliament proceedings which are the custodians of Human Rights. The Roles enacted by the individuals in social contexts stimulate social interactions and observations of social behavior .These help students to find ways of solving problems in conflict resolutions (Shafter et al-1982; Joyce and Weil- 2006)

3. Jurisprudential Inquiry Method

This is also referred to as Case study method (Oliver and Shaver-1966, Oliver and Shaver- 1971; Shaver- 1995). The Teacher introduces a case (ongoing or outdated case) .All aspects of the case are made familiar to the students. The students take sides and justify their stand or position taken. Finally students identify factual assumptions and determine their relevance. Many current and social events can be used to highlight issues related to Human

Rights Eg., A lesson on communicable disease or viral diseases can incorporate legal cases related to Education of students suffering from AIDS/HIV. A lesson on role of various institutions in society can include legal cases pertaining to school related issues viz., Dress code to be followed in Educational Institutions, singing of National Anthem, tackling student misbehavior in the class.

Implications of the Study

The right approach to realize the objective of Human Rights Education is not by creating a separate syllabus, separate curriculum or a separate time schedule for imparting Human Rights Education but to incorporate it within the Time Table and in the syllabus. Human Rights Education forms a hidden curriculum of Social Science Education so, aspects concerning Human Rights issues can be addressed within the classroom in the course of teaching of Social sciences. Imparting the right perspectives of Human Rights Education can be achieved by use of proper instructional methodologies. The Models of teaching under the social family has a large number of appropriate instructional methodologies to realize the objectives of Human Rights Education.

REFERENCES

1. Indian Education Commission Report (1964-66): Govt. of India Publication.
2. Joyce and Weil, M. (2004): *Models of Teaching* (5th edn). New Delhi: Prentice Hall.
3. Oliver, D and Shaver, J P. (1971): *Cases and Controversy: A Guide to Teaching the Public Issues Series* Middletown: American Education Publishers.
4. Oliver, D and Shaver, J. P. (1974): *Teaching Public Issues in the High School*. Boston: Houghton Mifflin Publications.
5. K.S Pillai. (2001): *Module of Human Rights Education,* Trivandrum: Kalanikethan Publishers.
6. Shaftel, F and G. Shaftel (1982): *Role Playing of Social Values: Decision making in the Social Studies*. New Delhi: Prentice –Hall India Pvt Ltd.
7. Shaver, J.P., (1995): Social Studies in G. Cawelti (Ed.) *Handbook of Research on Improving Student Achievement,* Arlington: Educational Research Service.

26

Corruption and Human Rights

Neena Thomas

Introduction

The vice of corruption is more dangerous than the viruses of AIDS or SARS. Corruption causes massive human deprivations and creates sudden and extreme income inequalities; it introduces uncertainties into the economic environment and forms webs of illegal obligations. Extortions, robberies, assaults, crimes on women, children and the weak and even all that is associated with terrorism and under-world are some of the outward expressions or manifestations of corruption that hurt human beings and their rights deeply and more. As corruption leads to discrimination and arbitrariness in decision-making, established rules, regulations and procedures become meaningless; peoples' fundamental rights to corruption- free services from public institutions and Governments get trampled mercilessly. The sum of all these, rise as notorious impediments against protection and promotion of human rights and ultimately violates a very wide spectrum of human rights. In India, the judiciary system is relatively clean compare to all other areas but there self bribes estimated annually is around Rs. 2,630 crore parted 61% to lawyers, 29% to court officials 5% to judges and 5% to middlemen.

Concept of Corruption

The dictionary meaning of 'corruption' is *'decomposition, moral deterioration'* etc. The Encyclopedia Americana gave a very broad definition of corruption as 'the *unsanctioned use of public/political resources and/or goods for non-public ends.*' It is a general concept describing any organized, interdependent system in which part of the system is either not performing duties it was originally intended to, or performing them in an improper way, to the detriment of the system's original purpose. Corruption certainly stings the public more and the poor most.

Specific types of corruption include:

- *Political corruption,* corruption of a political system where public officials seek illegitimate personal gain through actions such as bribery, extortion, cronyism, nepotism, patronage, graft, and embezzlement. Misuse of government power for other purposes, like repression of political opponents and general police brutality, is not considered political corruption.
- *Police corruption* is a specific form of police misconduct sometimes involving political corruption, and generally designed to gain a financial or political benefit for a police officer or officers in exchange for not pursuing, or selectively pursuing, an investigation or arrest.
- *Data corruption,* the receiving of data which is different from that which was transmitted or otherwise intended.
- *Tempting* is an act that looks appealing to an individual. It is usually used to describe acts with negative connotations and as such, tends to lead a person to regret such actions, for various reasons: legal, social, psychological (including feeling guilt), health, economic, etc. Temptation also describes the coaxing or inducing a person into committing such an act, by manipulation or otherwise of curiosity, desire or fear of loss.

Human Rights

It is the concept of human beings as having universal natural rights, or status, regardless of legal jurisdiction or other localizing factors, such as ethnicity, nationality, and sex. As is evident in the United Nations Universal Declaration of Human

Rights, human rights, at least in the post-war period, are conceptualized as based on inherent human dignity, retaining their universal and inalienable character.

The existence, validity and the content of human rights continue to be the subject to debate in philosophy and political science. Legally, human rights are defined in international law and covenants, and further, in the domestic laws of many states. However, for many people the doctrine of human rights goes beyond law and forms a fundamental moral basis for regulating the contemporary geo-political order. For them, they are democratic ideals.

The idea of human rights descended from that of natural rights; some recognize no difference between the two and regard both as labels for the same thing while others choose to keep the terms separate to eliminate association with some features traditionally associated with natural rights.

Types of Human Rights

Human rights are sometimes divided into *negative and positive rights*. Negative human rights denote actions that a government should not take. These include right to life and security of person; freedom from slavery; equality before the law and due process under the rule of law; freedom of movement; and freedoms of speech, religion, assembly, and the right to bear arms for collective and individual defense.

Positive human rights denote rights that the state is obliged to protect and provide. Examples of such rights include: the rights to education, to a livelihood, to legal equality.

Justification of Human Rights

Several theoretical approaches have been advanced to explain how human rights become part of social expectations. The *biological theory* considers the comparative reproductive advantage of human social behavior based on empathy and altruism in the context of natural selection. Other theories hold that human rights codify moral behavior, which is a human, social product developed by a process of biological and social evolution or as a sociological pattern of rule setting. This approach includes the notion that individuals in a society accept rules from legitimate authority in exchange for security and economic advantage.

On the other hand, *natural law theories* base human rights on the "natural" moral order that derives from religious precepts such as common understandings of justice and the belief that moral behavior is a set of objectively valid prescriptions. Some have used religious texts such as the Bible and Qur'an to support human rights arguments. However, there are also more secular forms of natural law theory that understand human rights as derivative of the notion of universal human dignity.

Ultimately, the term "human rights" is often itself an appeal to a transcendent principle, not based on existing legal concepts. The term "humanism" refers to the developing doctrine of such universally applicable values. The term "human rights" has replaced the term "natural rights" in popularity, because the rights are frequently seen as requiring natural law for their existence.

Criticism of Human Rights

One of the arguments made against the concept of human rights is that it suffers from cultural imperialism. In particular, the concept of human rights is fundamentally rooted in a politically liberal outlook which, although generally accepted in Western Europe, Japan, India and North America, is not necessarily taken as standard elsewhere. The cultural imperialism argument achieves even greater potency when it is made on the basis of religion. Some histories of human rights emphasize the Christian influence on the agenda and then question whether this is in keeping with the tenets of other world religions. For example, in 1981, the Iranian representative to the United Nations, Said Rajaie-Khorassani, articulated the position of his country regarding the Universal Declaration of Human Rights by saying that the UDHR was "a secular understanding of the Judeo-Christian tradition", which could not be implemented by Muslims without trespassing the Islamic law.

If all viewpoints and moral frameworks are equally valid then one cannot condemn any behavior, however outrageous or horrific. In practice, human rights offer a basis to criticize such behavior or conduct, including imperialism. As such, human rights can be a transformative tool for determination. One way out of the cultural imperialism and relativism debate is to argue that the body of human rights exists in a hierarchy or can undergo *derogation*.

Violations of Human Rights Results on Corruption

Human rights Violation is abuse of people in a way that it abuses any fundamental human rights. It is a term used when a government violates national or international law related to the protection of human rights. According to the Universal Declaration of Human Rights, fundamental human rights are violated when, among other things:

- A certain race, creed, or group is denied recognition as a "person". (Articles 2 & 6)
- Men and women are not treated as equal. (Article 2)
- Different racial or religious groups are not treated as equal. (Article 2)
- Life, liberty or security of person is threatened. (Article 3)
- A person is sold as or used as a slave. (Article 4)
- Cruel, inhuman or degrading punishment is used on a person (such as torture or execution). (Article 5)
- Punishments are dealt arbitrarily or unilaterally, without a proper and fair trial. (Article 11)
- Arbitrary interference into personal lives by agents of the state. (Article 12)
- Citizens are forbidden to leave or return to their country. (Article 13)
- Freedom of speech or religion is denied. (Articles 18 & 19)
- The right to join a trade union is denied. (Article 23)
- Education is denied. (Article 26)

Relation Between Corruption and Human Rights

"It is a timely coincidence that 9th December, International Anti-Corruption Day, is followed on 10th December by International Human Rights Day, because corruption is a human rights issue. Corruption denies people the fundamental economic and social rights guaranteed to them by the Universal Declaration of Human Rights. Corruption leads to a violation of human rights in at least three respects: corruption perpetuates discrimination; corruption prevents the full realization of economic, social, and cultural rights, and also leads to the infringement of numerous civil and political rights. Most of the human right violation scenarios are resulted from corrupted environment and it is obviously contradicting human rights. For example, Supreme Court verdict on Gujarat communal riots (2002) and Nandigram mishaps (2007) exposed the Government machinery's malfunctioning in preventing miscarriage of justice by acquainting persons close to the ruling party.

Corruption Supports Human Rights

The linkage between various rights is complex since it can be argued that some are mutually reinforcing or supportive. For example, political rights, such as the right to hold office, cannot be fully exercised without other social and cultural pre-requisites, such as a decent education. Whether the latter should therefore be included as a first-generation right is a debated point. Execution of one person's rights may hinder the adequacies of another being. The acceptance of a deed basically depends on the thinking strategy of a person. So we cannot say human rights are always morally justifiable.

Another important philosophical criticism of human rights is their presumed bias in morality. If moral beliefs are fundamentally expressions of individuals' personally held preferences then the objective morality upon which human rights are founded is rejected. Richard Rorty has argued that human rights are not based upon the exercise of reason but a sentimental vision of humanity.

Final set of debating points revolves around the question, 'who has the duty to uphold human rights?' Human rights have historically arisen from the need to protect citizens from abuse by the state and this might suggest that all mankind has a duty to intervene and protect people wherever they are. Divisive national loyalties, which emphasize differences between people rather than their similarities, can thus be seen as a destructive influence on the human rights movement because they deny people's innately similar human qualities. But others argue that state sovereignty is paramount, not least because it is often the state that has signed up to human rights treaties in the first place. Commentators' positions in the argument for and against intervention and the use of force by states are influenced by whether they believe human rights are largely a legal or moral duty and whether they are of more cosmopolitan or nationalist persuasion.

Corruption Model

Politicians and public officials cannot be allowed to hold themselves above the law, a point clearly demonstrated by a new global public opinion survey conducted by Transparency International. The TI Global Corruption Barometer 2004 reveals that political parties were deemed to be the most corrupt institution worldwide, followed equally by the police and the judiciary.

In 36 out of 62 countries surveyed, political parties were considered the institution most affected by corruption, faring most poorly in Ecuador, followed by Argentina, India and Peru. Corruption is universally evaluated at two levels –Grand and Petty level. It is often argued that 'petty' or small scale corruption - for instance at the level of the school or hospital - cannot be evaluated on the same scale as 'grand corruption' relates to the accumulation of very large sums from backhanders related to big projects. In the case of petty corruption 'those who receive bribes do so as a result of their meagre incomes and low standard of living - and what they receive only helps make ends meet'. In contrast 'the second type of corruption involve(s) high level leaders and public servants whose involvement is a result of excessive greed for wealth, accumulation and money'. But both affect the lives of common.

Counter Measures

"We are responsible for what we are, and whatever we wish ourselves to be, we have the power to make ourselves. If what we are now has been the result of our own past actions, it certainly follows that whatever we wish to be in future can be produced by our present actions; so we have to know how to act'.

—*Swami Vivekananda*

The scriptures in all the religions and classics of all the societies have treated *Education* as an aspect of the constitution, preservation and maintenance of society itself. There is urgent need for all right minded citizens worldwide to join hands for ensuring eradication of the seemingly uncontrollable monster of corruption and help mankind live free from anarchy and violations of human rights. There is also a greater need to understand that combating corruption is not just about punishing corrupt politicians and bureaucrats but about saving human lives, human rights and peace everywhere.

Another measure is to increase the *Punishment* for those corrupted selves. Actions must be taken without any consideration so that no one further dare about such an act. As well as being a new international framework for tackling domestic and foreign bribery in the public and private sectors, the UN Convention signed by 95 countries, creates a global framework within which civil society can continue its important work, in particular in the new areas of asset recovery, of mutual legal assistance and also in the recognition of the need for information exchange and technical assistance to those signatories states that do not have the resources to live up to the requirements of this convention.

An environment characterized by poor governance offers greater incentives and more scope for corruption, so it is a must to avoid such ministries who are unable to direct state matters in appropriate manner. It is to promote good governance in all its aspects, by ensuring the rule of law, improving the efficiency and accountability of the public sector and tackling corruption, as essential elements of a framework within which economies can prosper, since mostly corruption are economic in nature. We have to provide assistance to strengthen administration of those areas that is susceptible to corruption. In this Globalization era, its better to improve the transparency and accountability of decision making by adopting internationally recognized standards and codes that cover government, the financial sector, and the corporate sector.

The public needs reliable access to information pertaining to laws related to human rights. Along with that to protect human rights civil society organisations can contribute by understanding the issues related to judicial corruption and monitoring the incidence of corruption, as well as potential indicators of corruptions such as delays and quality decisions.

The existing educational system succeeds in its mission of awareness about human rights against corruption. Continuous interaction with the society enables the youth to be conscious about the impact of corruption. So they can protect themselves from the iron hands of this malicious infection. Otherwise it affects the base of human rights itself; even the concept of human right will be ruined in the future.

Conclusion

Human Rights fundamentally enforce citizen's rights and probity in public sector. Civilian societies should adopt more active role in educating the Press about the human rights, with a view to promote more accurate coverage and to follow up the cases, and to move beyond sensationalized reporting mania. The new pattern for ethics within offices could play a role in cleaning up the broader existing system by promoting a cultural shift in all public offices. The constitutional quest to develop human rights against corruption goes beyond demanding that the government respect the rule of law. Everywhere the rule of law may be respected, the humanitarianism of human rights under the constitution must also provide the positive rights as well as the negative rights, which it serves to provide equality, concern and dignity for the citizens. A corruption free service offered is meant to provide all the human rights.

REFERENCES

1. Steiner, Henry J. & Alston, Philip. (1996). *International Human Rights in Context: Law, Politics, Morals,* Clarendon Press, Oxford.

2. Donnelly, Jack. (2003). *Universal Human Rights in Theory & Practice.* 2nd ed.:, Cornell University Press, Ithaca & London.

3. Forsythe, David P. (2000). *Human Rights in International Relations,* Cambridge University Press, Cambridge.

4. Ignatieff, Michael. *Human Rights as Politics and Idolatry,*: Princeton University Press, Princeton & Oxford.

5. Axel Dreher, Christos Kotsogiannis, Steve McCorriston (2004), *Corruption Around the World: Evidence from a Structural Model.*

6. Kimberly Ann Elliott,(1997)-Corruption and the Global Economy

7. Edward L. Glaeser and Claudia Goldin, eds, (2006)- *Corruption and Reform: Lessons from America's Economic History* U. of Chicago Press,. pp. 386.

8. Arnold J. Heidenheimer, Michael Johnston and Victor T. LeVine (eds), (1989)- *Political Corruption: A Hanbook* 1017 page.

9. Robin Hodess ,Victoria Jennett, and Diane Mak (2007)Global Corruption Report 2007-Cambridge University Press, New York.

10. Johann Graf Lambsdorff (2007), *The Institutional Economics of Corruption and Reform: Theory, Evidence and Policy* Cambridge University Press, Cambridge.

27

Mounting Corruption

A Challenge to Human Rights

Justin Thomas Panachakel

Introduction

'Manjunath's sacrifice a beacon of light' was a major caption of the 'The Hindu' daily on December 4, 2005. The report continues, Mr. Upendra Verma, the Director, Vigilance and Anti-Corruption Bureau (Kerala), said Manjunath had given his life in the battle against corruption. Manjunath Shanmugham, a young Indian Institute of Management (IIM) graduate, hailing from Kolar, Gold Field, Karnataka, who was killed on November 18, 2005 by miscreants allegedly employed by an Indian Oil dealer in Lakhimpur Kheri District, Uttar Pradesh. Manjunath, an employee of Indian Oil Corporation tried to prevent large scale adulteration of diesel by a few dealers in the area. This incident is not a lone case and it highlights the fact that corruption leads to violation of human rights in the extreme form. The IIM graduate's fundamental right to live was terminated by the heinous action of the corrupt oil dealers. The Manjunath incident highlights the most vulgar face of corruption, which poses a challenge to the basic human right, i.e., the right to live. A similar case was reported from Bihar in 2003. An IIT qualified engineer, S.K. Dubey was murdered on November 27, 2003 in Bihar, for trying bring out the corruption involved in the Government project he was working on. (S.K. Dubey Foundation – 2005).

Corruption is not a new phenomenon. It existed in public life even before Christ. Biblical narrations dating back to BC 750 describes about corruption. 'You are building Jerusalem on a foundation of murder and corruption' (Micah – 3:10). 'How terrible it will be for you build cities with money gained by murder and corruption?' (Habakkuk – 2:12). Kautilya (Chanakya) in 'Arthashastra' wrote '...just as it is impossible not to taste the honey or poison, one may find at the tip of one's tongue, so it is impossible for one dealing with Government funds not to taste at least a little bit, of king's wealth' (World Bank -2000) Kautilya stated 'forty' ways of embezzlement by Government officials. Even though the repercussions of corruption are mostly economic in nature, until 1980's, scholarly research on corruption was largely confined to the fields of Sociology, Political Science, History, Public Administration and Criminal (Woods, B.–2002).

This article attempts to analyse corruption from the viewpoint of violation of human rights. The first part of the article deals with typology of corruption. The second part shows how corruption leads to the violation of human rights.

Typology of Corruption

The Merriam-Webster Dictionary defines corruption as 'impairment of integrity, virtue or moral principle, or moral principle or inducement to wrong by bribery or other unlawful or improper means'. In India, the most significant law concerning corruption – Prevention of Corruption Act, 1947(amended in 1988) – defines it primarily as an action involving a public servant in taking gratification other than legal remuneration in respect of an official act (Prevention of Corruption Act-1947 (1988)). Corruption involves behavior on the part of officials in the public sector, whether politician or those close to them, by misuse of power entrusted to them (Marshall, I. E.-2001). Different types of corruption often tend to intersect and any specific act of corruption is usually a hybrid of certain basic kinds of corruption. Corruption originates not in any system but it is an integral part of the mindset of man himself. Some of the important types of corruption are:

1. *Bribery*: The penal laws of most countries include the offence of bribery, where private parties offer or promise money or advantages to officials in order to influence their decisions. Variations exist as to the attempt, promise, giving, solicitation or acceptance of a bribe (active and passive bribery). A sub-kind of bribery is extortion in which the public official forcefully takes bribes from a party. One of the main sources of recent global initiatives springs from the concern that public officials in many countries accept illicit payments or other advantages in order to extend contracts or offer business deals to particular corporations (United Nations-2005). In addition to usual laws governing bribes, an indirect way in which such practices are dealt with is by resorting to unfair trade or anti-trust regulations.
2. *Fraud*: Fraud is basically cheating government through deceit. It is very hard to prove cases of fraud as in this form of corruption, as corrupt intentions are not very easy to establish. Criminal deceptions that constitute fraud occur in many forms. Common examples are the overpricing of a project due to the effort of a company to recuperate the cost of bribes, cases of providing work of inferior quality than that specified in the contract, charging for goods or services never delivered, altering the specifications or the timing of completion etc.
3. *Embezzlement*: Stealing of government funds or property is one of the most prevalent kinds of corruption. The direct and immediately visible effects of this form of corruption are relatively larger.
4. *Nepotism*: Favoritism shown by authorities to friends and relatives is another major issue. Appointment of friends and relatives at high posts ("back door appointments"), leniency towards them while granting contracts licenses etc are examples of nepotism and cronyism. But favoritism shown to friends, who are qualified, during appointments etc, need not necessarily be cronyism.

Based on the public office held by the person committing corruption, it can be classified under two heads:

1. *Administrative corruption*: It is type of corruption that seeks to manipulate the way public policy is implemented at bureaucratic level. An example could be administrative level manipulations for granting licenses to an unqualified firm.

2. *Political corruption*: This type of corruption tries to manipulate the formulation of public policy, rules, regulations etc itself. It usually requires the participation of elected representatives or political leaders.

Heidenheimer et al (Heidenheimer, Arnold J., Michael, Johnston and Victor, T. Le Vine –1989) classified corruption into three groups – 'public office centered, market centered and public interest centered'. Public office centered corruption includes such behavior as bribery, nepotism and misappropriation (Nye, J. S. – 1967). Van Klaveren conceives market-centered corruption in terms of a civil servant who regards his public office as a business, the income of which he will, in the extreme case, seek to maximize. The office then becomes a 'maximizing unit'? (cited in Heidenheimer et al-1989). The public interest centered definition views corruption as existing whenever a power holder who is charged with doing certain things, i.e., who is a responsible functionary or office holder is by monetary or other rewards not legally provided for, induced to take actions which favour whoever provides the rewards and thereby does damage to the public and its interests (Friedrich, C. J. –1966).

Another important classification of corruption is as 'grand corruption' and 'petty corruption'. Grand corruption has been defined as the misuse of public power by heads of state, ministers and senior officials, for private pecuniary gain (Moody, S.G. - 1994). Petty corruption is the solicitation or extortion of small payments by low level officials in order to expedite business by cutting through red tape; or to do what they are supposed to do anyway. Petty corruption, in this form, is often referred to as 'speed' or 'grease' money. It is no less significant precisely because it bears most heavily on the poorest and the weakest sections of society who can least afford to make payments for services to which they are any way entitled (Doig, A. and Theobald, R. – 2000).

Heidenheimer et al (1989) categorise corrupt behavior into 'petty corruption', 'routine corruption' (including acceptance of gifts by public officials, nepotism, and graft) and 'aggravated corruption' (including kickbacks and organized crime).

Corruption As Violation of Human Rights

'Universal Declaration of Human Rights' adopted on the 10th of December 1948, by the General Assembly of United Nations, called upon the member states to ensure the effective implementation of rights and freedoms set forth in the Declaration. The Right to Life is an important human right. As noted in the earlier part of this article, there are several cases in which many warriors like Manjunath and Dubey who fought against corruption were killed by the 'mafia' of the corrupt.

Right to life need not be understood in a narrow sense. Absence of resources or denial of access to resources is also cases of violation of the fundamental human right – the right to life. Corruption make the misallocation of resources worse by transferring resources in favour of the rich, because corrupt officials are likely to press for change in the regulations from which they get rich. It also aggravates income inequality and poverty. It is rightly recognized that poverty is a violation of human rights (Sengupta, A. K.-2005). Corruption tends to shift Government spending away from socially beneficial investments, such as health, education, good roads and communication towards unneeded, high-cost, least-beneficial projects, which are not benefiting to the poor.

In India, consumption-expenditure has been made the basis for the measurement of poverty (Agrawal, A.N.-2001). The poverty-norm is anchored in terms of daily intake of 2400 calories in rural areas and 2100 calories in urban areas. Poverty in India has an institutional dimension. The people are not only poor but they suffer various social and economic handicaps (Dandeker, V. M. –1990). The socially and economically backward sections are worst affected by corruption. Corruption denies the poor from access to resources. For instance, when staff of public health care system (Government hospitals) demand bribe for services provided by them, the poor are the most affected and for all practical purpose, it is denial of the service to such people for whom it is intended. Similarly when Government and aided educational institutions demand for bribe in the pretext of donation or Parent Teacher Association (PTA) fund it virtually driving out the poor from the service and preventing their access to resources. The above sited two instances are often viewed as a normal thing, but we should reconcile with the fact that they are clear cases of human right violation.

Corruption is rampant in many Government offices, which provided direct services to people, like Village Offices, Panchayat Offices, Regional Transport Offices, etc. it is interesting to note that majority of the victims of corruption are poor people. In Trivandrum district, Kerala, twelve cases of corruption were registered in 2003 by Superintendent of Police, Vigilance and Anticorruption. Out of the twelve cases, six were trap cases, in which the officials involved in corruption demanded and accepted money from the affected party.

Corruption causes massive human deprivations and creates sudden and extreme income inequalities; it introduces uncertainties into the economic environment and forms webs of illegal obligations. Extortions, robberies, assaults, crimes on women, children and the weak and even all that is associated with terrorism and under-world are some of the outward expressions or manifestations of corruption that hurt human beings and their rights deeply and more. As corruption leads to discrimination and arbitrariness in decision-making, established rules, regulations and procedures become meaningless; peoples' fundamental rights to corruption-free services from public institutions and Governments get trampled mercilessly. The sum of all these, rise as notorious impediments against protection and promotion of human rights and ultimately violates a very wide spectrum of human rights, deeply.

Corruption is an obstacle to development. Article 3, Clause 3 of the UN Declaration on the Right to Development (4 December 1986) reads as follows:

'States have the duty to cooperate with each other in ensuring development and eliminating obstacles to development. States should realize their rights and fulfill their duties in such a manner as to promote a new international economic order based on sovereign equality, interdependence, mutual interest and cooperation among all States, as well as to encourage the observance and realization of human rights'.

Poverty eradication is a major human rights challenge of the 21st centaury. A decent standard of living, adequate nutrition, health care, education, decent work and protection against calamities are not just developmental goals; they are also human rights. Corruption shows down the development of the economy and the poor/marginalized are major victims of this artifact in the development initiative. Corruption is unfair to common man. Social costs of corruption are obvious. It is commonly accepted that corruption is not socially good (Panachakel, J. T. and Thomaskutty, P. G. 2005). Political and bureaucratic corruption at different levels of the Government has been seen as plaguing the implementation of development programmes and policies (Kohli, Sumesh 1975).

REFERENCES

1. Agrawal, A.N. (2001) , *Indian Economy*, Vishwa Prakashan, New Delhi.
2. Dandeker, V. M (1990) , *Agriculture, Employment and Poverty*, in the Indian Economy, Lucas Robert E.B. and Papanek Gustav, F. (eds.) Oxford, Delhi.
3. Doig, A. and Theobald, R. (2000), *Why Corruption' in Corruption and Democratization*, (eds.) Alan and Robin, Frank Cass, London, p. 5.
4. Friedrich, C.J. (1966), *Political Pathology*, Political Quarterly, 37, p. 74.
5. Heidenheimer et al (1989), *Political Corruption: A Handbook*, Heidenheimer, Arnold J., Michael, Johnston and Victor, T. Le Vine (eds.) New Brunswick, NJ: Transaction Book.
6. Kohli, Sumesh (1975) , *Corruption in India*, Chetan Publications , New Delhi.
7. Marshall, I.E. (2001), *A Survey of Corruption Issues in Mining and Mineral Sector"*, (15) Mining, Minerals and Sustainable Development 2, 48.
8. Moody, S.G. (1994) , Grand Corruption in Third World Development, Transparency International, Berlin.
9. Nye, J.S. (1967) , Corruption in Political Development: A Cost-Benefit Analysis, American Political Science Review, 61, June p. 417.

10. Panachakel, J.T. and Thomaskutty, P.G. (2005), *Economics of Corruption*, Paper Presented in International Conference on A Decade of Decentralisation in Kerala: Issues, Options and Lessons , 7-9 October 2005, Trivandrum, india.

11. Sengupta, A.K. (2005) , *Poverty is a Violation of Human Rights*; The Hindu, Thiruvananthapuram, November 18.

12. Woods, B. (2002), *Governance, Corruption, & Economic Performance*, George T. Abed and Sanjeev Gupta (eds.), International Monetary Fund, Sept. 23.

13. World Bank (2000), *Reflection on Corruption in Indonesia*, the Quality of Growth, 135, Oxford University Press.

Web Sites

1. *http://www.pegasus.or.id/Reports/29)%20Reflections%20on%20Corr.pdf* (July 15, 2005).

2. *http://www.imf.org*/external/pubs/nft/ 2002/govern/#chp1 (July 5, 2005).

3. www.transparency.org/working_papers/mining_mineral/survey _of_corruption_ marshall.pdf July 27, 2005.

4. *http://www.skdubeyfoundation.org/index.php* July 10, 2005.

5. *http://www.uncjin.org/Documents/corrupt.htm* July 15, 2005

28

Rights to Education As Human Rights

Bisni Gopalakrishnan

Introduction

'...All human rights depend on the basic right to know, to demand accountability. In India, the feudal social fabric has exploited the formal democratic system to its advantage because the literate are too busy building careers and empires to bother about social inadequacies...'

Aruna Roy[1]

Democracy is no longer perceived as a form of government where the participation of the people is restricted merely to periodic exercise of the right to franchise, with the citizens retiring into passivity between elections. It has now a more positive and dynamic content with people having a say in how and by what rules they would be governed. Meaningful participation of people in major issues affecting their lives is now a vital component of the democratic governance and such participation can hardly be effective unless people have information about the way government business is transacted[2]. Democracy means choice and sound and informed choice is possible only on the basis of knowledge.

Therefore right to information is a condition precedent to honest and accountable governance. It guarantees that every citizen will have a right to know how powers and functions of the State are being performed. For example, how is development plans made? How are discretionary powers exercised? What are criteria for giving contracts, licenses and largess? How do various Departments spend money allocated to them? All these questions will have to be answered promptly by the government .Thus right to information acts as a deterrent against abuse of power and corruption.

Right to Information—Tracing Out Its Development in India

The movement for right to information started when a group of farmers from Rajasthan were cheated of their wages by the government for work they had rendered during a famine in mid 1990's. Routinely government officials denied the poor and illiterate workers of their wages, on the ground that their records did not contain proof of their work. As these records were kept classified the workers felt that making these records available to public scrutiny would solve their problems. The villagers' anger and determination to hold the government accountable for its denial sparked the Right to Information movement which subsequently snowballed into forcing the government to enact the recently passed Right to Information Act 2005.

They united and formed the Mazdoor Kisaan Shakti Sangathan (MKSS) in 1990.MKSS demand for transparency led to an official enquiry which reported that a bogus company had received illegal payments for labour that had never been rendered. The MKSS transcribed the details of the enquiry report and through door to door visits made the enquiry findings public. This immediately led people to mobilize.

The movement was met with the governments determined efforts to stifle the campaign. Giving into the effective protests and campaigning, the Chief Minister established the Committee on Transparency to study the feasibility of supplying photocopies of bills, vouchers and muster rolls. However when the Committee recommended that it was practical the State Government declared the Committees findings secret.

Legislative Initiatives to Ensure Right to Information

Our age old Official Secrets Act 1923 was a colonial version of the English Official Secrets Acts 1911 which were very restrictive of the use and dissemination of governmental information. It was a hasty piece of catch all legislation which made a criminal offence of all unauthorized disclosure of information from official sources regardless of the question whether the public interest really demands secrecy.

The law was used more often for restricting the freedom of expression and inhibiting exposure of the illegal acts of the government. We continued with this colonial tradition of secrecy pretty long and the legislation became a handy tool to withhold information from the people. The government officials easily took shelter under the Act and withheld almost all kinds of information by classifying information into Top Secret, Secret, Confidential and Restricted. The need for a comprehensive law on the right to information which will make information available for the asking was felt through out the country.

Continuous complaints against the law led to the appointment of a committee of inquiry which condemned the main provisions of the 1923 Act and recommended a milder legislation. In 1977 a Bill to amend the Official Secrets Act was introduced but in many respects it was no improvements over the previous one. In 1995 the Press Council of India headed by Justice P.B.Sawant drafted the Freedom of Information Bill which was comprehensive and powerful. This was followed by many States enacting laws on its lines including the States of Rajasthan, Madhya Pradesh, Maharastra , Goa, TamilNadu, Karnataka, and Delhi though none of them accepted the PCI's Bill in its entirety.

By 2003 the Government of India finally yielded to the pressures and passed the Freedom of Information Act 2003.But cleverly in another bid to delay a provision was added providing that it would not come into force until a notification issued by the Central Government bringing it into force. As expected no such notification was passed. After all these long journeys of denials The Right to Information Act 2005 has been passed to secure citizens access to information under the control of public authorities in order to promote transparency and accountability in the working of every public authority.

Right to Information Act 2005- Salient Features

The Right to Information Act 2005 received the assent of the President on 15th June 2005, and came into effect on 12th October 2005. It promises a new era where all citizens are ensured right to information.

1. Access to Information

It firmly affirms that furnishing information to citizens who need them is essential in a democracy. This is because an informed citizenry and transparency of information are vital to the functioning of democracy and also helps to contain corruption and to hold Governments and their instrumentalities accountable to the governed.

With the enactment of the Act the citizens can secure access to information under the control of public authorities. A public authority is clearly defined by the Act to mean any authority or body or institution of self government established or constituted by or under the Constitution, by any other law made by the Parliament, by any other law made by State legislature or by notification issued or order made by the appropriate Government. It also includes any body owned controlled or substantially financed; non-government organization substantially financed, directly or indirectly by funds provided by the Government. Here one can find that there is an omission as far as private institutions is considered. In the wake of globalization when state making its withdrawal from all the welfare sectors and the private institutions is stepping into the shoes of the public institutions why is there a reluctance to rope in the private institutions also into the ambit of the Act?

The Act also defines the term information and right to information. Information means any material in any form including records, documents, memos, e-mails, opinion, advices, press releases, circulars, orders, logbooks, contracts, reports, papers, samples, models, data materials held in any electronic form and information relating to any private body which can be accessed by a public authority under any other law for the time being in force. Where as right to information means the right to:

- inspection of works, documents, records;
- taking notes, extracts or certified copies of documents or records; and
- taking certified samples of materials; obtaining information in the form of diskettes, floppies, tapes, video cassettes or in any other electronic mode or through printouts where such information is stored in a computer or in any other device.

2. Obligation of Public Authorities

Once a Right is being assured in naturally imparts certain obligations on the public authorities. The Act has neatly chalked out the same. It asserts that within 120 days from the enactment of the Act every public authority shall publish the particulars of its organization, functions and duties , the powers and duties of its officers and employees, the procedure followed in the decision making process, the rules regulations instructions, manuals, and records held by it or under its control or used by its employees, a statement of the categories of documents that are held by it or under its control, a directory of its officers and employees, the monthly remuneration received, the budget allocated to each of its agency, the manner execution of subsidy programmes, particulars of recipients of concessions, permits or authorizations, details in respect of the information available to or held by it, the names, designations and other particulars of the public information officers, etc.

Every public authority shall also maintain all its records duly catalogued and indexed in a manner that facilitates right to information.

3. Exemption from disclosure of information

This Act also excludes certain information from the purview of disclosure. For example information that pertains to those affecting the sovereignty and integrity of India, security, strategic or economic interests of the State; information expressly forbidden to be published by any court; information , the disclosure that would cause a breach of privilege of parliament or the State legislature; commercial confidence, trade secrets or intellectual property the disclosure of which would harm the competitive position of a third party; information available to a person in his fiduciary relationship; information received in confidence from foreign Government; , cabinet papers including deliberations of Council of Ministers ; information that would impede the process of investigation, personal information and the like.

4. Request for Obtaining Information

A person who desires to obtain any information shall make a request in writing or through electronic means in English or Hindi or in the official language of the area. The application must accompany with the prescribed fees. Where a request has been rejected the Central public information officer or state public information officer as the case may be shall communicate to the person making the request the reasons for such rejection, the period within which an appeal against such rejection may be referred and the particulars of the appellate authority.

5. Time limit for providing information

The information requested must be expeditiously provided and the maximum time that a concerned authority can take is 30 days.

6. Third party information

The Act also provides provisions to obtain information concerning a third party. The only limitation is that where a central public information officer or a state public information officer intends to disclose any information which relates to or has been supplied by a third party and has been treated as confidential by that third party, the Central Public Information Officer or the State Public information Officer shall within five days form the receipt of request give a written notice to such third party and of the fact that the concerned authority intends to disclose the information or record, and invite the third party to make a submission in writing or orally regarding whether the information should be disclosed and such submission of the third party shall be kept in view while taking a decision about disclosure of information.

7. Purposeful non disclosure of information.

If the request for information is malafidely denied or knowingly incorrect incomplete or misleading or destroyed information a penalty of two hundred and fifty rupees each day can be imposed on the concerned authority till application is received or information is furnished. However the total amount of such penalty shall not exceed twenty five thousand rupees.

8. Regulatory Bodies

The Act has also provided an elaborate set of regulatory bodies like the Central Information Commission and State Information commission. The Central information Commission shall consist of the Central Information Commissioner and such number of Central Information Commissioners as may be deemed necessary, The State Information Commission shall consist of the Sate Chief Information Commissioner and such number of State Information commissioners as may be deemed necessary.

Conclusion

There is little doubt that the RTI Act 2005 is one of the most important and revolutionary pieces of legislation enacted in independent India. Some would regard it as the most important since no other law has the potential to change the work culture of practically the entire Indian society; its impact is also the most widespread as it places an instrument in the hands of every citizen of the country irrespective of any category or classification. However there are certain apprehensions that have to be spelt out.

- Many persons view right to information and the information commissions as agencies for redressed of their grievances which they are not. The regulatory bodies has no power to intervene either in a dispute or order an erring official to attend to matters he is supposed to unless it involves providing access to the information sought for by the complainant.

- There may be persons who may ask for information only for the hack of it. They could at times prove to be of great nuisance.
- The time taken for providing information is often taken as 30 days and efforts are not made to provide information within it.

What is important is that for the first time in history an instrument of great power has been placed in the hands of ordinary citizen. He can now question beaurocratic and political masters which can go a long way in curbing corruption and making the entire administration more responsible transparent and responsive to public needs. The government of the day has to see that the RTI Act is not weakened in any manner. If there are loopholes in any manner that must be attended to and rectified. Earlier the talk of amendments such as closing of file notings or not revealing names of officials has finally died down. Our RTI act is one of the powerful acts and should remain as such.

REFERENCES

1. Aruna Roy: This Reputed Social Activist had Quit Civil Services to take up Social Work Initially with the Social Work and Research Centre (SWRC) in Tilona, Rajasthan.
2. Report of the Working Group on Right to Information and Promotion of Open and Transparent Government, Govt. of India.

29

Human Rights Education As Human Rights

Santhosh Areekuzhiyil

Introduction

Human rights refer to the concept of human beings as having universal rights, or status, regardless of legal jurisdiction or other localizing factors, such as ethnicity and nationality. As is evident in the United Nations Universal Declaration of Human Rights, human rights, at least in the post-war period, are conceptualized as based on inherent human dignity, retaining their universal and inalienable character. Human rights are intented to empower the people. The existance of human rights as it is does not result in achievement of its purposes. There must be conscientiousness among the people for which human right education is very essential. There lies the significance of human rights education.

What is Human Rights Education?

Human rights education is all learning that develops the knowledge, skills, and values of human rights. The United Nations Decade for Human Rights Education (1995-2004) has defined Human Rights Education as "training, dissemination, and information efforts aimed at the building of a universal culture of human rights through the imparting of knowledge and skills and the molding of attitudes which are directed to:

(a) The strengthening of respect for human rights and fundamental freedoms;

(b) The full development of the human personality and the sense of its dignity;

(c) The promotion of understanding, respect, gender equality, and friendship among all nations, indigenous peoples and racial, national, ethnic, religious and linguistic groups;

(d) The enabling of all persons to participate effectively in a free society;

(e) The furtherance of the activities of the United Nations for the Maintenance of Peace." (Adapted from the Plan of Action of the United Nations Decade for Human Rights Education [(1995-2004), paragraph 2].

Human rights education cannot be reduced to the simple introduction of human rights content in already overburdened curricula. It brings about a profound reform of education, which touches upon curriculum in-service and pre-service training, textbooks, methodology, classroom management, and the organisation of the education system at all levels. Human rights education implies the learning and practice of human rights. A holistic approach to human rights education means that human rights are implemented at all levels of the education system, and that they are taught through both content transmission and experiences.

Therefore, human rights education should not only be theoretical but should also provide opportunities for young people to develop and practice the skills to respect human rights and citizenship through "school life", i.e. all aspects of school as a living, social environment with its collective rules, interpersonal conflicts, time and opportunities for co-operation, and through opportunities for spontaneous initiatives by the pupils outside the actual teaching activities.

Human Rights Education As a Human Right

Education in human rights is itself a fundamental human right and also a responsibility. The Preamble to the Universal

Declaration of Human Rights (UDHR) exhorts "every individual and every organ of society" to "strive by teaching and education to promote respect for these rights and freedoms." The International Covenant on Civil and Political Rights (ICCPR) declares that a government "may not stand in the way of people learning about (their rights)."

Although news reports refer to human rights every day, "human rights literacy" is not widespread in our country. Students of law and international relations or political science may study human rights in a university setting, but most people receive no education, formally or informally, about human rights. Even human rights activists usually acquire their knowledge and skills by self-teaching and direct experience.

Rights, Responsibilities and Action

Integral to learning about one's human rights is learning about the responsibilities that accompany all rights. Just as human rights belong to both individuals and society as a whole, the responsibility to respect, defend, and promote human rights is both individual and collective. The Preamble of the UDHR, for example, calls not only on governments to promote human rights, but also on "every individual and every organ of society." Human rights education provides the knowledge and awareness needed to meet this responsibility.

The responsibilities of all citizens in a democratic society are inseparable from the responsibility to promote human rights. To flourish, both democracy and human rights require people's active participation. Human rights education includes learning the skills of advocacy – to speak and act every day in the name of human rights.

Human rights education also provides a basis for conflict resolution and the promotion of social order. Rights themselves often clash, such as when one person's commitment to public safety conflicts with another's freedom of expression. As a value system based on respect and the equality and dignity of all people, human rights can create a framework for analyzing and resolving such differences. Human rights education also teaches the skills of negotiation, mediation, and consensus building.

People who do not know their rights are more vulnerable to having them abused and often lack the language and conceptual framework to effectively advocate for them. Growing consensus around the world recognizes education for and about human rights as essential. It can contribute to the building of free, just, and peaceful societies. Human rights education is also increasingly recognized as an effective strategy to prevent human rights abuses.

The Goals of Human Rights Education

Human rights education teaches both about human rights and for human rights. Its goal is to help people understand human rights, value human rights, and take responsibility for respecting, defending, and promoting human rights. An important outcome of human rights education is empowerment, a process through which people and communities increase their control of their own lives and the decisions that affect them. The ultimate goal of human rights education is people working together to bring about human rights, justice, and dignity for all.

Education about human rights provides people with information about human rights. It includes learning about the inherent dignity of all people and their right to be treated with respect, about human rights principles, such as the universality, indivisibility, and interdependence of human rights, about how human rights promote participation in decision making and the peaceful resolution of conflicts, about the history and continuing development of human rights, about international law, like the Universal Declaration of Human Rights or the Convention on the Rights of the Child, about regional, national, state, and local law that reinforces international human rights law, about using human rights law to protect human rights and to call violators to account for their actions, about human rights violations such as torture, genocide, or violence against women and the social, economic, political, ethnic, and gender forces which cause them and about the persons and agencies that are responsible for promoting, protecting, and respecting human rights.

Education for human rights helps people feel the importance of human rights, internalize human rights values, and integrate them into the way they live. These human rights values and attitudes include "strengthening respect for human rights and fundamental freedoms" (UDHR Article 30.2), nurturing respect for others, self-esteem, and hope, understanding the nature of human dignity and respecting the dignity of others, empathizing with those whose rights are violated and feeling a sense of solidarity with them, recognizing that the enjoyment of human rights by all citizens is a precondition to a just and humane society, perceiving the human rights dimension of civil, social, political, economic, and cultural issues and conflicts both in the US and other countries and valuing non-violence and believing that cooperation is better than conflict.

Education for human rights also gives people a sense of responsibility for respecting and defending human rights and empowers them through skills to take appropriate action. These skills for action include recognizing that human rights may be promoted and defended on an individual, collective, and institutional level, developing critical understanding of life situations, analyzing situations in moral terms, realizing that unjust situations can be improved, recognizing a personal and social stake in the defense of human rights, analyzing factors that cause human rights violations, knowing about and being able to use global, regional, national, and local human rights instruments and mechanisms for the protection of human rights, strategizing appropriate responses to injustice and acting to promote and defend human rights.

Who Needs Human Rights Education?

Human rights should be part of everyone's education. However, certain groups have a particular need for human rights education: some because they are especially vulnerable to human rights abuses, others because they hold official positions and upholding human rights is their responsibility, still others because of their ability to influence and educate. Among these groups are the following:

Administrators of Justice

- law enforcement personnel, including police and security forces

- prison officials
- lawyers, judges, and prosecutors

Other Government and Legislative Officials

- members of the legislature
- public officials, elected and appointed
- members of the military

Other Professionals

- educators
- social workers
- health professionals
- journalists and media representatives

Organizations, Associations, and Groups

- women's organizations
- community activists and civic leaders
- minority groups
- members of the business community
- trade unionists
- indigenous peoples
- religious leaders and others with a special interest in social justice issues
- children and youth
- students at all levels of education
- refugees and displaced persons
- people of all sexual orientations
- poor people, whether in cities or rural areas
- people with disabilities
- migrant workers

Human rights is not a subject that can be studied at a distance. Students should not just learn about the Universal Declaration, about racial injustice, or about homelessness without also being challenged to think about what it all means for them personally. As human rights educators, we must ask our students and ourselves, "How does this all relate to the way we live our lives?" The answers to this question will tell us much about how effectively we have taught our students.

Why Human Rights Education?

(a) *Human rights education* declares a commitment to those human rights expressed in the Universal Declaration of Human Rights of 1948, the UN Covenants, and the United States Bill of Rights. It asserts the responsibility to respect, protect, and promote the rights of all people.

(b) *Human rights education* promotes democratic principles. It examines human rights issues without bias and from diverse perspectives through a variety of educational practices.

(c) *Human rights education* helps to develop the communication skills and informed critical thinking essential to a democracy. It provides multicultural and historical perspectives on the universal struggle for justice and dignity.

(d) *Human rights education* engages the heart as well as the mind. It challenges students to ask what human rights mean to them personally and encourages them to translate caring into informed, nonviolent action.

(e) *Human rights education* affirms the interdependence of the human family. It promotes understanding of the complex global forces that create abuses, as well as the ways in which abuses can be abolished and avoided.

Conclusion

Knowing about human rights makes people better able to participate in the social and political life of their communities. However, it is important to distinguish between political and analytical skills and party politics and political ideology. Educators have a great responsibility not to become propagandists or to push students towards a specific political position or party. Human rights education must be exploratory, open-ended, and problem solving. It should also call on the learner to identify and strive to eliminate injustice.

Human rights education should not focus only on rights abuses, which can be disturbing and dismaying to people of all ages. While human rights education may include teaching about violations, it also provides a value system that condemns those actions and upholds human dignity. Human rights education also offers people the skills to take action to prevent such abuse, as well as to advocate for the realization of human rights.

Indeed, educators need to shield children and some adults, such as former victims of abuse, from the brutality of human rights violations. However, everyone can be inspired by the vision of a world built upon principles of human dignity, respect, and justice where such abuses do not occur.

Human rights should be part of all these educational movements!

REFERENCES

1. Donnelly, Jack. (2003): *Universal Human Rights in Theory & Practice*. 2nd ed. Ithaca & London: Cornell University Press.
2. Forsythe, David P. (2000): *Human Rights in International Relations*. Cambridge: Cambridge University Press.
3. Ignatieff, Michael, (2005): *Human Rights as Politics and Idolatry*. Princeton & Oxford: Princeton University Press.
4. Landman, Todd (2006): *Studying Human Rights*, Oxford and London: Routledge
5. Weston, Burns H.(2006): *Human Rights* in Encyclopedia Britannica Online, p. 2, Retrieved May 18.

30

Meaningful Inculcation of Human Rights Education Through Classroom System

T. Ravichandran

Introduction

Education is the most powerful instrument that can bring about and inculcate valuable changes and perception in human right and its meaning to the younger generation. The basic rights and freedoms, to which all humans are entitled, often held to include the right to life and liberty, freedom of thought and expression, and equality before the law.

Human Rights Education

Human rights education is not only education about, but also for human rights. Education is a human right with immense power to transform. On its foundation, rest the corner stones of freedom, democracy and sustainable human development.

Human rights education is all learning that develops the knowledge, skills and values of human rights. Human rights education affirms the interdependence of the human family in the universe, irrespective of color and race, creed and sex. It promotes understanding of the complex global forces that create abuses, as well as the ways in which abuses can be abolished and avoided.

The UN Decade for Human Rights Education (1995-2004) has defined HRE as training, dissemination and information efforts aimed at the building of a universal culture of human rights through the imparting of knowledge and skills and the molding of attitudes which are directed to the strengthening of respect for human rights and fundamental freedoms, the full development of the human personality and the sense of its dignity, the promotion of understanding, respect, gender equality and friendship among all nations' indigenous peoples, and social, national, ethnic, religious and linguistic group and the enabling of all persons to participate effectively in a free society.

Human Rights Education (HRE) helps prevent violations, strengthens actions and campaigns, creates a space for dialogue and change, and encourages respect and tolerance, integrating the principles of human rights into everyday life. The Universal Declaration of Human Rights embodies a set of guarantees enabling one not just to live but to live with dignity. It aims at to develop fully and use one's human qualities, intelligence, talents, and conscience; and to satisfy one's physical, mental, social, and spiritual needs.

The Goals of HRE in the School System

Its goal is to help people understand human rights, value human rights and take responsibility for respecting, defending and promoting human rights. The ultimate goal of human rights education is people working together to bring about human rights, justice and dignity for all. Human rights education teaches both about human rights and for human rights. Human rights education is about acquiring not only knowledge but also skills and the ability to apply them; it is about developing values, attitudes and behaviour that uphold human rights but also about taking action to defend and promote them. It involves learning about human rights through the practice of human rights".

To achieve a meaningful effect the educational program needs to be sustained over a period, involve direct and constant interaction between the trainers and the trainee, and include practical, hands on learning. HRE teaches both about human rights and for human rights. It translates and sandwiches the need, its importance and use of human rights in associated manner. Its goal is to help people understand human rights, value human rights and take responsibility for respecting, defending and promoting human rights.

Human rights education is learning and participatory process by which we understand together our common responsibility to make human rights a reality in our lives and in our communities. Its fundamental role is to empower individuals to defend their own rights and those of others. It is education for action, not only about human rights but also for human rights.

Dimensions of Human Rights Education

Human rights education is multi-dimensional. It aims at strengthening respect for the human personality. That is, fully developing the human personality and its dignity. It intends to promote understanding, tolerance, gender equality, and friendship among all nations, indigenous people and racial, national, ethnic, religious, and linguistic groups. It plans to enable all persons to participate effectively in a free society; and furthering the activities of the United Nations to maintain peace (Guidelines for national plans of action for human rights education-UN-A/52/469/ Add.l.)

Principles of HRE

As HRE is a global concept to meet the demands of the society as a whole, all dimensions and every one should be included. Following are the main principles underlying HRE.

1. HRE must involve every one: It is a responsibility for every one-government, industry, the media, educational institutions, and community, right down to the level of the individual.

2. HRE must be life long: Information about human rights problems is forever improving, as we learn from our experiences and mistakes. As we develop and apply better technologies, the ability of society and individuals to respond effectively also improves.

3. HRE must be holistic and about connections: In order to address global changes in human relations through technologies, we need people who think broadly and who understand systems, connections, patterns, and causes and improvement and betterment of universal human beings.

4. HRE must be practical: One of the most fundamental defining characteristics of effective HRE is that it must lead to actions that result in better human potential outcomes.

5. HRE must be in harmony with social and economic goals: Effective HRE must also encourage the pursuit of environmental goals in harmony with other powerful and legitimate social and economic goals.

Need for Human Rights Education

Teaching pupil how to respect and protect rights is the need of human rights education. The important needs of HRE may be listed as follows:

- *Awareness rising:* It is the HRE which may raise awareness about the human rights, protect from any sort of discrimination and provide democratic structure, values as well as individual freedom.

- *Feeling of oneness:* HRE contributes towards the development of global wide perspectives, insights into the idea of international society and community.

- *Creating respect among human:* It ensures essential respect for human rights in a democratic and multi-cultural society where tolerance and patience inevitable for all.

- *Protection of basic rights:* HRE protects from infringement of rights of racial, ethnic and religious groups in any country or area through inculcation of global awareness and mutual understanding among the citizen.

- *Remove the fear:* It is possible to remove the fear of war in future through eradication of human rights abuses, social justice, human selfishness and self-orientedness.

The Components of HRE

The evolution of HRE has required closer and renewed investigation into learning process. It has become customary to define the components of learning relevant to struggle for existence and sustainability of human population. Awareness rising is not just a matter of shaping attitudes; it must also be about the development of knowledge. Without appropriate and helpful underlying values and attitudes, HRE is bound for failure. These values include respect for and appreciation of the interdependence of all life forms, appreciation of the dependence of human life on the finite resources of the earth and appreciation of the role of human ingenuity and creativity in ensuring survival. It has been noted that the types of knowledge needed to participate effectively in HRE are wide ranging and not confined to any particular discipline. HRE is not a passive process. In response to the new levels of awareness, knowledge and skill, and based on evolving values and attitudes. It is about changing behavior, whether one's own or as part of larger community changes.

Certain Practical Activities of HRE

Human rights are both inspirational and practical. Human rights principles hold up the vision of a free, just and peaceful world and set minimum standards for how individuals and institutions make aware of importance of human rights.

- *(i)* *Blood donation camp:* The school authorities and teachers should arrange blood donation camps and motivate the students to donate blood in order to save a prestigious life of another person. Thus, the students are being aware of human rights.
- *(ii)* *Celebration of human rights day:* In every school, December 10 need to be celebrated as human rights day with special talks, seminars and related activities.
- *(iii)* *Arrangements of periodical hospital visit:* The students are adviced to visit the nearby hospitals in order to see the affected individuals, analyze their home condition, and find the nature of suffering.

(iv) *Conducting quiz programs* in connection with human rights to inculcate knowledge about human rights and its importance.

(v) *Establishment of donation stations inside the school:* All the students are asking to donate some amount, which they are spending unwantedly, to the poor funds.

(vi) *Making awareness about environmental pollution:* It is the right of every citizen to respiring pure air drinks good water and dwell in decent land. However, this is not possible because of over exploitation of the nature by the dominant group.

(vii) *Try to eat vegetarian food as possible:* All the students are advice to take vegetarian food to eat to protect wild life and to save endangered species.

(viii) *Daily Morning Prayer in the school:* The teachers are asking the students to pray for the world, neighbors, diseased person and world peace.

(ix) *Establishment of human rights movement in school:* in every school, a human right movement is organizing in the form of helping poor, making possible campaign regarding voting, making use of government resource etc.

Factors that will Promote HRE in School System

In schools, human rights education should take account of the developmental stage of children and their social and cultural contexts, in order to make human rights principles meaningful to them. Teachers, administrators, outside resource persons and parents should be involved in this process as well as the students themselves. The "human rights climate" that exists in the classroom and the school is also important: it should be based on reciprocal respect between all parties involved. The incorporation of human rights education in national educational legislation will be of great use. Appropriate provision for human rights issues in curricula and textbooks should be provided. Pre-service and in-service training for teachers on human rights and human rights education methodologies should be made compulsory. The organization of extracurricular activities, both at the school level and reaching out to the family and the community will be found advantageous. The development of educational materials, the establishment of support networks of teachers and other professionals from human rights groups, teachers' unions, non-governmental organizations or professional associations are also essential.

Human Rights Education and Curriculum

Highlighting the need to strengthen national identity, the National Curriculum Framework for School Education (NCERT 2000) reaffirms the 10 core components identified in the National Policy on Education (1986). They are:

(i) the history of India's freedom movement;

(ii) Constitutional obligations;

(iii) the content essential to nurture national identity;

(iv) India's common cultural heritage;

(v) egalitarianism;

(vi) democracy and secularism;

(vii) equality of the sexes;

(viii) protection of the environment;

(ix) removal or social barriers;

(x) Observance or small-f1mily norms.

Human Rights Education and the Elementary-Level Curriculum

The major subject areas relevant to human rights at the lower-primary stage are social studies, environmental studies, and languages. Human rights issues are integrated into environmental studies, starting with the child's immediate environment and gradually taking the child to the study of the district, state, country, and the world. Narratives and biographies of men and women from the history of India and of the world, India's freedom struggle, and certain aspects of the Indian Constitution should be included in this course. The language curriculum should focus on the development of compassion, tolerance, and sympathy, through stories and poems. Environmental studies dealing with family, neighborhood, relations, food, clothing, shelter, religious festivals, and national heroes expand the knowledge of and respect for diversity and human equality. The human right, dimension lies in providing a critical understanding of Indian society through the ages, with focus on the position of women and the inequalities created by the caste system. Children should be made aware of legislative reforms and the role of international organizations in uplifting women and children. The course in geography helps children develop an appreciation for different ways of living, interdependence, and sharing of common values by diverse cultures.

Civics helps promote values of democracy, secularism, socialism, and national integration. It also includes the study of issues relating the environment, arms race, and human rights. Children develop a perspective of these problems in an international context. It is possible to introduce the student to a more comprehensive view of the concept of human rights and the interconnection between the ideals of secularism and democracy.

Human Rights Education and the Secondary Curriculum

Secondary schools offer a much wider and varied range of opportunities to teach human rights and to practice and observe rights and duties. A literature course may offer the opportunity to study the rights of children and young people. Literature and language classes can be used to promote cultural exchanges with schools in other countries as well as to promote social relations, peace, freedom, and justice. At this stage, "the global perspective" and" major concerns" are integrated into the social sciences. Human rights can be taught in the context and understanding of family, school, community, country, and State. It should also deal with the forms of government; democratic, dictatorship and parliamentary. There should be mention of the United Nations, the world today-East-West problems, armaments, events, and personalities in International affairs; the religion and philosophy of life, analysis of different religions, traditional beliefs, and practices.

Methodology, Approaches, and Strategies of HRE

Human rights education can be incorporated into the school curriculum in several Ways:

- *The formal curriculum:* Schools may choose to examine their present curriculums and identify areas where themes and elements of human rights education already exist. Human rights education is considered the most important part of the core curriculum of good general education.
- *The informal curriculum:* Human rights education can also be promoted through the extracurricular and co-curricular activities of the school.
- *The hidden curriculum:* Human right education should also address the far-reaching hidden curriculum of the school to create a school atmosphere that truly reflects respect for human rights. Values, attitudes, knowledge and patterns of behavior should be integrated into the student's personal experiences in order to help them to view reality critically.

Conclusion

In the globalization scenario, much importance is given to non-material resources and welfare of individual potential. Therefore, it is the duty of education system as a whole to think of positive approach in human rights awareness and its importance to human being. In a complex country such as India, violations of human rights at all levels necessitate human rights education at all school levels in general and teacher education in particular. Hence, human rights education should find its rightful place in the school curriculum, teacher-training courses (pre- and in-service), textbooks, supplementary reading materials, educational policies, and school administration. Human rights education must exert its influence from early childhood education onward and through a broad range of disciplines to build a human rights culture.

REFERENCES

1. Bhaskara Rao D., (2005): Human Rights Education, Journal of Edutracks , Neel Kamal Publications Pvt Ltd PP 14-18, Vol. 5 No. 2.

2. Jagannath M., (2005): Teaching of Human Rights , New Trend and Innovations , Deep and Deep Publications Pvt. Ltd , New Delhi.

3. Naseema.C, (2002): Human Rights Education, Kanishka Publishers, New Delhi.

4. Pathak. C.K., (2004): Human Rights Education, Rajat Publications, New Delhi.

5. Qureshi M., (2004): Education and Human Rights , Anmol Publications Pvt. Ltd., New Delhi.

6. Rameshwari D., (2004): Human Rights in Modern World, Mahamaya Publishing House, New Delhi.

7. Vanaja .M., (2003): Context and Constructs of Human Rights Education, Edutracks, Neel Kamal Publications Pvt Ltd. Vol. 3 No. 4. pp. 9-15.

31

Human Rights in Education

Aneeshya. S.S.

Introduction

"O my Lord of Light and Love, fill my heart with light and love
O my Lord of Bliss and Joy, fill my heart with bliss and joy
O my Lord of Truth and Peace, fill my heart with truth and peace
O my Lord of Transcendental Virtues, fill my heart with those virtues".

–R.P. Dhokalia

Every women, men, youth and child has the human right to education, training and information, and to other fundamental human rights dependent on realization of the right to education. The right of all persons to education is explicitly set out in the Universal Declaration of Human Rights; the Convention on the Rights of the Child and other widely adhered to international human rights and Declarations. Universal Declaration of Human Rights – Article-26 states that "Everyone has the right to education... Education shall be directed to the full development of human personality and to his strengthening of respect for human rights and fundamental freedoms. it shall promote understanding, tolerance and friendship among all nations, racial or religious groups, and shall further the activities of the United Nations for the maintenance of peace." Human rights education is an integral part of the right to education and has gained of late greater recognition as a human right in self. The knowledge of the rights and freedoms, of oneself as much as of the others, is considered as a fundamental tool to guarantee the respect of all rights for each and every person.

Concept and Aim of Human Rights in Education

The concept underpinning human rights education is that education should not only aim at forming trained, professional workers, but also at contributing to the development of individuals who possess the skills to interact in a society. Human right education aims at providing pupils and students with the abilities to accompany and produce societal changes. Education is seen as a way to empower people, improve their quality of life and increase their capacity to participate in the decision making processes leading to social, cultural and economic policies.

Purpose of Human Rights in Education

Three particular components of many a school curriculum contain Human Rights education as an explicit or implicit goal. These are global education, moral education, and social and civic education.

Global Education

Global education focuses broadly on "...people as individuals and as a society and how they relate to the world's physical conditions, human institutions, social and economic systems, and interconnecting world problems and developments" (US Commission of Education, 1979). It is to "...contribute to the development of mutual respect for the human dignity of all peoples, cultures, and civilizations, at home and abroad" (US Commission of education, 1979). Global education thus incorporates multicultural education and peace education. Education for global perspectives also addresses such transactional concerns as the environment and energy resources and the examination of related critical ecological problems which demonstrate the interdependence of the world's people (US Commission of Education, 1979).

The issue of Human Rights pertains to global education in more than one respect.

The Universal Declaration of Human Rights begins. "All human beings are born free and equal in dignity and rights" (Universal Declaration, Art 1). The Declaration in subsequent articles mentions, among others, legal rights, rights of persons including; freedom of movement (Art,. 13), right to employment (Art. 23), to a family (Art,. 16, #1), to practice religious beliefs (Art. 18) and to adequate health (Art. 25) . These examples are congruent with the purpose of global education which is intended to create sensitivity to human concerns around the globe.

Moral Education

Human Rights education may also be related to moral education. The latter is formalized in Koranic schools in many countries as well as in the formal school curriculum of different nations in the subject, religion. In England, for example, students spend time comparing and contrasting the major religious faiths in the worlds represented among the nation's multiracial society (Hampshire Education Authority, 1978). In West Germany where religion is also a school subject a similar exploration is conducted in classrooms (Etzold, 1984) *The Religious and Moral Education Syllabus* for Zimbabwe's Junior Certificate speaks of students learning to accept responsibility and to help others in the community (Zimbabwe, Ministry of Education and Culture, 1984b). In other words, moral education as well as religious education introduces the learner to the moral principles, or ideals and related formalized codes of conduct which have been incorporated into tribal and societal law. Human Rights agreements belong to these codes.

Social and Civil Education

Human Rights education can be effectively introduced as preparation for citizenship and social responsibility. In the British Hansard Society's instructional guide on "Political Dilemmas". Students are asked to *consider power and authority* as used by the State and also the use of violence as compared with peaceful means of influencing governments or persons (Stradling, 1980). In the United States the *US Constitution*, including the *Bill of Rights* or first ten amendments, is studied both in the required US

History Class (grade II) and American Government Class (grade 12). Holocaust studies have been included in World History and US History Courses.

Role of Human Rights Education

One body that has engaged in curriculum development entered on Human Rights education is the Council of Europe. Founded in 1949, the Council is a direct outgrowth of the lessons drawn by Westerm Europe from the inter-war years and World War II itself. The 21 member nations, that is the democratic countries of Western and Southern Europe, together have stressed the importance of Human Rights beginning wit their *Convention for the Protection of Human Rights and Fundamental Freedoms* (Council of Europe, 1953). Through the Council of Europe's Council for Cultural Cooperation (CDCC), education about Human Rights has developed into a major project in order to give young people knowledge and understanding of the concepts (of democracy and freedom), but – more importantly – also some real experience of them so as to create a deeper personal appreciation of their importance" (Council of Europe, 1984).

In the course of the Council of Europe's meetings on human rights education, primary and secondary teachers emphasized this very point. They agreed that the teaching about Human Rights is important but to be meaningful it must be followed accompanied in secondary schools" by greater democratization of school life and of relationships between pupils an d the administration and teachers(Council of Europe 1981). Schools their personalities and to tolerate other people's ideas and conception, that is, to practice Human Rights" (Council of Europe, 1981). The human right to education entitles every woman, man, youth and child to: The human right to free and compulsory elementary education and to readily available forms of secondary and higher education.

National Center for Human Rights Education (NCHRE)

National Center for Human Rights Education (NCHRE) provides the following education services to promote human rights in education.

- Assists communities in taking action on human rights concerns,
- Trains people, who in turn train others in human rights knowledge.
- Builds collaborative relationship across issues of race, gender, ability, class and sexual orientation.
- Fights directly against the spread of hate groups and bigotry.
- Develops new educational strategies for diverse culture groups.
- Functions as a clearing house for resource information on human rights education.

Vision and Mission of Human Rights and Education Network

- To promote the universal understanding, tolerance, interactive co-operation and equality.
- To sensitize individual organizations groups and communities on human rights and intercultural relationships.
- To promote the intercultural understanding for all communities.
- To promote the mutual congruity.
- To act as a platform for exchanging ideas and experiences on human rights, civil society and intercultural education.
- To mediate and to provide services.

Governments' Obligations and Commitments for Ensuring the Human Rights Education

"Everyone has the right to education. Education shall be free, at least in the elementary and fundamental stages. Elementary education shall be compulsory. Technical and professional education shall be made generally available and higher education shall be equally accessible to all on the basis of merit ... Education shall be directed to the full development of the human personality and to the strengthening of respect for human rights and fundamental freedoms. It shall promote understanding tolerance and friendship among...racial or religious groups..." – (Universal Declaration of Human Rights, Article 26).

"The States Parties ... recognize the right of everyone to education...Education shall enable all persons to participate effectively in a free society, promote understanding, tolerance and friendship among...racial, ethnic or religious groups...Primary education shall be compulsory and available free to all... Secondary education ... including technical and vocational secondary education shall be made generally available and accessible to all...Higher education shall be made equally accessible to all..." – (International Covenant on Economic, Social and Cultural Rights, Article 13).

"State Parties undertake to prohibit and to eliminate racial discrimination... and to guarantee the right of everyone, without distinction as to race, color, or national or ethnic origin, to equality before the law... in the enjoyment of ... the right to education and training..." –(Convention on the Elimination of All Forms of Racial Discrimination, Article 5).

"States parties recognize the right of the child to education, and shall make primary education compulsory and available free to all; ...make [secondary education] available and accessible to every child..' make higher education accessible to all.... Make educational and vocational information and guidance available and accessible to all ... children...; take measures to encourage regular attendance at schools and the reduction of drop-out rates...States Parties agree that the education of the child shall be directed to;.. the development of the child-personality, talents and mental and physical abilities to their fullest potential; the development of respect for human rights... - (Convention on the Rights of the Child, Articles 28 and 29).

"Education is a fundamental right for all people, women and men of all ages, throughout the world...Every person – child, youth and adult – shall be able to benefit from educational opportunities designed to meet their basic learning needs...To be able to survive, to develop their full capacities, to live and work in dignity... To improve the quality of their lives, to make informed decisions..."- (World Declaration on Education for All, Preamble and Article 1).

Human Rights Education in Schools, Colleges and Universities

Human Rights education in educational institutions can play a very important role in inculcating human rights and values in students. Towards this goal the following steps have been suggested.

(i) Generating awareness and reach through media advocacy to the deprived and special target group of children that a Right to Basic Minimum Education is their human right.

(ii) Introduction of human rights issues in the school curricular at primary as well as at secondary level and preparation of appropriate course material for this purpose in a way to make it part of the

(iii) Devising a plan of action for training the teachers on human rights/values in collaboration with State Education Departments/SCETs/NCTE.

(iv) Introducing courses on Human Rights at the under-graduate and Post-graduate level, including either a compulsory/special paper at under-graduate level.

(v) Introduction of short-term/long-term courses on human rights through the distance education programmes. IGNOU and other premier universities should be encouraged by UGC to take up these courses by liberal funding of these courses.

(vi) There is a dearth of books as well as research material on human rights. Universities should therefore, encourage research on human rights by liberally instituting scholarships and internships on issues pertaining to human rights.

(vii) To bridge the gap in the availability of research material on human rights, a National Resource Centre for documentation, training, research and education in human

rights is to be set up in one of the premier Universities/ research organization under Ministry of HRD.

(viii) Gyan Darshan and Gyan Vani the dedicated video/audio channels for education under Prasar Bharati could be put to effective use for spreading human rights education.

(ix) Colleges and universities should be encouraged to hold seminars/workshops/debates on issues of human rights. Associations and unions in the colleges/University could be given financial assistance for such activities. Project base learning should be encouraged. Assignments and field activities like data collection, event organization, camp activities, social service events during distress situation, etc., may be integrated into courses designing and performance evaluation.

(x) Being out a booklet containing the basic instruments of Human Rights for public distribution.

(xi) As the subject of human rights is a matter of changing attitude, the audio visual medium of imparting education has better impact than the class room type of learning. Accordingly, more stress need be on preparation of course material in multimedia forms – like videos, CDs and films in addition for mass propagation and mass education.

Role of UGC in Promoting Human Rights Education Through Universities and Colleges

In 1985, the UGC prepared a blueprint for promotion of Human Rights teaching and research at all levels of education. The blueprint contained proposals for restructuring of existing syllabi, and introduction of new courses and/or foundation courses in Human Rights. This was for students of all faculties at the under-graduate, graduate and post-graduate levels for both professionals and non-professional education.

During the year 1997-98, the Commission framed "UGC IX plan Approach for the promotion of Human Rights Education (HRE) in Universities and Colleges" with an objective to promote Human Rights and Duties Education through the Universities and Colleges and spreading awareness about the Human Rights and Duties Education amongst the teachers and students. For this purpose, the Commission has been providing financial assistanfe to Universities and Colleges for introduction of PG Degree, UG Degree, Diploma and Certificate Courses in Human, Rights and Duties Education. It is also providing financial assistance to Universities and Colleges for spreading awareness about the Human Rights and Duties Education amongst the teachers and students. For this purpose, the Commission had been providing financial assistance to Universities and Colleges for introduction of PG Degree, UG Degree, Diploma and Certificate Course at PG level in Human Rights and Duties Education. It is also providing financial assistance to Universities and Colleges for holding seminars symposia and workshops in Human Rights and Duties Education.

The following are the objectives and strategies of UGC for promoting Human Rights Education and Duties in Universities and Colleges:

- Mere Knowledge about human rights is not sufficient. An understanding as to how human rights can easily become vulnerable to abuse of various structures and processes of Power is crucial. It may be added that understanding of abuse and misuse of power alone serves no purpose unless people in general and professionals in particular are imparted skills for protection and enforcement of these rights.
- Human Rights Education does not merely mean imparting knowledge in the class-room, but it also has to cover all modalities (formal, non-formal and informal) which could sensitise a person, awaken his/her conscience and develop an attitude of mind imbibing respect for human rights of others.
- Human Rights Education cannot merely be an intellectual exercise alone. It requires building linkages between what happens in the society and what is transmitted in the classes to the students. It requires capturing actual experiences of violation of human rights and denial of human dignity. This kind of education needs field experience and action oriented ways of learning and teaching.

- Human Rights Education requires building strong linkages and networking between colleges/universities and various NGOs and other groups working in the field and community. Building these linkages would go a long way in giving. Human Rights Education a grass-root orientation. Collecting, collating and classifying the data and experiences that NGOs and groups working in the field have already acquired can be an important aspect of human rights education and may lead to create new knowledge and research.
- Human Rights Education must encompass in it a strong research component. Any teaching of or about human rights need to be backed up by strong multi-disciplinary research on various aspects of human rights and their complexities.
- Training and public information are the indispensable components of human rights education. As such for carrying out awareness and other programmes, audio-visual aids and distance mode of education need to be used amongst other tools and inputs,
- Extension work has long been recognized by the University Grants Commission (UGC) as an equally important for University and Collegiate Education, besides teaching and research. National Service Scheme (N.S.S.), Women Studies Research Centre, adult education and population education programmes, and continuing education are some area specific modalities. These along with field action, need to be utilized for extending the scope and access of human rights programmes to the grass-roots level.
- The extension programmes in the colleges need special attention and emphasis with a view to giving them Human Rights orientation.
- The legal aids programmes in the colleges could be more vigorously utilized by the law schools for the benefit of the needy to render legal advice and assistance for human rights enforcement.

- National Human Rights Commission is now a statutory institution with responsibility amongst others, "to spread human rights literacy and promise awareness of the safeguards "Co-ordination with and by the National Human Rights Commission for a more purposeful use of extension programmes of the universities and colleges is necessary. Modalities for the same need to be worked out through joint consultation between the University Grants Commission and the National Human Rights Commission.

- Three alternative approaches for promoting human rights education be pursued simultaneously, viz. (a) introducing separate courses on Human rights; (b) Human Rights issues to be incorporated in courses already being taught; (c) Reorientation of all courses so that the human rights component is not seen as an adjunct to the existing syllabi, instead the academic packages should be so offered as to have "people" as the central theme. The advantages of such a strategy are obvious. It is highly flexible and can accommodate the needs, pace of growth and extent of commitment to human rights education, of each institution.

- It is basic to the promotion of human rights education in universities and colleges that the students after training could expect decent employment. Presently, no such avenues exist apart from extremely limited slots available in teaching and research institutions and in the media.

- Perhaps the setting up of the proposed human rights courts in each district all over the country could open up avenues of self-employment for a substantial number of students. Inclusion of human rights as one of the subjects to national competitive examinations also observes consideration., Other avenues too are needed to be explored by all agencies and institutions interested in the promotion of human rights education, including the National Human Rights Commission and the University Grants Commission.

- There is a need to convince all Union and State Governments and departments especially those which provide service to the people like the railways, the post and telecommunications and electricity as well as all law courts and prisons and law enforcement agencies to appoint human rights experts as advisors and trainers.

The Content of Human Rights Teaching

Closely related to issues that result from different interpretations of Human Rights are questions about what constitutes the cognitive and affective content of Human Rights that prospective teachers should learn,. One approach, influenced by the lead taken by faculty of law throughout the world, emphasizes the legal basis of Human Rights. The documents, resolutions and the interpretations given to them in the context of the historical, philosophical, and legal traditions of different societies are emphasized.

The social science approach to Human Rights content draws relationships between rights statement and major contemporary problems and intellectual events. Teaching about Human Rights is closely associated with development, peace and disarmament education and specific topics of Human Rights violations, eg. Apartheid, racism, colonialism, terrorism, and poverty and starvation (UNESCO, 1978: UNESCO, 1982. UNESCO, 1983).

Emphasis in successful programmes is also given to affective content. Tolerance, mutual respect, commitment to the proposed new international economic order, special empathy with the most desperate victims of Human Rights violations, yearning for Human Rights objective, "human-centered concern" are but a few of the affective objectives that different projects recommend that students should learn (Churchill and Omari, 1981).

Methods of Human Rights Teaching

In addition to acquiring the skills to foster critical thinking, beginning teachers would need to learn numerous methods thought to be critical in Human Rights teaching, They should learn how to lead and participate in open discussion: involve students in the creation of curricula; establish classroom climates conducive to equal participated by all students, encourage expression of opinions about social and economic problems and government's actions to resolve them; emphasise student opportunities to exercise judgements and solve problems (Kidd. 1968; Leming, 1982. Torney-Purta, 1983).

Teachers would learn about the need for a staged introduction of Human Rights concepts from preschool through adulthood; and how at each stage to connect them with personal situations and experiences.

Things We can do to Promote Human Rights in Education

Get to know our human rights. Look up the Universal Declaration of Human Rights and other international human rights agreements at our local library, where we may be able to search the internet for the documents. Get involved and become a Human Rights Educator. Reach out and share our human rights learning with others working for economic, cultural, social, civil, and political human rights. Use the human rights framework and language to describe, defend, and define our social justice issues. Remember, we can all be ambassadors for each others issues! Launch a local Human rights Coalition to celebrate the Anniversary of the Universal Declaration of Human Rights on December 10 every year. Put human rights language to work for social justice. The issues affecting us and our community are human rights issues. Help hold us federal, state, and local governments accountable to human rights standards.

Be heard! Always put human rights on the agenda at conferences, in literature, and at meetings, Human rights is not a single issue, but al our issues combined. Find creative ways to communicate social justice issues in our community as human rights issues, such as media strategies, open hearings, telling the stories, etc. Focus on the ways the global human rights movement affects people in our community. Join efforts to have the United States ratify the International Covenant on Economic, Social, and Cultural Rights, the Convention on the Rights of the of the Child, and the Convention on the Elimination of Discrimination against women. Ensure that our organizing efforts and events are universally accessible, including disability access and culturally sensitive places to hold events. Contact the National Center for

Human Rights Education for information, materials, training, technical assistance, or support. Schedule a training or workshop for our community.

Implementation of Human Rights in Education

Human rights education cannot be reduced to the simple introduction of human rights content in already overburdened curricula. It brings about a profound reform of education, which touches upon curriculum in service and pre-service training, textbooks, methodology, classroom management, and the organization of the education system at all levels.

Human rights education implies the learning and practice of human rights. A holistic approach to human rights education means that human rights are implemented at all levels of the education system, and that they are through both content transmission and experiences.

A new vision of quality education is essential and current events around the world have demonstrated that quality is not only about literacy and numeracy. There is a growing consensus at all levels that quality education cannot be limited to increasing the material inputs into the school systems or enhancing school effectiveness, important as they are. Quality education has both to be based on a human rights approach, and to address new areas including but not limited to, cultural diversity, multilingualism in education, peace and non-violence, sustainable development, life skills.

A quality education based on the human rights approach means that the rights are implemented throughout the whole education system and in all learning environments. It means that the education system is oriented towards human values allowing the realization of peace, social cohesion and the respect for human dignity. This implies reforming national education system to include fundamental change of education structures, the management of the education system, the teaching/learning practices, the revision and adaptation of learning materials, the adequate preparation of educational personnel, etc. this was also reaffirmed by the CRC;' every child has the rights to receive an education of good quality which in turn requires focus on the quality of the learning environment, of teaching and learning process and materials and of learning outputs'.

National Education Reforms to Implement Human Rights in Education

- Improving the quality of the curriculum by integrating human values for the realization of peace, social cohesion and respect for human rights and human dignity.
- A more participatory process of curriculum development is essential.
- Changing traditional teaching methods in order to make them more participatory and democratic.
- Making teacher training consistent with the educational objectives.
- Democratizing the internal structure of the school and its management.
- The participation of children in school life, the creation of school communities and student councils, peer education and peer counseling.
- The involvement of children in school disciplinary proceedings should be promoted as part of the process of learning and experiencing the realization of rights.
- Increasing opportunities for parents and teachers to take decisions on school issues.
- Creating mechanisms to foster cooperation and mutual appreciation among all members of the school community and thus promote better relations between teachers and pupils.
- Ensuring constructive communication and appreciation of diversity.
- Providing the opportunity to practice through real life examples and activities.
- To link the school with local community and to promote extracurricular activities.

Conclusion

"The great aim of education is not knowledge but action".

Herbert Spencer

Human rights education should not only be theoretical but should also provide opportunities for young people to develop and practice the skills to respect human rights and citizenship through "school life", i.e. all aspects of schools as a living, social environment with its collective rules, interpersonal conflicts, time and opportunities for co-operation, and through opportunities for spontaneous initiatives by the pupils outside the actual teaching activities. Thus human rights in education provide the full development of the child's personality and the development of respect for human rights and fundamental freedoms.

REFERENCES

1. Goel, Aruna & Goel, S.L., (2005) – 'Human Values and Education', New Delhi: Deep & Deep Publications.
2. Symonides, Janusz (2005) – 'Human Rights, International Protection, Monitering, Enforcement', New Delhi: Rawat Publications.
3. Brownlie, IAN & Goodwin – Gill, (2002) – 'Basic Documents on Human Rights' , New York: Oxford University Press.
4. http: / /www.search.yahoo.com
5. http: / /www.search.google.com
6. http: / /www.humanrights.gov.au./info-for teachers/index.html
7. http: / /portal unesco.org/education/en.php-URLI id=1920 & URL ID=1920 & URL-DO=DO-TOPIC & URL-SECTION=201.HTML
8. http: / /www.hrea.org/education
9. http: / /www.nchre.org/education
10. Batra, B.B., (2004) – 'Encyclopaedia of Human Rights', New Delhi: Reference Press, Vol. IV.

32

Terrorism in Kashmir
A Human Rights Perspective

Rekha Nair R.

Terrorism and Violence

Terrorism is a reality in most of the world today. Although it is not new in history, in contradiction to older precedents, extra legal violence below the level of traditional warfare in the past three decades has marked a new phase posing new challenges to contemporary societies. Today we find that terrorism is also escalating into the spectrum of conflict, as slow intensity, low level warfare, as a form of strategic surrogate warfare. The small groups with the direct and indirect support of states are able to conduct political violence on regional, national and international levels even altering the balance of power and international order to a certain extent.

What distinguishes terrorism from other acts of violence is its fundamentally and inherently political nature. Looking at terrorism from another angle it may be said that it is concerned with the pursuit of power, the acquisition of power and the use of power to achieve political change.

Terrorist violence naturally creates revolution and anger; but law makers should not be carried away by feelings of revolution and anger and use them as a justification for dispensing with all safeguards in our criminal justice system. Terrorism and human rights cannot coexist. They are all mutually destructive of each other. Where there is terrorism, there are no human rights; there can be no respect for human dignity, life and democratic values. Terrorism not only affects human rights of many about also hinders the resolution and settlement of disputes and conflicts by civilized methods.

A major obstacle in the way of a global strategy to stem terrorist violence is summed up in the new familiar saying one man's terrorist is another man's freedom fighter. Violence is of two types – violence which is used to fight and perpetuate injustice, oppression and inequality; violence which is used to fight and defeat injustice oppression and inequality. Here it is of first one.

"Terrorism and Insurgency are specific violations of human rights". The notion of human rights is the most precious legacy of the classical and contemporary human thought to culture and civilization. Although Human Rights have been guaranteed as Fundamental rights under Indian constitution and various other laws, in practice it is not in that way. Human Right situation is and prevalent state of affairs can be termed as "the crisis in Human Rights." In India the institutions of a strong press and Judiciary with substantive power have not succeeded in extending effective protections to hundreds of citizens who have died by torture and ill-treatment at the hands of the police.

Human rights are a human creation they grow out of the feeling of injustice which human beings experience in their bodies and minds when their humanity is abused or denied. Human rights introduced the idea that justice in the natural order of the world, thereby giving human existence a higher sense and purpose. The first and foremost human rights is the right to existence or right to life.

According to traditional concept of international law, human rights are protected and violated by states; generally speaking, human rights involve obligations of states towards individuals. The whole movement for the protection of human rights arose as an attempt to redress the balance between the power of the state to impose duties on individuals and the powerlessness of the individuals to ensure correlative respect for their rights. While the international law of human rights is, indeed addressed to the behaviour of states and deals with acts or commissions of government officials or agents modern developments of international humanitarian law, recent authoritative pronouncements and a respectable body of theory tend to embrace elements leading to some modification of the traditional position that private individuals or groups are not capable of violating human rights. The issue of the responsibility of non state actors as perpetrators of human rights abuses has thus become important. In that context it is being pointed out that it was somewhat ironic to talk about the enjoyment of Human Rights in conditions of massive killings by terrorist groups.

At the same time it is said that it is the gross denial of human right that forces the sections of people to resort to terrorist activities because otherwise they are not heard. In other words terrorism is projected as a form of protest movement against gross handedness of the authority or rulers of the state. In that sense terrorists are considered to be committed to greater cause. They work for personal gain is benefit but for the interest of community. At times terrorism is applauded by sections of suffering people who feel that the adversaries have been punished by the terrorists. However, in most cases it has been observed that even these terrorist movements which start. With high ideals and commitment for supreme sacrifice, degenerate into purposeless killings and provide a rendezvous for meaningless unsocial activities and activists. Terrorists acts and methods do abuse the human rights of innocent people. At the same time they do provoke or give an exercise for serious violations of human rights and fundamental freedoms by the Governments which feel threatened by terrorism. The problem of is compounded as some states may react against real or perceived internal terrorism with counter terrorism campaigns, resulting in serious human rights violations.

Terrorist violence aims at the destruction of human rights, in order to create fear and provoke conditions that are proportions to the destruction of the prevailing social order. Killing innocent people, destroying properly and fostering an atmosphere of alarm and terror amount not merely to a violation of the rights of the victims but a solicitation of further serious of human rights; in fact, because of the terrorists despicable conduct and the threat posed to society, the authorities of the states which are responsible for bringing the terrorist violence to an end are entitled to respond with counter –terrorist measures and may not be constrained by the normal limits of official measures for the prevention of ordinary crimes. Thus there is a real danger that the state will one react to the threat of terrorism and slide towards repression and violation of the human rights not only of the terrorists but of the rest of the society whose rights and liberties might be diminished in the course of discovery, apprehending and convicting the terrorist.

The actual and potential effects, then of terrorism become obvious in the internal or domestic legal sphere. Nonetheless, terrorism is an international as well as a domestic phenomenon. In this age of increasing internationalization and interdependence, the national and international dimensions of terrorism are but two facets of the same dangerous social phenomenon which infringes upon the interest of all states, not only as an assault against there public order and institutions that protect the liberty and security of their citizens but, at the same time, as a serious danger to peaceful international relations and cooperation, which in our day is clearly understood as encompassing human rights and values, as well as the principles of equal rights and self determination of peoples.

Human Rights Violation in Kashmir

All values-based violences, which contravenes generally accepted norms of social order, human behaviour and right to life and equality of all men, are retrogressive. Terrorism is a negation of life, and violation of the norms of human behaviour recognized by all civilized people of the world.

Since 1947, Pakistan has been fomenting trouble in the state of Jammu and Kashmir. Having failed in her attempt to annex the state in the wars of 1948, 1965 and 1971, she started exporting terrorism from across the border through the ISI Agency, widely known as the ISI. Pakistan also started using the human rights card to denigrate and defile India. She tried to promote the theory of self determination for the people of the state conveniently forgetting that the people had exercised their franchise in the many dictions held for the state Assembly and the union parliament.

Political terrorism even if it is for religious crusade is as heinous as crime as any other crime against humanity. All political terrorism is organised crime. Terrorist violence cannot be justified on the ground of its political and ideological motivations of value-basis. There is a growing corpus of Municipal as well as International Law and precedent to deal politically motivated terrorism. The civil jurisprudence and international law generally identify political terrorism as a crime, more serious traditional, civil and international crime Murder of innocent people, torture deaths, kidnappings, abduction and rape of women are heinous crimes which do not come within the traditional definitions of crime.

The Muslim terrorist crusade in Jammu and Kashmir is aimed to merge the state into the Muslim nation of Pakistan on the basis of its Muslim majority, to convert it into a Muslim state governed in accordance with the religious precepts of Islam and to restrict human rights of all ethnic and religious minorities within the injunction of the Muslim state.

The crusade is a negation of human rights. All religious crusades which seek to establish religious precedence including Muslim Jihad and the militarization of the Pan-Islami fundamentalism violate the Declaration of Human Rights. The rights envisaged by Declaration of Human Rights are irreconcilable to all political regimes which are based on religious precept and precedent. Fundamental Rights, including human rights, conflict with restricted citizenship and all forms of religious protectorate.

The protection envisaged by human rights imposes limitations on the arbitrary exercise of state power, it also imposes a limitation on the exercise of authority by all regimes including instruments of social control, private citizens, foreign states and international organizations. The terrorist organizations in the state, the Muslim crusade for a second partition of India and the state of Pakistan cannot escape the liability for the violation of human rights in the Jammu and Kashmir state.

The responsibility of violation of human rights in the Jammu and Kashmir state rests upon all the terrorist organizations in the state, all the Muslim organizations and the para-military outfits which aid and support terrorism, all the political regime in the part of Jammu and Kashmir occupied by Pakistan and all the state of Pakistan.

Political terrorism is condemned by the UN as a crime against the rights of man. Terrorist killings, kidnappings, torture, hostage taking, abduction are listed as grave crimes against humanity. The Jammu and Kashmir Government and the Government of India have failed to take adequate and necessary measures to suppress terrorism in the state. In spite of increasing terrorist violence during the fall of 1989, the state Government stubbornly refused to take any action against the growing terrorist menace. During 1989, sixteen hundred violent incidents including 351 bomb blasts took place in Kashmir province.

The terrorist violence spread deaths, and hundreds innocent Hindus were moved down by the terrorist bullets but none of the high officials of the state Governments was brought to book for having abetted the terrorist assault on human rights.

Terrorist crime is still dealt with as an ordinary crime. Trial procedures have not been changed to meet the threat of crimes committed by the terrorist; no special anti-terrorist organizations have been instituted with in the police department or within the security structures of the state.

Thousands of innocent lives could have been saved, if the state and Union Government had taken adequate measures which the world community, the civilized nations have adopted to deal with the political terrorism. The local newspapers are a testimony to the death and destruction of Hindus and other innocent civilians who have been victimized by the various terrorist flanks and who could be saved if powers were given to the security forces to take pre-emptive action. Thousands of innocent lives have been taken by the terrorist and thousands of Hindus have been uprooted from their homes. They are languishing in refugee camps in Jammu and other parts of India.

Terrorism in Jammu and Kashmir motivated by ideological commitments to a Muslim crusade is a greater violation of human rights. There is an imperative necessity for a bold and unconventional endeavor to identify the content and contours of violence which has ravaged Jammu and Kashmir State and describe the perspectives in which the infringements of human rights deserve to be assessed. There is always a danger in shifting parameters and judgements in respect of human rights are incompatible with and destructive of the universality of such rights. It will be a travesty of human history to ignore the crucial factor of terrorist violence in Kashmir which must ultimately determine the context in which the violation of human rights has taken place.

An inquiry into human rights violations in Jammu and Kashmir cannot be confused with narrowly local and narrowly dated frames of reference. The terrorist violence unleashed in Jammu and Kashmir by various terrorist organizations and the state of Pakistan, is by itself a violation of human rights. The Muslim crusade seeks to exterminate the religious and ethnic minorities.

Terrorist violence in Jammu and Kashmir has several dimensions which have a direct bearing on human rights in the state. In the first place, terrorism in Jammu and Kashmir is a process of political violence which has specified political commitments aimed to separate Jammu and Kashmir State from India and secure its annexation to Pakistan. It is the culmination of the Muslim struggle in pre-partition India for the homeland of Pakistan, which claimed Jammu and Kashmir on account of the Muslim Majority character of its population.

It is a religious crusade to complete the partition of India which it is claimed is "incomplete, 'so long as Jammu and Kashmir is not merged with Pakistan. It must clearly be understood that this terrorist violence is not aimed at effecting any change in the existing political system, economic organisation or social relationship. It is neither an expression of political dissent, nor is it apolitical movement aimed to replace the existing sets of political instruments in the State. It has an international content as it is aimed at cutting off a part of the Indian nation and secure its annexation to the State of Pakistan.

The Kashmir Valley is in grip of terrorist trauma engineered by Pakistan. In fact, it is a low cost proxy war declared by Pakistan against India to grab Kashmir. The grimmest fall out of these atrocious Pak operations is the total exodus of the Hindu minority from Kashmir Valley. It has threatened the unity of India and the very survival of Kashmiri Hindu minority. They have been uprooted from Kashmir Valley.

The future is bleak and their existence is in danger. At present about 78,000 families are either residing in temporary relief camps at Jammu, Delhi, Chandigarh or Amritsar or have made their own arrangements in various parts of India. This figure of over 300,000 excludes over 10000 Muslims, who also have been forced by the denial of free expression and circumstances to leave the Valley of Kashmir to seek refuge in India.

The political content of the terrorist violence has a direct effect on human rights as it involves militants' strategies which cannot but infringe the principles which form the basis of human rights. A major dimension of terrorism in Jammu and Kashmir is the terrorists aim to exterminate Hindu population in the Kashmir Valley because Hindus do not accept the secession of the State from India and its annexation to Pakistan nor do they accept to be governed by the authority which derives its sanction from the law and precedent of Islam.

The most crucial aspect of terrorism in the State is the participation of Pakistan in the terrorist violence. The human rights violation by Pakistan in Jammu and Kashmir in the name of terrorism attained great significance. There is enough proof of the complicity of Pakistan in the terrorist activity in Jammu and Kashmir which cannot be disregarded.

The induction of terrorism in Jammu and Kashmir by Pakistan is its third attempt to cut off Jammu and Kashmir from India and annex it to its territories.

The terrorist violence in Kashmir has involved mass massacre of the people of the State, destruction of their property and genocide of Hindus and their exodus from Kashmir. The death and destruction of innocent people, genocide of minorities and conduct of a war of attrition in violation of the laws of war are crimes against humanity and international law, besides being violation of human rights.

The terrorist violence in Jammu and Kashmir on a well designed pattern, has led to several consequences which are inextricably inter linked with the violation of human rights. The pattern in which terrorism has manifested itself in Jammu and Kashmir has several aspects, some of which are characteristically original to the political violence unleashed by the various terrorist organisation and Pakistan in Jammu and Kashmir. These are mass massacre, genocide of Hindus - genocide is the destruction in the whole or in part of a national, ethnic or religious group and atrocities committed by terrorists.

Terrorists targeted not only Hindus but also Muslims who are opposed to secession.

The Kashmir conflict not only continues to raise the spectre of war between India and Pakistan, but it also continues to produce serious human rights violations: Summary executions, rape and torture by both sides. In their effort to curb support for pro-independence militants, Indian Security forces have resorted to arbitrary arrest and collective punishments of entire neighborhoods, tactics which have only led to further disaffection from India.

The Indian Security forces also engage in brutal forms of torture which like wise has the sanction of senior officials. The latter privately justify the practice on the grounds that there is no other way to obtain information from a suspect. Indian security faces have raped women in Kashmir during search operation, particularly in remote areas outside of major cities and towns. The difficulties inherent in documenting such attacks on women are many. The victims are unlikely to seek medical attention unless their injuries are severe and are reluctant to report their assaults because of the shame and stigma that they may bear as a result. Significantly army authorities have demonstrated some concern about rape and have initiated a number of courts martial of soldiers for rape. However many reports of rape particularly by feudal or local police forces are never investigated. Prosecutions of security personnel responsible for abuses are rare. The State Human Rights Commission which is mandated to investigate complaint of human rights violations and make non-binding recommendation to the government began its work in early 1998 and by November of that year had undertaken investigation in some 200 cases.

TADA has been widely used in Kashmir against persons suspected of having ties with militant groups. The act authorizes administrative detention without formal charge or trial for up to one year. It virtually criminalizes free speech. Under the TADA, anyone who knowingly facilitates the commission of any disruptive activity or any act preparatory to a disruptive activity shall not be less than three years but which may extend to a term of life and shall also be liable to fine". How far TADA is effective is yet to be decided.

The Indian Army, Special Task Force, Border Security Force and state sponsored, paramilitary groups and village defense committees the principle government forces operating in Jammu and Kashmir have systematically violated these fundamental norms of international human rights law. Under international law, India's state sponsored militia is State agents and therefore must abide by international human rights and humanitarian law. Human Rights Watch makes the following recommendations for action to be taken by the government of India, the militant forces in Kashmir, the government of Pakistan, and the international community to address thee human rights crisis in Kashmir.

To the Government of India

The government of India should disarm and disband all State-sponsored militias not established and regulated by law and prosecute members of such groups who have been responsibilities for extra judicial killings, "disappearances", assaults, and other abuses. State authorities and the headquarters of the army and paramilitary operation in Kashmir should issue public statement affirming the security of human rights defenders. The statements should include explicit guarantees for the security of human rights monitors to investigate incidents of abuse, record the statement of witnesses, publicize their reports, and petition the courts.

To the Militant Organisations

Militant groups should immediately stop all attacks on civilians, including kidnappings and assassinations. Militant groups should abide by human rights norms.

To the Government of Pakistan

The government of Pakistan should end all support for abusive militant organizations in Kashmir. It should not provide indiscriminate weapons, such as landmines to such groups.

To the United Nations

The General Assembly should condemn abuses by both security forces and militants in Kashmir and urge India to permit relevant U.N working group and special rapporteurs to visit Kashmir. The High Commissioner on Human Rights should visit Kashmir and conduct an investigation into abuses by all parties to the conflict. The findings and recommendations should be reported to the Security Council and the General Assembly and should be made publicly available.

To the International Community

France, Germany, Russia, the U.K, the U.S and India's other leading partners should suspend all military aid and sales and all programs of military corporation with India, including joint exercises, until India provides greater accountability on cases of "disappearances", torture and summary killings by its forces in Kashmir and disarms all state-sponsored paramilitary groups operating in Kashmir. The International Community should condemn Pakistan's support for abusive militant groups operating in Kashmir and make any future arms sales or military cooperation agreements contingent on an end to Pakistan's support for abusive militant groups.

These suggestions are very much important with regard to the human rights situation in Jammu and Kashmir. Human Right violations from the part of terrorist as well from the Indian army should be avoided. Terrorism surfaced in the Kashmir Valley culminating in making more than three lakhs Hindus to flee from their own homeland and suffer as refugees in their own country and is deprived of the basic human rights.

What is being done in Jammu and Kashmir to Protect Human Rights?

(a) Whenever complaints of violation of human rights and excess committed by the security forces are received, they are promptly enquired into by responsible authorities and the results are communicated to the complaining party.

(b) The National Human rights Commission often takes cognizance of media reports of both of Indian and foreign origin and initiates enquiries in respect of them, if there is any substance the concerned are punished.

(c) Human Rights education has been made compulsory for the Army and Para-military forces operating in the States.

(d) International NGO's foreign diplomats and officials have been given freedom to visit the State and have free access to information and they are meeting and have met many of the so-called militants.

(e) International Committee of the Red Cross has been given permission to visit all places of detention and meet with detainees.

India's Commitment to uphold the Human rights in the most laying circumstances in the State has been very much appreciated by the International Community. Day by Day, Pakistan is finding herself isolated and is unable to derive mileage from the false propaganda of Human Rights violations in Kashmir.

REFERENCES

1. Vinod Sharma, *Human Rights Violation. A Global Phenomenon* APH Publishing Corporation, New Delhi, 2002.

2. Krishna Mohan Mathur, *Challenges to Police, Human Rights and National Security,* Kalpaz Publications, Delhi, 2003.

3. Narang, A.S., *Terrorism and Human Rights,* A.S.Narang, Pramila Srivastava (eds) *Terrorism—The Global Perspective,* Kanishka Publishers, New Delhi, 2001.

4. Website :-http/www.yespakistan.com/kashmir/human rights violation in kashmir asp, dated 6/3/2006.

5. Singh Sehgal, B. P., (ed), *Human Rights in India Problems and Perspective,* Deep and Deep Publications, Delhi, 1999.

6. Subramanian, S., Forward by Justice Ranganath Mishra, *Human Rights-International Challenges,* Manas Publications, New Delhi, 1997.

7. Jayakumar, N.K., *Terrorism Rule of Law and human rights*. Dr. G. Gopakumar (ed), International Terrorism and Global Order in the 21st century, Kanishka Publishers, New Delhi, 2003.

33

Human Rights Violations and Beedi Workers

Muralidharan Nambiar. M

Introduction

Beedi manufacturing is one of the traditional and largely home based industries in India. It is highly labour intensive and engages about 4.4 million workers; of them nearly two third are women and one percent children. It does not involve any machinery at any stage by and large it is producing in unorganised sector. It is labour intensive. No other foreign exchange is involved in this sector. Besides the experience labourer's skill, the only equipment requires worker's hand, sieve and a pair of scissors. All these belong to the workers only. Unlike any traditional industries, beedi industry is not subject to competition from modern technology.

Beedi rolling began in the organised sector during the early 20th century but gradually shifted to unorganised sector consisting of house holds, small unincorporated units and worksheds. At present hardly 10 percent of the beedi manufacturing takes place in the organised sector. There are about 80 thousand beedi workers in North Malabar under organised and unorganised sectors. Of this 25 percent belong to organised sector and the rest 75 percent are under unorganised sector.

Statement of the Problem

The economic status of the beedi worker has been poor although some improvements were observed once the organised sector began to function. There exists variety of reasons for the pathetic conditions of the industry. Variety of reasons can be attributed for this plight - low - resource base, low education, under employment and low income generation etc. Not surprisingly, it is found that prospect of employment and means of living are the two major reasons given by workers for their performance of this occupation. The beedi workers are exploited in different stages and the human rights violations prevailing in beedi industries especially in the unorganised sector.

The impact of privatisation, liberalisation and globalisation adversely affected the beedi sector also. The Central Government issues the license for multinational companies for establishing trade and industries and even allowed the manufacturing of mini cigarettes. As their mini cigarettes are machine made, its manufacturing cost is very low. In certain states of USA, the prohibition of the entry of Indian beedies is enforced on the ground that beedies are rolled by small children and therefore child is exploited.

There is no direct relationship between the owners and the workers. The work is given through contractors or agents. The beedi leaf and tobacco are distributed through the branches from where the beedies rolled by the workers are collected. The government fixed the minimum wages much lower than of that fixed for unskilled workers in other industries in that states.

System of Work

There are three major system of work in beedi industry

1. Factory system;
2. The contract system;
3. The outdoor system or pass book system.

The Factory System

In the factory system of beedi making there is direct relations between the producer and the worker. Under this system of work, beedi workers sit and roll beedies in a common place provided by the employer for the purpose. This common place of work is generally referred to as the 'factory'. The Factories Act of 1948 is applicable to producing units employing 10 or more workers using power and those employing 20 or more workers without using power. Generally they are not allowed to take the raw materials to their residence[1]. Therefore it may appear that the workers employed under the factory system of beedi production are able to employ all facilities and benefits envisaged in the various legislations relations to the conditions of employment, place of work, none-wage benefits and other aspects of production. But investigations regarding the working of the beedi factories and interview with workers in those factories have revealed that in reality, the labourers are desired even fair wages and other benefits and facilities by the employers resorting to different methods. Though actually a large number of workers are employed under this system only 932 workers were reported to be employed in 1977 in the Factory Sector[2].

The Contract System

Under the contract system of beedi production, which became rampant in all the beedi producing states in India circumvent the factories Act 1948, raw materials are supplied to the workers through intermediaries known as contractors or agents. There exist no direct relationship between the producer proper and the worker. The workers work under the control and suspensions of paid or commission agents. The producer provides tobacco and *tendu* leaves to the agents. Apart from the commission borne by the employees, the workers are paid only low wage, by the contractors or branch managers[3]. The producer need not bother about providing the benefits and other amenities to the workers prescribed by the various legislations passed in different periods. Even the big well organised firms resorted to the practice of getting a part of their output produced through appointing contractors or agents at various places. Even the organised firms run on factory based system are found to be running branches in other parts of the district or state through contractors or branch managers. The contract system can assume the form of either a factory based or a home based system[4]. The contractors can also manipulate almost every part of the production process- from the price at which they sell wrapper leaves and tobaccos to the workers, to the price they pay for the finished beedi to the weighing of the leaves, to the "quality checks" and rejection rates.

Outdoor System (Pass Book System)

The outdoor or pass book system of production is different from the contract system in the sense that under the former the producer supplies raw materials direct to the workers and allows them to take the materials to their residence and roll beedies, while under the latter the raw materials are supplied through an intermediary. The workers under this system are provided with leaf and tobacco and have to return a specified number of beedies as per the norms of the company. Any shortfall in production involves a penalty in the form of deductions in the piece wage rate.[5]

Under the outdoor system workers are not employees of the producer; they are self employed workers. The raw materials are generally supplied on the basis of a standard regarding the number of beedies to be rolled from a given quantity of raw materials. Some firms sell the raw materials to the workers and purchase the beedies produced at a fixed price. Since the pass book is issued to record the transactions and identify the workers, this system of work is also known as the 'pass book system'. As per the norms of the sale and purchase practice, there is no fixed wage system. What is left after deducting the cost of the raw materials has to be accepted as wage by the worker. The pass book system of work is resorted to by some producers through contractors or branches or agents also.

These two-home based systems together the unorganised sector which have been growing in since 1930s[6]. These indirect systems of work have resulted in an enormous increase in the volume of women and children labour in beedi industry. The helpers, mostly children have to spend five to ten years in this way before becoming full-fledged laboures. While labourer is exploited by the firm or the intermediary, they in turn exploit the helpers. This was evidenced by a recent procession of more than a thousand helpers with several years of experience employed in a leading private firm in Cannanore[7]. Since there is no used to attend the factory and since work can be carried on at the premises of the residence, the women folk finds it more attractive and convenient to work under the indirect system. The indirect system has actually enabled the producers to shift the work site to the residence of the worker whereby they can avoid investment for constructing and maintaining work sites.

In addition to this, beedi is also produced on self employed basis. Here workers are procuring the necessary raw materials from the market, produces the beedi and finally they themselves are selling the finished products in the market. Workers are finding the livelihood in this system is mainly seen in the old Travancore area which includes the Southern districts of Kerala.[8]

Production Relation and Exploitation

The complication of indirect system of work arises mainly due to the thoroughly informal relations between the principal employer and workers and the unorganised and scattered nature of the workers. The wage and non- wage benefits available to the workers and the scope or otherwise for exploitation primarily depend on the nature on which the industry is organised. The factory system, by and large provides higher wages and better conditions of work and life free from exploitation by middlemen.

Highly exploitative production relation exist in the indirect unorganised sector of the beedi industry. Many kinds of exploitation have been reported under the indirect systems of work including sexual exploitation. The checkers in beedi factories prefer women to make the daily delivery trips because they are easier to cheat and can have a lot of 'man handling' while bundles of beedies, tobacco and *tendu* change hands. Young women silently suffer these to prevent the checker from rejecting more beedies.[9]

It has also been brought to light that the workers work in ill-ventilated unsanitary places.[10] Another report examined in detail the conditions of work in beedi industry and brought out the unhealthy working conditions, long hours of work, miserable conditions of women and child labour and above all the exploitation of labour.[11] The big manufactures of beedi evade legal obligations and limitation of space, the absence of ventilation and light, exploitation of women and children-these are the methods that the employers put into practice through the domestic system of beedi manufacture.[12]

Information provided by the respondents and discussions with knowledgeable persons have revealed the existence of large scale exploitation of beedi workers in the home based system of work by the middlemen. A two tier exploitation by the contractor as well as the producer exists in the beedi industry. The producer exploits the contractor who in turn exploits the workers mercilessly.[13]

Why do women allow themselves to be exploited in such an inhuman manner? Whenever they question the agent or the contractors on the quantity of beedi leaf or the identity cards or ask for an increase the wages, they are threatened with loss of work. They are in the constant fear of losing even that meager income to maintain their families. Wherever they are trying to get organised, the owners are stopping to give them work on the false plea that they are not having a good market for their beedies. So they don't want to make them. At the same time, the work is given through contractors to some other workers. The beedies are made without any label, so that the women don't know for whom they are making them, then taken away to some other place where they are labeled and sold. At such places the wages are very low and they don't have any other benefits.

Conclusion

In Kerala, beedi workers as an organised working group could be mostly found in Kannur and Kasaragod districts partly because of their proximity to the neighbouring districts of Karnataka and partly because of skills already acquired by these workers. This means that the beedi owners started beedi industries in these districts because of the proficiency in beedi of the people in these districts. Female members in Kerala like other parts of India mainly dominated this industry. Initially, the beedi workers were exploited by the beedi owners from Karnataka. But by the emergence of co-operative societies in beedi sectors, reduced the exploitation and inhuman activities of the beedi owners maximum.

Even though the government has fixed the minimum wages for rolling 1000 beedies, the beedi workers never got the statutory wages from the owners or agents. The agents continue to exploit the beedi workers in two ways. One, while supplying the raw materials i.e. leaves and tobacco to make 1000 beedies, they always provide insufficient quantities to make the fixed quantity. So being forced by the agents to produce the fixed quantity of beedies, they invariably purchase raw materials from the market to meet the scarcity. As a result, the beedi workers would have to spend from their own pockets. Unless they produce the fixed quantity, the agents besides rejecting the finished products, would refuse to make supplies of raw materials in future. Second, while taking back the finished products, beedies are rejected in the name of 'quality checks'.

This is a violation of right to live in dignity. The right to freedom is also curtailed by denying bargaining power and organisational activities.

References

1. M. Mohandas, *Beedi Workers in Kerala: Conditions of Life and Work,* EPW Vol. 15, No. 36, 6th September 1980, p. 1517.
2. Ibid. p. 1717.
3. M. Mohandas *Beedi Workers in Kerala: Conditions of Life and Work,* EPW Vol. 15, No. 36, 6th September 1980, p. 1517.
4. M. Mohandas and P.V. Praveen Kumar, *Socio-Economic Conditions of Beedi Workers in Kerala,* EPW Vol. 15, No. 26, 27th June 1992.
5. Ibid.
6. M. Mohandas *Beedi Workers in Kerala: Conditions of Life and Work,* EPW-1980,Vol. 15, No. 36, p. 1518.
7. Report in Chintha Weekly, October 10, 1978.
8. C. Kannan, *Beedi Industry in Kerala and Benefits Achieved by the Beedi Workers,* Souvenir All India Beedi Workers conference Kannur, 1993.
9. Anil Awachat, *'Beedi Workers of Nipani'*- EPW November 1980.
10. Report Commission Report on Beedi Industries, 1934.

11. Regay Committee Report, Government of India, 1944.
12. Report of National Labour Commission, 1966.
13. Udaya Kumar Varma and M.M Rahman *Tobacco, Tendu Leaf and Beedi workers in India - Problems & Prospects*. Shipra Publications, New Delhi, 2005, p. 24.

Index

H

I

J

K

M

R

❑❑❑